Stages of Struggle

D1607725

Stages of Struggle

*Modern Playwrights and
Their Psychological Inspirations*

JOHN LOUIS DIGAETANI

McFarland & Company, Inc., Publishers
Jefferson, North Carolina, and London

Except where otherwise noted, photographs are provided by
the Billy Rose Theatre Division, the New York Public Library for
the Performing Arts, Astor, Lenox and Tilden Foundations.

LIBRARY OF CONGRESS CATALOGUING-IN-PUBLICATION DATA

DiGaetani, John Louis, 1943–
　　Stages of struggle : modern playwrights and their
　psychological inspirations / by John Louis DiGaetani.
　　　　p.　　　cm.
　　Includes bibliographical references and index.

　　ISBN 978-0-7864-3157-1
　　softcover : 50# alkaline paper ∞

　　　1. American drama — 20th century — History and criticism —
Theory, etc.　2. English drama — 20th century — History and
criticism — Theory, etc.　3. Dramatists, American — 20th century —
Psychology.　4. Dramatists, English — 20th century — Psychology.
5. Autobiographical memory in literature.　6. Subjectivity in
literature.　7. Playwriting.　8. Drama — Technique.　I. Title.
　PS352.D54　2008
　822'.909353 — dc22　　　　　　　　　　　　　　　2007045987

British Library cataloguing data are available

On the cover: Jessica Lange and Alec Baldwin star in Tennessee
Williams' *A Streetcar Named Desire* at the Barrymore Theatre
(photograph 1992 by Brigitte Lacombe)

Manufactured in the United States of America

*McFarland & Company, Inc., Publishers
　Box 611, Jefferson, North Carolina 28640
　www.mcfarlandpub.com*

For Jim Hohman

Acknowledgments

I would like to thank Hofstra University for granting me a sabbatical leave and travel funds to work on this book. I would also like to thank Jim Hohman and Branko Rieger for encouragement with this project.

I would also like to thank Tom Lisanti and Jeremy Megraw of the New York Public Library for permission to use the photos from its archive in this book — and Martha Swope and the other photographers whose work is contained in the archive of the New York Public Library's Performing Arts Collection. Those photographers include Jos Abeles, Hunt/Pucci, Friedman-Abeles, Paul Kolnik, Richard Feldman, and Brigitte Lacombe.

Finally, I would like to thank Winnie Klotz of the Metropolitan Opera for the use of her excellent photos of the Britten operas.

Table of Contents

Preface

Theater has changed drastically in terms of audience appeal. For most of its history, theater remained the most popular of the literary forms — even people who would not read a poem or a novel would go to a play. Theater was the medium for everybody, though intellectuals often sneered at the cheap popularity of the theater of their time. Intellectuals of the Elizabethan period did not think much of Shakespeare or his contemporary playwrights. For one thing, they wrote in English, while Latin remained the language of the church and the intellectuals.

But theater was a literary form for the populace, and popular actors became celebrities in their own time — people like Fanny Kemble, Henry Irving, and Macready. Once journalism became popular in the 19th century, actors and actresses were photographed or daguerreotyped and appeared often in the popular press.

But new technological developments in the 20th century altered theater forever and served to rob it of much of its audience. Cinema in the early years of the century made actors like Buster Keaton, Charlie Chaplin, and Lillian Gish more popular than theater could have ever made them. Films became the theater of the everyman — silent and in black and white, yes, but available in every small town and not just places like New York and London. Then after World War II, television took over the popularity of radio and became everyman's every night theater. Many wildly popular radio programs simply moved to television and came to resemble theater more, since television was visual, unlike the radio. Radio shows like *Charlie McCarthy* and *Burns and Allen* joined Milton Berle and Steve Allen as stars of the new medium of television. Actors like Milton Berle, who had started in vaudeville, found themselves appearing on television in their old vaudeville routines (which resembled commedia dell'arte skits). Soon, television was even broadcast in color — also like theater.

In the early years of the 21st century, most people are not much interested in theater — unless we are talking about a Broadway musical — but are very interested in television and the movies. Have these new media destroyed theater? Well, they have certainly changed theater from being the most popular of literary forms to being a much more elitist form. These days mostly well-educated and well-heeled people go to the theater; it has become much less popular and frankly more intellectual. Common, ordinary people feel uncomfortable going to the theater — it is very expensive, unlike movies and television, and seems forbiddingly highbrow. With the singular exception of Broadway musicals — available only in very large cities, by and large — theater has become an elitist art-form.

But are the new media of television and movies really enemies of theater, or only kin? What is a film or television script other than a play that will be photographed? Many very popular plays like *A Streetcar Named Desire, Night of the Iguana, A Chorus Line, Cat on a Hot Tin Roof,* and *Amadeus* have, after their Broadway runs, become popular movies. Most situation comedies on television resemble commedia dell'arte skits turned into one-act plays with lots of commercial interruptions. *The Honeymooners, All in the Family,* and even *Will and Grace* reflect the comic situations and repetition of character types of commedia dell'arte. The use of clever one-liners often robs these shows of credible characters, but those very clever one-liners also add to the shows' popularity.

Early in the 21st century, theater has become a kind of Ur-theater — an old-fashioned but often avant-garde form of theater which is elitist but still vital and fascinating. Its new sister forms of media — film and television — learn from the art of Ur-theater, or live plays. The legitimate theater, as it was called when movies first appeared, remains as legitimate as ever. Most film and television actors (sometimes even feeling like bastard children) seek their validity as actors by appearing in theater — the Ur-theater of the several contemporary forms of theater. If that Ur-theater has become avant-garde and cutting-edge, daring to go places that movies and television avoid, then that adds to its legitimacy and its excitement. Part of that excitement involves the willingness to examine various forms of insanity by contemporary playwrights and even contemporary audiences.

If theater has lost an audience of quantity, it has now gained a higher quality audience. Revolutionaries like Richard Wagner have even changed the way audiences behave in a theater. Before Wagner's revolutionary theater in Bayreuth, Germany, the house lights were always kept on so that audience members could chat during a performance and examine what other audience members were wearing and who they were sitting next to. Wagner wanted his audience to sit in total darkness, stop talking, and concentrate on what was happening on the stage before them, and that is precisely what most contemporary audiences are now completely willing to do. Theater behavior has changed for the better, but playwrights have examined new issues.

There was a time when playwrights tried to reflect the truths of their religion — as with the ancient Greeks — or tried to reach their own versions of morality, especially in the 18th and 19th centuries. By the late 19th century, playwrights like Ibsen and Shaw created a more political theater dedicated to examining important social and economic issues. There was also a philosophical theater with playwrights like Strindberg and opera composers like Richard Wagner.

Now, psychological issues have become more often presented and examined on the contemporary stage, and that is the main theme of this book, which tries to understand theater in terms of a playwright's own psychological troubles, or at least those which interest him. While this of course is not completely new, a new focus for the theater has clearly developed by the early years of the twenty-first century, and this book will examine the new psychological realities of contemporary theater. Since it is not only playwrights who suffer with psychological anguish, we can all feel attracted to such a theater. Such a theater driven by these issues will also influence significantly the more popular forms of theater, the movies and television.

Introduction

The Germans have a word for it: *Theaternarr*, or a fool for the theater; that person who is obsessed with the theater and its performers, who identifies completely with a particular actor or a play. The performing arts can produce a kind of neurotic adulation so that some audience members become obsessed with a particular playwright, actor, or performance. We also use the term *Stendhal effect* for the case of a person who can be overwhelmed by a work of art. Identification with actors can cause people to see the same play or actor over and over again. I have a friend who saw Barbra Streisand in *Funny Girl* over one hundred times when it was on Broadway despite being a poor student at the time. I have another friend who will go anywhere around the world to see Wagner's *Ring* cycle — these people are known as Ringheads these days. They are like the Deadheads who will go anywhere to hear the Grateful Dead perform.

A neurotic identification also can occur with some fans, who fantasize a performer singing or acting just for them. When Ralph Fiennes performed *Hamlet* on Broadway, one of my friends was so nervous for his favorite actor at the premiere that he could not eat dinner before the performance. This kind of identification with a particular performer makes many people question the sanity of some audience members. To think and to feel for a particular performer so that the fan's own life becomes affected would cause many Germans to use the word *Theaternarr* for such a malady and such a person.

In turn, some playwrights can be seen as neurotic, and their plays tend to focus repeatedly on a particular neurotic obsession. This book will analyze the neurotic undercurrents of many of the major modern dramatists since the beginnings of the 20th century. This study will analyze how an author's personal mental problems can appear in his or her work, and also how the playwright can observe mental problems in the people he or she knows personally and dramatize them. We will also understand how those very mental problems can both repel and attract audiences to that playwright's particular brand of theater.

Whether it is Pirandello's images of schizophrenia or Tennessee Williams's recurrent examples of sibling rivalry leading to mental collapse, many modern playwrights have dramatized their own personal obsessions with a particular neurosis or even psychosis. Perfectionism can be seen as a personality problem, but in the case of Stephen Sondheim perfectionism can also be seen as the basis for his repeated experiments with form for the musical theater. Even so painful a topic as pedophilia can appear in a work of art, and can enrich a play or opera while it can poison the life of an artist like Benjamin Britten. Alcoholism, one of the most tragic of addictions, appears repeatedly in the life and plays of Eugene O'Neill, Tennessee Williams, Edward Albee, Brian Friel, and Martin McDonough.

This book will analyze drama and creativity in terms of neurosis, and the results will exemplify some of the major trends in the modern theater. Since we are all, to a greater or lesser extent, neurotic, this book will enable readers to analyze both the plays and themselves in the plays. While we have been taught that the ultimate truths are philosophical, this book will argue instead that they are psychological, for as Freud once said, "Neurosis is the human condition." While some remain incapacitated by their neurosis, others can deal with it and even turn it into great art.

The special talent of the artist, it seems to me, is the ability to turn neurosis — his own or other people's suffering — into art. While most people suffer through their personal problems with Prozac and patience, with or without the help of a psychiatrist or psychologist, the artist can also use emotional problems as the raw material for art. A character in *Deconstructing Harry,* one of Woody Allen's movies, pulls a gun on a writer — accusing him of turning her anguish into bestsellers. It is this very phenomenon that I will be investigating in this book — where the neurosis occurs in the art, and whether the neurosis also occurred in the personal life of the artist. Such an investigation should give us an insight into both the nature of the dramatic art and also some of the main issues in modern theater.

I have also been rather loose in my terminology — using *neurosis, mental problems,* and *mental conflicts* in a rather informal way. This informality has been intentional since I want to be as inclusive as possible in my discussions of various mental problems and various plays. This book will, as a result, be helpful I hope to the student (and fan) of modern drama as a way of approaching and understanding how many aspects of modern theater work their magic on contemporary audiences — and how modern and contemporary theater differ from classical drama.

Twentieth century drama in both America and Europe has created theatrical excitement for contemporary audiences, and the presentation and examination of psychological problems act to entice audiences to a window into their very souls. Such a theater can provoke fascination from an audience as well as fright and repulsion. While earlier playwrights felt that theater could cure moral problems, modern playwrights would probably find this approach rather naïve and instead want a theater which can explore human complexity in the hope of pointing out and maybe even curing neuroses both in themselves and their audiences. And maybe that is naïve too. But being able to expose and explore psychological problems enables both the playwright and the audience to understand better, and knowledge and power have a legendary attraction which can certainly become dramatic.

Since we all have our own forms of neuroses, we can relate easily to neuroses both in a playwright's life and when those very neuroses appear in his or her plays. Neurosis is the human condition, and such a theater can help us better to cope with our own problems when we see those very problems on stage. And theoreticians on the arts have connected artistic abilities with mental problems, from the French Romantics of the 19th century to the present through aesthetic theoreticians like Foucault and Derrida. These writers have repeatedly connected artists, especially writers, with madness and mental illness; here dramatic theoreticians connect in an interesting way with the popular view of the artist as a crazy person, believing that normal people do not become writers and artists. But then who is normal?

If all theater is a footnote to Shakespeare and the ancient Greeks, then all these problems also appear earlier in their plays. Shakespeare's Othello becomes a prime example of neurotic jealousy, and his Hamlet exemplifies an inability to act despite the end of all doubt. *Antigone* presents us with a wonderful example in the title character of both a victim and a neurotically angry teenager. But while these neurotic problems appear within another context, a very ancient one, modern playwrights can present peculiarly modern problems in a contemporary context, our own times. The psychological problems of contemporary playwrights then become the central concern in their theater, a concern central to each of our lives.

1

George Bernard Shaw
The Gay Subtext

George Bernard Shaw had a very peculiar sex life according to his biographers. The definitive biography by Michael Holroyd, in three long volumes, describes Shaw as a young man in London at the end of the 19th century having a series of affairs with older women and then finally marrying Charlotte Townsend-Payne in a peculiarly Platonic agreement — she insisted and he agreed to a marriage that would include absolutely no sex. Shaw married Charlotte on June 1, 1898; according to Michael Holroyd, after he married at the age of 42 he did not have a sexual life at all, which also seems peculiar, and he was apparently a happily married man after that. Critics have often wondered why he was satisfied with such a frustrating relationship, but some critics have argued that as Charlotte was a very wealthy woman and he was a very poor writer from an impoverished background, she offered him the financial stability which any writer longs for — especially one who had written so much but had had so little financial success at that point in his career. Shaw had once said that those who can, do; but those can't, teach — his variation for himself seems to be those who can do, those who can't, marry into money. It is interesting here that the playwright did exactly what his own father George did in marrying his mother Lucinda, thinking that she was from a very wealthy family which would provide for him. Once Bernard Shaw had married the rich Charlotte he never again had to worry about money but could live like a wealthy man and write whatever he wanted regardless of the financial considerations. But were his only reasons for such a marriage purely financial ones? Was he happy in his asexual but faithful marriage to his Irish wife? And was he so faithful to her given her insistence on no sex? He had long and loving correspondences with several actresses, including Mrs. Patrick Campbell, but were these also asexual?

Sally Peters's *Bernard Shaw: The Ascent of the Superman* answered the common critical belief in Shaw's asexuality by arguing that Shaw might well have been a closeted homosexual, which would explain why he was content with his Platonic marriage to the motherly but very wealthy Charlotte. But Peters was unable to prove conclusively that he practiced homosexuality, though she suggests that he had a brief affair with a director, Harley Granville-Barker, who became the great love of his life. But Peters's provocative argument lacked sufficient evidence of homosexuality and failed to explain his many involvements with women, especially actresses like Florence Farr, Janet Atchurch, and Mrs. Patrick Campbell. Peters failed to provide any written evidence for his alleged homosexuality though there exists much documentation of his sexual interest in women. Shaw had sexual relationships with several women, especially Jenny Patterson, before he married in his 40s, so it is hard to prove that he was a closeted homosexual, but there is no doubt that he had an intellectual interest in homosexuality since it was the great unmentionable of the Victorian period.

Shaw himself often suggests that the most interesting people are effeminate men and masculine women, which was certainly a provocative concept at the time and also suggested an interest in homosexuality since many (but not all) effeminate men are homosexual, as are many (but not all) masculine women. But his interest in these people — people that were only joked about at the time — indicates something about the ideology of Shaw's theater. Repeatedly in Shaw's plays, the main characters become variations of two of Shaw's favorite character types: masculine women and effeminate men.

Certainly homosexuality was much in the news at the time of his youth and maturity in London. It was during the Victorian period that homosexuality was given a scientific name. The terms homosexuality and heterosexuality, originating in Germany, came into use for a reality which only had nasty slang terms to describe it — terms like sodomite or pederast or even fop. Finally, homosexuality had a scientific explanation of sorts and a scientific terminology. In Tom Stoppard's play *The Invention of Love*, which concerns the poet and classics scholar A.E. Housman, who was a closeted gay man, the character is horrified when he first hears this term. As he says: "That is a mixture of Latin and Greek!!" — which indeed it is. This play also contrasts a closeted gay man, Housman, with a flamboyant gay man, Oscar Wilde, who paid a terrible price for his flagrant homosexuality — four years at hard labor in prison and death soon afterwards.

The notorious trial of Oscar Wilde in 1895 was the sensation of London, and Shaw was in London at the time. Indeed, he knew Oscar Wilde personally; Wilde was of course Irish as Shaw himself was, and both men were born in Dublin, Wilde being two years older than Shaw. Wilde's father was a wealthy physician and Oscar was raised in the wealthiest part of Dublin, while Shaw was the son of an impoverished drunk from the poor part of town. Shaw remembered that Wilde's mother was especially kind to him and invited the impoverished Irishman to her house for receptions and dinners. Shaw's was also the only negative review of Wilde's smash hit *The Importance of Being Earnest* when it opened in the West End in 1893. Almost one hundred years later, in 1982, a book was published which provides the correspondence of Shaw with Lord Alfred Douglas, who was Wilde's lover for a while, and it was Douglas's father whose charges of homosexuality led to Wilde's three disastrous trials for "gross indecency" and subsequent imprisonment. Shaw corresponded with Douglas for many years, and Shaw also contributed for many years to a society trying to legalize homosexuality in Britain, something which was not accomplished until 1967 — as a result of the Wolfenden Report, which recommended such a legalization — when it was approved by Parliament. The following year, in 1968, Great Britain abolished theater censorship.

Clearly Shaw was very sympathetic to Wilde and Lord Alfred Douglas, and he was also sympathetic to the movement for the legalization of homosexuality. As an enlightened, thinking man who supported progressive and even radical causes like the suffrage movement for women and socialism, and unlike many others, Shaw remained sympathetic to the suffering of gay people. Shaw undoubtedly read the newspaper accounts in the Victorian period and the early 20th century of gay people who were blackmailed because of their sexual secrets and then committed suicide. Indeed, Lord Alfred Douglas's own brother committed suicide over being blackmailed because of his own homosexuality and an affair he had with Lord Roseberry. As a dedicated Fabian socialist, Shaw was supportive of most progressive causes during the late 19th and early 20th centuries in Britain.

Shaw was also clearly interested in what defines masculinity and what defines femininity despite the Victorian strictures on rigid sexual roles. Since he fully supported the liberation of women and the suffrage movement (indeed his own mother Lucinda Shaw was a vocal spokesperson for women's liberation and suffrage since she was the victim of a drunken husband), Shaw absorbed from her his interest in women's liberation. Some liberated women of the period were also lesbians — or at least masculine women who refused the passive, wifely, and motherly role that Victorian culture assigned to them. His mother did not want to spend all her time raising children, and in fact she often neglected Shaw and his siblings to go to London to study music and perhaps had a long-standing affair with George Vandeleur Lee, her musical mentor, while she was still outwardly married to Shaw's father George, the drunkard. Was there a ménage à trois going on in Shaw's childhood home? We can never know the exact relationship of Shaw's mother to Vandeleur Lee, but it was hardly typically Victorian. So the questions of what constitutes normal male behavior and what constitutes normal female behavior were naturally confused in Shaw's own unhappy childhood house, since his mother seemed like the head of the household, often gone on mysterious trips to London with her friend Vandeleur Lee, and his father was passive and incompetent but a serious drinker.

All of these questions — from both his own experience of his parents' unhappy marriage and current new scandals in the Victorian newspapers — naturally would appear in his writings, and that is what I want to investigate in this chapter. The questioning of sexual roles despite Victorian stereotypes and the possible homosexuality of some of Shaw's characters remain connected with all these concerns. Shaw also insisted on being called Bernard by his friends — he hated his first name of George, probably because that was also the first name of both his father and Vandeleur Lee, whom he did not like at all — partially because of his father's alcoholism but also because of the bad relationship which existed between them.

We see all these issues in what some critics argue was Shaw's first major play, *Mrs. Warren's Profession*. Shaw completed the play in 1894 but it was considered much too shocking to win approval from the English censors. The play was first staged in public in 1902 in New York but not until 1925 in London, and was even then considered very shocking since Mrs. Warren's profession was of course prostitution. The play in its first scene presents us with the masculine woman and the effeminate man. Praed, an old friend of Mrs. Warren, meets Vivie, Mrs. Warren's young daughter, and modern audiences (and probably Victorian audiences as well) would have suspected that Praed was a gay man. He is the only male onstage who either has not had sexual relations with Mrs. Warren or did not want to. He seems like an amazingly asexual creature, and is the great defender of the arts in the play — in addition to being sensitive to people in a way that Mrs. Warren is not, least of all to her own daughter. Praed certainly has no success in interesting Vivie in any of the arts, and she describes her boredom with classical music and opera but owns up to a weakness for mystery novels.

Vivie, when she enters early in the first scene, seems like a very masculine woman — a college student at a new woman's college, Newnham, at Cambridge, who seems to be primarily interested in mathematics, money, and not much else. She is hardly the typical Victorian young ingenue — and in fact one of the running jokes in the play is that whenever any of the male characters shake her hand they have to rub it afterwards because of the power of her grip. She clearly has the handgrip of a strong man rather than the genteel little shake of a typical woman. The play is centrally concerned with her difficult relationship with her domineering and demanding mother, the former prostitute and now owner of a string of brothels in several countries in Europe. She clearly is a very successful entrepreneur in the sex industry, and her daughter Vivie is like her in the sense that she too is very interested in money and wants above all else to succeed in the man's world of business and not spend her time with what would have been considered normal women's work — being a proper Victorian wife and mother.

By the end of the play Vivie has severed all relationship with her mother and moved in with Honoraria Fraser, a female actuary and lawyer whom she knows and has apprenticed with. Vivie also severs all relationship with her seeming suitor Frank Garner, who seems interested in her primarily because of her money and her rich mother. Frank seems like a reverse of the female stereotype of a young woman looking for a rich husband — he is a lazy and penniless young man looking for a rich wife to support him, in other words, Shaw's rather effeminate young man. Shaw was often seen this way by his friends since they noticed his attraction to the very wealthy Charlotte Townsend-Payne.

But aside from Frank, why does Vivie end her relationship with her mother? There are several possible theories: One is that Vivie can understand her mother's becoming a prostitute when she was a poor woman trying to survive, but she cannot understand why her mother would continue in the sex trade after becoming wealthy in the profession and continue as a madame, exploiting other poor women. Another theory is that her mother wants her to become her nursemaid and marry one of her partners in the prostitution business, Sir George. In any case, the play ends with Vivie alone on stage and smoking a cigar and looking over some actuarial charts in Honoraria Fraser's office. Cigar smoking was then, as now, often seen as a suggestion of lesbianism in a woman, since it was such a typically masculine habit. The habit was also connected with the lesbian French writer George Sand. Does the play suggest that Vivie will now become a successful businessperson and a lesbian, having an affair with her new business partner Honoraria Fraser? It does! And the first name of her business partner, Honoraria, suggests that Vivie is doing an honorable thing. Such an ending would undoubtedly have added to the shock value of the play and explained why it had to wait thirty years for a professional production in Britain. The play's ending also implies a positive endorsement of lesbianism and a rejection of marriage and motherhood as desirable goals for every woman. Shaw clearly likes to reverse sexual roles and poke fun at the Victorian world's rigid concepts of masculinity and femininity. Here we have a young man looking for a rich woman to support him and a young woman determined to earn her own way and make her own millions in the world of business.

Vivie can also be seen as the daughter of her own mother, since Mrs. Warren hardly appears like a typical woman of the Victorian period. Instead, her pursuits seem typically masculine, since she wants social independence and wealth. Even when she becomes a wealthy woman, Mrs. Warren wants to continue her business career, like an obsessed businessman in love with the pursuit of money. She also wants her daughter Vivie to tend to her in her old age and marry one of her business cronies, George Crofts — but Vivie wants her own business career instead of tending to her aging mother.

Shaw's next play, however, was staged the same year it was written, 1894, and that play was *Arms and the Man* — and the play succeeded with the British public and went on to become a very popular Viennese operetta. Shaw's plays quickly became much-staged in German-speaking countries, thanks to Shaw's very good German translator, Siegfried Trebitsch, and Oscar Strauss turned this play into the operetta *The Chocolate Soldier*, which succeeded very well in Vienna, London, and especially New York. Shaw disliked this tuneful work since Strauss and his librettist used the comic situations but not the serious ideas in Shaw's intellectual comedy. But audiences at the time seemed to enjoy the operetta more than Shaw's original play.

One of the main ideas in the play is questioning the whole concept of masculinity — what does it mean to be a man? The very title of "Arms and the Man" (from Virgil's *Aeneid*) indicates the centrality of this theme, and right in the opening scene we have a sissy onstage. When Bluntschli enters he is unchivalrously invading a young woman's bedroom and threatening to kill her — and instead of having a loaded gun like a real soldier, all he has is some chocolate, a true son of Switzerland. Ethnic stereotypes are also being played with in this play, especially those of the Swiss and the Bulgarians — the Swiss as unemotional, rational business people and the Bulgarians and Serbs as incompetent and bloody bumpkins.

When this play was very successfully staged in Berlin, it was picketed by Bulgarian and Serbian students living there who accused the play of being racist. It undoubtedly is racist in its view of the Bulgarians and Serbs, but *Arms and the Man* remains such fun and is so playful that most audiences will undoubtedly forgive its stereotyping.

The apparent real man in the play is Sergius, the fiancé of the young woman, Raina, and Sergius is always armed (unlike Bluntschli) and a true masculine hero. But Bluntschli's rather cold-blooded efficiency gets his masculinity attacked by Sergius as well, who calls Bluntchli "a machine rather than a man." But by the end of the play, Bluntschli's Swiss efficiency saves the naïve Bulgarians, and Sergius ends the play by pointing to the Swiss and saying "What a man!" Clearly Bluntschli is the real man by the end of the play. The play plays with stereotypes of Europeans, presenting the Bulgarians as bloodthirsty, provincial boobs — as western Europeans and Americans tended to see them when the play was written. The play was picketed by angry Balkan students when it was very successfully staged in Berlin and Vienna, but aside from the comic racism of the play, it also asks if a sissy is a real man or a homosexual. Since this issue recurs in the theater of GBS, it must have been central to Shaw's concern as a man.

Shaw had more success with *You Never Can Tell*, which was first staged in London in 1898, and here he seems to put his own family on the stage. The play centrally involves a broken marriage and the parents' attempts to come to an agreement for the sake of the three children, who are now grown up. There is much comedy in the play, with its opening in a dentist's office and an ineffectual young dentist called Valentine — a wonderfully obvious name for the young male lead who falls in love with the young female lead, also comically called Gloria. Shaw opens his play in a dentist's office and gives the best part and the best lines to a waiter — a recipe for theatrical disaster, one would think, but Shaw's theatrical acumen proves that prescriptions for the theater can safely be ignored by a genius.

Shaw's presentation of Valentine is another Shavian reversal of a comic stereotype — here we again are presented with a handsome but penniless young man, a failed dentist, who seems to be looking for a rich woman to support him since he seems rather incompetent. As a sincere feminist, Shaw often presents his audience with powerful women like Mrs. Warren or Gloria, and even some men like Valentine, incompetent despite his attractive and affable name. Clearly Shaw enjoyed reversing theatrical and social stereotypes to indicate his view of how complicated people and social realities really were, even in Victorian England.

What has caused the parents to have lived separately for so many years? In fact, the children do not remember ever meeting their father before, an incident which also occurs in a later play, *Major Barbara*. The mother in *You Never Can Tell* is a suffragette and feminist author who has left her husband and raised her three children in her concepts of enlightenment, though her daughter Gloria ends the third act by saying, "Mother, you have taught me nothing!" She has just fallen in love with Valentine, appropriately enough, and is angry that her mother's modern theories about education and liberation did not explain the thorny topic of love and sexuality.

The father of the family seems very aggrieved that his wife and children have left him, but he also seems like a very conservative old Victorian, and also probably a drunkard—in short, Shaw's own family. But a type of reconciliation occurs at the end, though Valentine seems like an effeminate man since he is so ineffectual as both a dentist and provider and is clearly looking for a rich woman to support him, and the mother seems like a masculine woman who wants to dominate her family according to her own modern theories of liberation. The father in the family seems to be sullen and angry and a drinker—based on Shaw's own father George.

In 1903 *Man and Superman* was first staged in London, and here too Shaw has fun with typical Victorian views of masculinity and femininity. Ann Whitefield pretends to be a delicate Victorian virgin who claims to be utterly helpless and needs some man to direct her life, especially now that her father has died. Jack Tanner knows this is all a pose and says she pretends to be helpless but really manipulates all the men around her to do her bidding. In her way, Ann is much more masculine and calculating than any of the other men on stage.

Jack Tanner makes an interesting foil to Roebuck Ramsden, the elder Victorian gentlemen who cherishes all the clichés of the period, especially about sexual roles and the helplessness of women. Jack's cynicism about women and their alleged helplessness and need of a man become reinforced when we finally get to see Ann Whitfield on stage. The audience soon sees that she cleverly pretends to be a helpless Victorian virgin in order to manipulate the naïve men around her to do exactly what she wants.

Despite Jack's own insights into Ann, whom he calls a boa constrictor (she enters the play wearing a feather boa), Jack himself falls in love with her and agrees to marry her by the end of the play. The play also includes Octavius—the helpless, effeminate man who clearly needs some woman to direct his life. Octavius's sister Violet is an example of the masculine woman, who seems like the helpless female pregnant and without a husband but is actually completely in control and after her husband's father's money. She is clearly hard as nails, as one of the characters say, and hardly the Victorian image of the helpless female—and she does not pretend to be, unlike Ann. Violet refuses to disclose who she is married to lest her husband lose his father's substantial wealth—and she wants that money desperately, and gets it by the end.

Major Barbara was first staged in 1905. Here, too, Shaw plays with concepts of masculinity and femininity. The title character, Barbara, appears to be a masculine woman—she first enters the play in the masculine military uniform of the Salvation Army and clearly rejects the Victorian role of woman as weak helpmate to some man. But by the end of the play, she marries Adolphus

Cusins but clearly wants to spend her life helping the workers on her father's company town rather than taking care of her own children. Her sister marries an effeminate man, Cholly, who is silly and comic and clearly needs some forceful, rich woman to direct his life. But Shaw also draws the Nietzschean distinction between mensch and ubermensch in the play — the natural leaders like Adolphus, Andrew Undershaft, and Barbara versus the more common types who think in clichés, people like Lady Britomart and her son Stephen. In these last two roles, Shaw also enjoys satirizing the typical British upper classes, who think in clichés and have a naïve assumption of their own superiority, morality, and intelligence. Shaw's play also indicates that although he claimed to be a Fabian socialist and a Marxist, he has a grudging but keen admiration of the entrepreneurial capitalist, who remains bloodthirsty in his determination to make money. Andrew Undershaft runs a munitions factory and will sell arms to anyone who can pay, and this is the man who is the real hero of the play. It is the capitalist Undershaft who is the original thinker and who really helps poor people, since his prosperous company (and not the local Socialists) has eliminated poverty in the company town.

Shaw as an outspoken member of the Fabian socialist party declared himself a dedicated socialist, but the play's most mesmerizing character is Sir Andrew Undershaft, the rich munitions manufacturer. Shaw gives him all the best lines in the play. When a character asks him what his religion is, Undershaft says, "I am a millionaire, that is my religion." He gets the best speeches as well as the best lines. Shaw the Fabian socialist seems to be violating his own beliefs here, and the play seems to be glorifying entrepreneurial capitalism rather than socialism. We know that Shaw's repeated defenses of individualism made his Fabian socialist friends Sidney and Beatrice Webb uncomfortable, since Shaw's speeches seemed to violate socialism's concepts of collecticism and collective social changes. But Shaw remained a defender of individualism and also a lover of money and wealth. He seemed to have a fascination with the rich entrepreneur who could become a millionaire. Shaw also admired the person who could make a lot of money on his own, perhaps because Shaw owed his own wealth to his shrewd marriage to the wealthy Charlotte. Shaw very early realized the power of money in society and had a keen admiration for people who could earn it themselves.

After *Major Barbara*, a major play, Shaw wrote what is now considered a minor play, *Getting Married,* which was published in 1908. Here Shaw names one of his major characters Lesbia, a woman who wanted a child but would not get into bed with her suitor. Her masculine behavior in the play, plus her character's very name, clearly suggests that Shaw wanted her presented as a lesbian who was repelled by the idea of sex with a man. Such a character would certainly have been exceedingly shocking in 1908, which explains why the play had to wait for its first production in London. Clearly here too in *Getting Married* we see Shaw questioning sexual roles and presenting closeted characters — people who are homosexual but having to pretend to be heterosexual for the sake of society's demands. Shaw clearly indicated his interest in hidden sexual desires and the neurosis of hiding and lying which society's stupidity about homosexuality forced upon many of its citizens.

In 1912, just before the beginning of World War I, Shaw's *Androcles and the Lion* was written. It was first staged in London the following year. Here again we have Shaw using the effeminate man, or rather the sissy Lion who does not want to go into the coliseum and fight the Christians. The effeminate man (or lion) is the central character here and Shaw creates great comedy from it — and he also uses the play to question the whole rationale of Christianity and why the Christians resisted what was essentially a pro forma ritual by the Romans. Shaw presents as foils contrasting kinds of men — the aggressive warrior and the passive sissy, though it is the sissy who succeeds by the end, as with Bluntschli in *Arms and the Man. Androcles and the Lion* allows Shaw to toy with concepts of masculinity and how they interact with Christian charity and passivity.

Perhaps the play which most clearly questions masculinity and suggests the taboo topic of homosexuality remains *Pygmalion*. This premiered in 1913 at the Hofburg Theater in Vienna but opened in London the very next year — clearly by now Shaw had many German fans who were eager to see his new plays, more eager than his English audience. In fact, Shaw's plays often succeed more in German-speaking lands than in English-speaking ones, thanks to Siegfried Trebitsch's translations. Another factor was undoubtedly English censorship of Shaw's plays, while in Germany they could be staged without the Victorian censorship legal in London during Shaw's lifetime. Theater censorship was not eliminated in Britain until 1968 — long after Shaw's death in 1956.

One of the central questions in the play is why Henry Higgins does not want to marry Eliza Doolittle at the end of the play. He seems to want her to live in his house, he seems to love her, he even says he has grown accustomed to her face. Is he just a confirmed old bachelor and likely to remain so? One of the implications that a close reading of the play suggests is that Henry Higgins is a gay man who is very aware of the law. In the first scene he meets Colonel Pickering and immediately invites him to move into his house. By the last scene, he tells Eliza that she can stay in his house — along with him and Pickering. He even dances with Pickering at one point to teach Eliza how to dance.

My Fair Lady (film), 1964; Audrey Hepburn as Eliza Doolittle and Rex Harrison as Professor Higgins.

It seems to me that it is Pickering he is attracted to, not Eliza, and he cannot be completely frank with her about this because if he is he could be thrown in jail (or "gaol"), given the British legal system of the time. In the first scene of the play when Henry Higgins meets Pickering he immediately invites him to move in with him — strange behavior to a total stranger unless there was some sort of sexual attraction between them. Shaw in his introduction to the play tries to explain Henry Higgins in terms of an obsession with his mother — a mother so perfect that all other women pale in comparison. But when we see Higgins's mother, she seems rather cruel and neglectful of him; she tells him not to visit her when she is receiving company since he is always so rude to her company. By implication, his mother is telling him she would rather have company over than spend time with him. Shaw's own mother Lucinda Shaw was very neglectful of him; she often abandoned him in Dublin to go to London for musical events or to study singing, or to visit her lover, and he often felt abandoned by her as a child.

Once, when a friend accused Shaw of having a heart of stone, he responded, "It is a good thing I have a heart of stone or my family would have broken it years ago." Clearly he felt that both his parents were neglectful of his childhood needs, and this is indicated by the comic but also nasty mother of Henry Higgins in this play. We see this kind of mother-figure again in *The Devil's Disciple* when one of the characters tells his mother that he was raised in a house "of children's tears," clearly again implying that she was a horri-

My Fair Lady (based on Shaw's *Pygmalion*), original Broadway production, 1956; Julie Andrews and Rex Harrison.

ble mother who made him weep as a child. Shaw's experience with his mother and family life clearly left the playwright quite bitter about mothers in general and family life as well — which may have been part of his attraction to Charlotte since she wanted neither sex nor children. Did she become a mother-figure for him? Since he did not have a very good relationship with his own

Pygmalion, 1914; Mrs. Patrick Campbell as the original Eliza Doolittle.

mother, he seemed quite susceptible to the charms of older women. Many of his lovers were older than Shaw himself was.

In Shaw's Chekhovian comedy, *Heartbreak House*, we experience Captain Shotover and his two eccentric daughters, Hesione Hushabye and Ariadne Utterwood. The situation is a bit like that of King Lear and his own three

Pygmalion, 1945; Robert Massey and Gertrude Lawrence.

daughters, but here the daughters seem unhappily married and not much interested in men in general. The male characters, especially Mangan, seem incapable of directing events, though the daughters seem very domineering and demanding. All the characters, ultimately, seem incapable of avoid the coming catastrophe — a symbol in the play of the tragedy that was World War I.

Arguably the best of Shaw's late period plays remains *St. Joan*, which was first staged in New York in 1923 and then in London the following year. By the '20s Shaw had clearly developed an international reputation as a playwright and he had no trouble getting the play staged. The character of St. Joan is another one of his lesbian figures — if a saint can claim to have a sexual life, she seems like the model lesbian. Only two years earlier Joan had been declared a saint, so the whole saga of St. Joan and her trials was much in the public eye, and Shaw's lengthy introduction to his play indicates that he knew that long story and had read all the relevant historical documents. But the Joan that Shaw presents would be what most people would recognize as a lesbian. She dresses as a man and with a man's haircut, refusing to wear women's clothing or do anything that women were supposed to be doing in the fifteenth century in France or in fact even now. Instead she says in the first scene of the play (she appears dressed as a man) that she is trying to get armor and a horse so she can get together an army to drive the English out of France and get the French King Charles crowned in Rheims.

The play also shows that one of the reasons why she was burned for being a witch was that she acted like a lesbian — refusing to act and dress like a woman, cutting her hair short like a man, and insisting that she wanted to be a soldier to lead an army to drive the English out of France. Even when the Church orders her to desist, she refuses and instead has faith only in her voices — which makes her either a saint or a lesbian or a heretic or a Protestant (insisting on her right to approach God herself and without the intercession of the Church). Shaw clearly presents her as the first Protestant saint — and also a lesbian. She is certainly a liberated woman who does not want to play the submissive role of the typical female of the period — either medieval or Victorian or modern. But is St. Joan a lesbian? She does not have sex with women in the play, but she dresses and acts like a man rather than a woman — and she saves France at a time when no man could do that. A saint is not supposed to have a sexual life, but many aspects of St. Joan's character look much more like a homosexual woman than a heterosexual one. Here again Shaw suggests that society's rigid social roles for men and women fail to account for human realities.

Is King Charles a gay man? He is treated as a sissy and a fool for much of the play, and he is clearly presented as an incompetent and an effeminate man. Even his wife — not to mention his archbishop and his generals — has utter contempt for him. He certainly is not masculine and does not have the masculine attributes of a forceful king and leader for France. But Joan turns him into a man, and he becomes an anointed king and eventually helps to drive the English out of France — although his masculinity is always questioned in the play. Shaw suggests that he is perhaps a homosexual who is very uncomfortable with the hypermasculine role which his society has planned for him as the dauphin and eventually the king of France. It is the liberated woman, the lesbian Joan, who makes a man of him.

We see this same type of character in what is arguably Shaw's last important play, *The Millionairess*— which once again had its premiere at the Burgtheater in Vienna in 1936 but was not staged in London until 1944. Once again it was the German-speaking world, and Shaw's German translator Trebitsch, who made him an international success as a playwright. Here Shaw presents us with the woman as entrepreneur, determined to get rich and hardly interested in being a typical woman of even the '30s but instead wanting to be free and rich — and she succeeds by the end, though she does marry the Egyptian doctor she has fallen in love with. What does it mean to be male? What does it mean to be female? These are issues that Shaw wrestled with for his entire life — and the homosexual implications of these very issues were also very subtly addressed as a gay subtext in many of his plays. Shaw was a revolutionary of the theater in many ways, including in terms of wanting to examine the issue of homosexuality. Was he himself a homosexual? I do not think there is enough evidence to prove that, though there is much more evidence of his heterosexuality and his sexual interest in women, but clearly as an intelligent and progressive thinker he would hardly have been satisfied with the Victorian theories and taboos on the issue. The gay subtext of many of his plays proves that he was an enlightened social thinker, even on this pressing but quietly avoided issue of his times. Shaw's willingness to examine, even if by an oblique approach through subtext, the difficult issue of homosexuality perhaps helped him to be awarded the Nobel Prize for Literature in 1925.

There is a gay subtext to many of Shaw's plays, and that subject indicates his awareness of the neurosis of closeted homosexuality, and his sympathy for people who were forced to live dishonest and thwarted lives thanks to the stupidity of English laws of the nineteenth and most of the twentieth centuries. The concepts of masculinity and femininity which he absorbed from the Victorian culture of his youth clearly made him uncomfortable and left him questioning these complex issues in non-stereotypical ways which prefigure the gay liberation movement of the end of the twentieth century. Shaw's thinking remained consistently progressive, and he clearly dramatized in his plays that human realities about gender roles were much more complicated and flexible than the rigidity of British Victorian laws allowed. Neurosis, Shaw suggests, results from human beings forced into rigid sexual roles when human realities remain complicated and flexible.

Shaw clearly presents in his plays the madness of the Victorian view of rigid sexual roles for people. He states that people and social realities are much more complicated and that the really interesting people are the masculine women and the effeminate men.

Bibliography

Berst, Charles. *George Bernard Shaw and the Art of Drama.* Urbana, Ill: University of Illinois Press, 1973.

Davis, Tracy. *George Bernard Shaw and the Socialist Theatre.* Westport, Conn.: Greenwood Press, 1994.

Gainor, J. Ellen. *Shaw's Daughters: Dramatic and Narrative Constructions of Gender.* Ann Arbor: University of Michigan Press, 1991.

Gordon, David J. *Bernard Shaw and the Comic Sublime.* New York: St. Martin's Press, 1990.

Holroyd, Michael. *Bernard Shaw.* 3 vols. New York: Vintage, 1993.

Innes, Christopher, ed. *The Cambridge Companion to George Bernard Shaw.* Cambridge: Cambridge University Press, 1998.

Leary, Daniel. *Shaw's Plays in Performance.* University Park: Pennsylvania State University Press, 1983.

Meisel, Martin. *Shaw and the Nineteenth Century Theater.* Princeton, N.J.: Princeton University Press, 1962.

Mencken, H. L. *George Bernard Shaw: His Plays.* New Rochelle, N.Y.: E. V. Glaser, 1959.

Morash, Christopher. *A History of Irish Theater: 1601— 2000.* Cambridge: Cambridge University Press, 2002.

Peters, Sally. *Bernard Shaw: The Ascent of the Superman.* New Haven, Conn.: Yale University Press, 1996.

Reynolds, Jean. *Pygmalion's Wordplay: The Postmodern Shaw.* Gainesville: University Press of Florida, 1999.

Shaw, Bernard. *Bernard Shaw and Alfred Douglas: A Correspondence.* London: J. Murray, 1982.

Silver, Arnold. *Bernard Shaw: The Darker Side.* Stanford, Calif.: Stanford University Press, 1982.

Smith, Warren Sylvester. *Bishop of Everywhere: Bernard Shaw and The Life Force.* University Park: Pennsylvania State University Press, 1982.

Sternlicht, Sanford *A Reader's Guide to Modern British Drama.* Syracuse: Syracuse University Press, 2004.

_____. *A Reader's Guide to Modern Irish Drama.* Syracuse: Syracuse University Press, 1998.

Turco, Alfred. *Shaw's Moral Vision: The Self and Salvation.* Ithaca, N.Y.: Cornell University Press, 1975.

Valency, Maurice. *The Cart and the Trumpet: The Plays of George Bernard Shaw.* New York: Oxford University Press, 1973.

Weintraub, Rodelle, ed. *Fabian Feminist: Bernard Shaw and Women.* University Park: Pennsylvania State University Press, 1977.

Whitman, Robert F. *Shaw and the Play of Ideas.* Ithaca, N.Y.: Cornell University Press, 1977.

2

Luigi Pirandello

Schizophrenia

Schizophrenia was an immediate reality for Luigi Pirandello because he lived with a schizophrenic woman, his wife, Antonietta Portulano Pirandello, for most of his adult life. Even before this, while the playwright was still living at home with his parents, his sister went insane for a time and had to be put in an asylum; here too the illness was probably schizophrenia. Pirandello's daughter Lietta also had to be institutionalized for a period because of schizophrenia, so clearly there was a family pattern of severe mental problems. But Pirandello's most prolonged exposure to living with a person with severe mental problems came from his wife Antonietta, who was eventually diagnosed as a paranoid schizophrenic. Before then she and Pirandello endured a hellish family situation. He was often the victim of her accusations and hallucinations; at one point she even accused him of having an affair with their daughter Lietta, which almost drove the daughter to commit suicide.

Pirandello used the trauma he experienced with his wife and with his own family for his theater — writers, unlike the rest of us, do not waste their traumas (or other people's) on mere suffering but turn them into literature. Normal people suffer from these mental problem, but writers can turn them into gold. In Woody Allen's film *Deconstructing Harry,* the main character is a writer; one of his friends pulls a gun on him and accuses him of using all her misery in his new book, and he of course is guilty. The conflict between what is real and what is a hallucination, which is so much a part of the life of a schizophrenic, can be experienced by the rest of humanity as well. We have all had experiences which afterwards we realize did not really happen but were night dreams, day dreams, or fantasies. Pirandello uses this very schizophrenic problem in his plays *Six Characters in Search of an Author, Henry IV, Right You Are (If You Think You Are), As You Desire Me, and* other works. In all these plays, the problems of schizophrenia are presented in terms of the realities of everyday lives — lives we all live as allegedly normal people. What really happened during a particularly traumatic situation? Can we ever be sure of what really happened during that traumatic event or is what we think happened merely a product of our fevered imagination and fantasy life — fevered by the stress of the particular situation, or the stress of living with a particular family?

Very early in his life, and through much of his adulthood, Pirandello had the experience of dealing with schizophrenia within his own family, so he very soon knew what it was like to experience life through the schizophrenic mind — and that mind very early imposed itself on his own personal experiences within family life. In June of 1919 Antonietta Pirandello was sent to a mental institution and she died there thirty years later, but her insane hallucations and accusations had a lasting and traumatic effect upon her family, especially her husband.

Even before Pirandello started writing plays, he indicated an interest in the schizophrenic fantasy of a dual personality. His first major literary success, *The Late Mattia Pascal,* appeared in 1904 and became a comic masterpiece which gave Pirandello his first experience with international recognition. In that novel, the main character, Mattia Pascal, has a dual personality by the end of the comic novel. He returns home after a long time to find that his wife has announced his death and married someone else. He feels he has no choice but to avoid disturbing her new family so he attends to his grave and becomes another Mattia Pascal, referring to his earlier self as the Late Mattia Pascal. So who is the real Mattia Pascal? Pirandello ends this comic masterpiece with this comic question revolving around his main character's dual identity. Pirandello wrote this novel before he became so interested in theater and the writing of plays, but once that happened after World War I he immediately addressed the very same theme in a major way in his plays of that period.

In one of his first major successes, *Così è se vi pare (Right You Are If You Think So)*, we are immediately confronted with a family in confusion, especially confusion of its female members. There is a serious conflict between the woman known as the wife and her mother. What really happened? Mrs. Frola complains to her neighbors that she is not allowed to see her daughter, and we (and all the town gossips) wonder why this is the case. Why would a husband forbid his wife to visit her own mother? The townspeople in the play are clearly looking for some juicy gossip in this situation and find it, though they eventually discover that the situation is more complicated than they thought it would be.

By the last act of the play the husband, Signor Ponza, appears and complicates the situation even further. In the final scene of the play the daughter,

Signora Ponza, finally appears and complicates the situation more and adds even more confusion instead of clarifying things. By the end of the play, we are still confused about what really happened between these three characters. They clearly have completely different views of what happened — and by the end of the play we see all the characters defend the validity of their view with the most moving sincerity. One possible conclusion is that one of the three is schizophrenic and has fantasized or fabricated a reality that does not exist. Ultimately the play seems to suggest that life is essentially schizophrenic since everyone's reality is very real for that person and there is no such thing as an objective reality. Philosophically this becomes a particularly speculative view called solipsism — that objective reality is a fantasy and only one's individual reality is real, and by implication the schizophrenic's view of reality is just as real as anybody else's view. Or perhaps in a way we are all schizophrenic since we believe very sincerely in our perception of reality, but that perception is true only for us and certainly not for others. There is simply no objective reality outside the perception of one (and anyone's) individual mind. The play ends with the cynical laughter of Laudisi, the skeptical character who suggests that we can never know the truth since there is no objective "truth" out there. Laudisi laughs at the end, but what he is laughing about remains confusing as well — is it a sadly ironic laughter to a situation that is ultimately tragic? Of course the quality of that final laughter all depends on the actor who is doing the laughing, but Pirandello has certainly provided a situation fraught with both tragedy and comedy. Laudisi has often been called Pirandello's *raisonneur,* the most rational and yet the most cynical of characters. The *raisonneur* character remained isolated from the others, and his final laughs suggests all our attempts to get at the "truth" are doomed since there is no single truth but many of them, all from differing points of view, and all equally valid.

The play also makes fun of the comic townspeople who are so nosey about their neighbors' lives. They all seem to love gossip and trying to peek into other people's lives. In the midst of all the fun of gossip there is also the cynical observer Laudisi, who maintains a distance from all the other characters and is skeptical about both their motivation and their success in their attempts to find out the truth, and he suggests at the end of the play that finding out the "truth" is never really possible.

When *Six Characters in Search of an Author* premiered in Rome in 1921 many members of the audience, according to the reviews, thought that the play was the product of a lunatic. Several of the reviews stated that the play resembled nothing so much as a lunatic's view of reality staged in a lunatic asylum. Such a reaction was understandable given the innovative nature of

Six Characters in Search of an Author, American Repertory Theater, 1988; Pamela Glen as Step-Daughter, Priscilla Smith as Mother, Matthew Dundas as Little Boy, Dana Kelly as Little Girl and Alvin Epstein as Father (photograph: Richard Feldman).

this completely new form of experimental theater. The play begins as an apparent rehearsal of an older play by Pirandello (*Il Giuoco delle Parti*), and then all of a sudden six apparently insane or fantasized characters appear and ask for an author to write their play rather than the one the actors are rehearsing.

Such a lunatic situation can easily be seen as a schizophrenic fantasy. Schizophrenia is characterized by visual and auditory illusions — schizophrenic patients often complain of having auditory and visual fantasies, of voices telling them what to do. Such patients often report hearing voices from God or the president or the pope giving them orders. Pirandello's six characters — only four of whom actually speak, the two children being silent since they are "dead" during the time of the play — can easily be seen as products of a schizophrenic's fantasy life. Perhaps they are voices that Pirandello's wife heard — they are the imaginary wife and family which she often accused him to having, and of being unfaithful to her with. She often accused him of sleeping with other women — even his female students at the school he taught at in addition to their own daughter. Until she was finally hospitalized in

1919, she made his life a misery with all of her accusations of sexual infidelity. In addition, Pirandello often commented that when he was working on a play or a short story or novel he had the fantasy that the characters would appear in his study and demand that he tell their story so that they could live, and such an encounter with imaginary people could easily seem like his wife's schizophrenic delusions — or even his own. Such an imaginary situation could also be seen as schizophrenia on Pirandello's part since clearly these literary characters did not actually exist — depending on how "existence" is defined. If we have had similar experiences, does that mean that we are all schizophrenic, or have schizophrenic episodes? Perhaps. We have all had periods in our life when we had visual fantasies which we realized afterwards were only dreams or fantasies rather than reality.

Pirandello's next great play, *Henry IV*, also involves a mental patient. Henry IV seems to be living in a delusion of believing himself to be the historical Henry IV — often schizophrenic patients think they are Jesus or Moses or some other famous historical figure. But as the play progresses, the character of Henry IV reveals to his warders, who are costumed in period attire to aid his fantasized life, that he has been cured and that he knows that the situation is all a masquerade and that he knows he is not really the medieval king. But of course, after a while the audience cannot be sure if this is true

Henry IV, Shaw Festival, Ontario, 1991; Matthew Henry, Tony Munch and Peter Krantz as guards and David Schurmann as Henry IV.

Henry IV, 1948; Ian Keith in the title role; Brattle Theater, Boston.

or if the character is pretending to be sane to connect with and manipulate his warders and family members. One of the fascinating aspects of a Pirandello play is the confusion of what is happening — is the character insane or pretending to be insane? Of course Shakespeare does this very thing with his character

Hamlet — is he insane or merely pretending to be insane? The audience remains unsure for much of the play, clearly as intended by the playwright.

The play also presents the theme of role-playing, for if Henry IV is not insane, as he insists, he is playing the role of an insane person for a while. His role-playing becomes a method of survival for him, but of course the question is when does he become insane and when sane, and when is he playing the role of an insane person and when is he sane, if ever. Clearly the commedia dell'arte tradition of improvisation and role-playing is central to *Henry IV* since at times the character seems to be improvising to his warders.

As You Desire Me, one of Pirandello's late plays, also deals with the confusion between differing views of reality. The play was first staged in 1930, six years before the playwright's death and four years before he won the Nobel Prize. The play was clearly written for his current sexual obsession, the actress Marta Abba. Is the main character who she says she is or is she only pretending to be that character in order to achieve a position in a prominent family with much wealth? Or is she just trying to please the people around her by humoring their fantasies? The main character, called "L'Ignota," or the unknown woman, is a cabaret singer in Berlin in the first act but the lost member of a wealthy Italian family in the second act. Is she the family's long lost relative (lost because of World War I) or is she a fraud who is claiming membership in this prominent family because of its wealth and social status? Is she really Italian or a German fraud who happens to be fluent in Italian? Pirandello maintains the confusion in the hope of keeping the audience confused and fascinated with his play of complicated ideas. Even the woman's husband remains unsure if his long lost wife has finally returned to him or whether he is being fooled by a fraudulent social bounder. Pirandello certainly had a genius for turning profound philosophical ideas into exciting theater — not many playwrights can deal with philosophy in such a theatrically vibrant way. Audiences do not want philosophical lectures when they go to the theater, but that is precisely what Pirandello does not do.

Role-playing remains central to this play as well since L'Ignota seems to be playing a role, but which role? She seems to be improvising in the second act when she seems to be trying to make the people around her happy. Or is she role-playing in the first act when she is the cabaret singer in Berlin and really yearning to go back to her home in Italy? Here again the commedia dell'arte tradition of role-playing is used by Pirandello to indicate the confusion of our own reality — and the characters' realities in this play.

Pirandello became fascinated with the new invention of talking films in the '30s and attempted in both Germany and America to write for this new medium. One of his few successes was *As You Desire Me*, with Greta Garbo in the lead, though Pirandello did not direct the film himself. This film succeeded admirably in presenting Pirandello on film and with dialogue to an international audience. Pirandello kept trying to repeat this success with other films, but most of his other projects were doomed to failure since film then as now involves many powerful people in various fields and very large budgets.

Ultimately, Pirandello is asking the profound philosophical question of what reality is in *As You Desire Me.* Is the solipsist right, that we cannot be sure of what reality is because we all have our own voices and all hear what we think is the truth but may not be the truth? Are we all ultimately trapped in our own vision of reality which may or may not be reality? Does the schizophrenic experience an extreme version of what reality is really like? Is this an extreme form of solipsism — that we all hear our own voices and we all have our own version of the truth, but there is no such thing as an objective reality because of the power of those personal and individual voices which seem very real to each of us?

But the father in *Six Characters in Search of an Author* is also right when he says that the basic problem is words. We use them all the time in attempting to communicate with each other, but really important words have very different meanings for each of us. The various meanings and associations that we can have for especially charged words like "mother" and "father" and "daughter" complicate our attempts to communicate — Pirandello suggests — and perhaps also make real communication ultimately impossible. We all have a particularly psychological association with highly charged words, and that makes our whole response to those words charged with psychological realities which are unique to us and very different for other people. That reality, Pirandello suggests, makes communication virtually impossible on highly charged topics. We should not forget that the complexities of language and communication were early interests of this playwright. After all, Pirandello wrote his doctoral dissertation at the University of Bonn on the dialect of his home town, Agrigento, and his training at the University of Bonn included studies on the complex nature of language. In his dissertation, Pirandello wrote of the differences between the language of Agrigento and the rest of Italy, and those very differences suggest psychological realities for the speakers of the various languages and dialects under analysis.

Given the experimental nature of Pirandello's innovative theater, he himself was repeatedly accused of insanity. His was called the theater of the insane, but his theater could just as easily be seen as an early version of surrealism — a dream theater, reflecting Freud's theories about dreams and their relationship to the subconscious mind of the dreamer. In either a day dream or a night dream, the reality of the dreaming mind remains very powerful and seems disturbingly real. But it is a reality or only a dream? And "only a dream" perhaps too easily dismisses the power of our dream life. André Breton, in his famous Surrealist Manifesto, called for a new art—a new form of theater—which used Freud's *On the Interpretation of Dreams* to present us with the psychological realities of our dream life, which were the most important realities in our personal existences.

One can also see Pirandello's theater as an early product of existentialism — the dreaming mind can be seen as attempting to assert itself and connect with God. Kierkegaard's essays were available to most of Europe by the early part of the 20th century, and Pirandello certainly read Kierkegaard; several critics have noted how the plays reflect the philosophy of existentialism. Kierkegaard's brand of Christian existentialism was centrally concerned with the human being's efforts to connect with and communicate with God—who never responds to us. One possible view of Pirandello's Six Characters is as a metaphor for man's attempt to connect with God—we are all characters looking for an author, and that author is God. And just as the search of Pirandello's Six Characters is doomed to frustration and failure, so are we all doomed in our own searches for fulfillment? A theological interpretation is possible for this play, whether it be the Christian existentialist attempt to communicate with God or the ancient Sicilian gods and their foundations in ancient Greek theology, with their gods on Mount Olympus and attempting to influence human endeavors for their own purposes rather than the purposes of the human beings suffering on this planet. There are ancient Greek amphitheaters in Sicily, and some of Pirandello's theatrical innovations connect in a significant way with ancient Greek tragedy.

One of the many things which Pirandello is suggesting in his theater is that the schizophrenic's complex view of a complicated reality has become an insight into the reality of our own lives. "Objectivity" is the fantasy and what is real is what we think is real. In such a complicated and confusing world, one of the realities is human suffering and desperation in trying to cope and survive in such a complicated situation as real life. It is certainly understandable that human beings would appeal to God for help in the midst of such confusion, but the existential God in Pirandello's world never responds to us. Sigmund Freud would argue that there is no God; this became central to the thought of atheistical existentialism after World War II in the writings of people like Sartre and Camus. Pirandello's plays attempt to connect the schizophrenic view of the world with modern philosophical thought—not to mention exciting contemporary theater. His efforts resulted in his winning the Nobel Prize for literature in 1934, two years before his death, but his plays continue to fascinate because of the brilliance of his insights and the quality of his writing. That for a while Pirandello became a fascist and a defender of Mussolini (but only for a while) adds to the complex human and theatrical reality that was the playwright Luigi Pirandello.

But at the core of Pirandello's complex vision of reality and contemporary theater is the schizophrenic view of a fragmented reality, one that isolates Pirandello's characters from each other and makes communication ultimately impossible. He learned of that reality having to deal with the schizophrenia within his own family, particularly the tragic suffering of his own wife Antonietta, and her suffering became the basis of his own unique form of revolutionary new theater.

Schizophrenia becomes, then, a metaphor for Pirandello's complex view of reality — a kind of complex cubism with fragmentation as an image of a reality which varies with every person and communication often impossible because of the complex nature of reality and the complex nature of words and language, those messy tools which we are doomed to use in our attempts to communicate with each other. The schizophrenic becomes, in Pirandello's view, an extreme example of our own attempts to understand the nature of reality.

Our attempts to communicate with each other — and perhaps even with God — are frustrated and doomed to failure because of the complex nature of language and also because of the complex nature of human reality. Pirandello often presents people as trapped in their own futile attempts to communicate with other people, but communication rarely actually occurs because of the schizophrenic view of reality which Pirandello presents as our own reality. That those philosophical complexities can be mixed with political realities is apparent in Pirandello's own obsession with Mussolini, though this did not last very long in his long and distinguished literary career.

Bibliography

Barbina, Alfredo. *La Biblioteca di Luigi Pirandello.* Rome: Bulzoni Editore, 1980.

Bassnett, Susan, and Jennifer Lorch, eds. *Luigi Pirandello in the Theatre: A Documentary Record.* Switzerland: Harwood Academic Publishers, 1993.

Bassnett-McGuire, Susan. *Luigi Pirandello.* New York: Grove Press, 1983.

Bentley, Eric. *The Pirandello Commentaries.* Evanston, Ill.: Northwestern University Press, 1986.

Bini, Daniele. *Pirandello and His Muse: The Plays for Marta Abba.* Gainsville: University Press of Florida, 1998.

Bloom, Harold, ed. *Luigi Pirandello.* New York: Chelsea House, 1989.

Cambon, Glauco, ed. *Pirandello: A Collection of Critical Essays.* Englewood Cliffs, N.J.: Prentice-Hall, 1967.

Caputi, Anthony. *Pirandello and the Crisis of Modern Consciousness.* Urbana: University of Illinois Press, 1988.

Cometa, Michele. *Il Teatro di Pirandello in Germania.* Palermo: Novecento, 1986.

DiGaetani, John Louis, ed. *A Companion to Pirandello Studies.* New York: Greenwood Press, 1991.

First, Michael B., et al. *Diagnostic Criteria from DSM-IV-TR. Diagnostic and Statistical Manual of Mental Disorders.* Arlington, Va.: American Psychiatric Association, 2005.

Giudice, Gaspare. *Pirandello: A Biography.* Trans. A. Hamilton. London: Oxford University Press, 1975.

Matthaei, Renate. *Luigi Pirandello.* Trans. Simon and Erike Young. New York: Frederick Ungar, 1973.

Mignone, Mario, ed. *Pirandello in America.* Rome: Bulzoni, 1988.

Milioto, Stefano, ed. *Le Donne in Pirandello.* Agrigento: Edizioni del Centro di Studi Pirandelliani, 1988.

Nichols, Nina DaVinci, and Jana O'Keefe Bazzoni. *Pirandello and Film.* Lincoln: University of Nebraska Press, 1995.

Paolucci, Anne. *Pirandello's Theater: The Recovery of the Stage for Modern Art.* Carbondale: Southern Illinois University Press, 1974.

Pennica, Gilda, ed. *Pirandello e la Germania.* Palermo: Palumbo, 1984.

Ragusa, Olga. *Pirandello: An Approach to His Theatre.* Edinburgh: Edinburgh University Press, 1980.

Zangrilli, Franco. *Pirandello: Le Maschere del "Vecchio Dio."* Padova: Edizioni Messaggero, 2002.

3

Noel Coward

Narcissism

Narcissus was one of the most self-obsessed of the characters from Greek mythology, and it is from him that we get the image of the self-obsessed personality who cannot really see any point of view but his own and who cannot tolerate criticism of any kind. The narcissistic personality, as a result, sees only its own point of view, and becomes enraged when anyone points this out. Criticism of any kind cannot be tolerated by this personality type and any form of criticism produces rage in the narcissist — a long, enduring rage. Needless to say, actors, playwrights, and people in the world of the theater — and artists in general — have become famous for this kind of reaction. Actors and actresses have often been accused of being narcissists, though their defenders say that this is the kind of personality that is needed to survive in the fantastic and highly competitive world of the theater. This personality type prospers as well outside the world of theater, but the Greek myth of Narcissus has an unhappy ending since the poor, deluded, self-obsessed boy ends up drowned. One of Coward's most popular songs was "Mad about the Boy," which perhaps contains a hint of the obsessive self-love of this personality type so rife in the theater.

This was the world Noel Coward lived in, and so he could witness narcissism first hand, and in fact he was sometimes accused of it himself. He was raised by parents who were themselves self-obsessed, especially his mother, who was theatrical herself and tried to push her son into theater while he was still a child; as a result, Coward often felt neglected as a child since his mother especially wanted him to perform rather than just be himself. But his mother also told him repeatedly how absolutely perfect he was as a child and how supremely talented and so needed to be onstage. And this kind of loneliness often absorbed him as a child. His father was a musical salesman, and often Coward did not see his father because he was off selling musical instruments;

Coward's father did not seem to influence him much as a child but his attachment to his mother was quite intense. As a result of his victimization by his sometimes narcissistic and very ambitious parents, he was a keen observer of the narcissistic personality type, and that type often enters his plays.

Joseph Morella and George Mazzei, in comparing Coward with Cole Porter, had much to say about the narcissism which Coward absorbed in his childhood:"Noel Coward was a precocious child. If Cole Porter's mother developed her son's talents through intense effort in leading him, Noel's mother followed her little boy's lead. Noel seemed to know what he wanted as soon as his baby eyes saw the world.... According to legend he kicked and screamed to be allowed to entertain.... He was a natural entertainer. He needed no special coaxing from Violet (his mother) to fulfill her fantasy of him being a specially talented little boy. He performed because he loved performing almost as much as he loved the attention and applause" (Morella and Mazzei 21–22).

And Coward performed very early in life as a child actor. As Morella and Mazzei report: "In the 1920s the press called Noel Destiny's Tot, and surely he was.... Noel showed acting and performing talent early; more importantly he had drive and ambition, unusual in a boy of ten.... Noel was a professional actor by age ten. He never was without the inner goading desire to get there. The tantrums of his youth now manifested themselves in a highly nervous personality. Part of his general nervousness was that he wanted to be a full-blown star right away and was achingly impatient to achieve this goal" (22).

Because he was always the center of attention at home, he soon showed the signs of narcissism that characterized his personality for his entire life. As these same authors commented: "Noel, the hysterical, nervous actor was also often the nervous person with people who understood him, encouraged him, because he'd react hysterically whenever he ran into the slightest hint from his company that he wasn't wonderful and right all the time. Like Cole Porter in Paris, Noel Coward too had assembled his family or nurturers. His own real family had become somewhat of a drain" (Morella and Mazzei 76–77).

One of his first successes in the theater was the play *Hay Fever*, which was first staged in London in 1925 in the West End, and then moved to Broadway later that year. This play is rather a *drame à clef*, since the play resulted from something he had experienced when he visited New York the previous year. His friend the actress Laurette Taylor invited him to stay with her and her family in their large house on Riverside Drive in New York. While he was there, he got to see a family of narcissists in action, beginning with the actress and including her husband, a writer, plus their young adult children, a son and daughter. This traumatic experience became the basis for *Hay Fever*, which succeeded admirably both in London and New York.

Hay Fever, 1985; Robert Joy, Mia Dillon, and Rosemary Harris (photograph: Martha Swope).

As Morella and Mazzei summarize the story: "Noel made friends ... with Laurette Taylor, her husband, Hartley Manners, and their unusual family.... Laurette's husband, Hartley Manners, was an extremely conservative man in such issues as religion, politics, and sexuality.... Laurette, very theatrical, never hesitated to unsheathe her scathing wit and uninhibited humor. The family liked to play parlor games and Dwight and Marguerite, children by Laurette's first husband, would frequently argue about game rules with their mother and step-father. These regular battles would result in all family members stalemating and retreating upstairs to their separate quarters.... Noel later said he churned out *Hay Fever* in three days" (71).

The play involves a British family, the ironically named Blisses. The mother, Judith Bliss, remains the most famous member of the family, a thoroughly self-absorbed actress who has just retired from the stage but is clearly planning a return to the stage, her only proper milieu. We see her at her angriest when her daughter Sorel tries to criticize her behavior, and her immediate response of rage indicates her inability to tolerate any kind of criticism — typical of the narcissistic personality. "Are you criticizing me!" Judith Bliss responds in horror when her daughter tries to comment negatively on her behavior. Judith's husband is a fairly successful novelist, David Bliss. Their son Simon draws and clearly wants to be an artist of some kind. Their daughter seems interested in writing, especially poetry. When act I of the play opens, the family, especially the mother and the two siblings, seem to be bickering with each other, but are basically loving to each other as well. From this family situation, Coward creates some truly hilarious comedy which adds to the pleasure of seeing this play.

As the various family members appear and discuss their various plans for the weekend, it soon transpires — to the vast amusement of the audience — that each of the four family members has invited a friend to visit the family on the weekend but not informed anyone of the invitation. So the family has to face putting up four weekend guests even though they have only one guest room. And to complicate the comic situation even further, each of them is clearly sexually interested in the guest he or she has invited. The possibilities of adultery in addition to the burden of four houseguests in one weekend clearly create the kind of comic situations that Coward was to become famous for. In the over fifty plays he wrote, designing and developing comic situations remained one of the characteristics of his genius.

Hay Fever, Broadway, 1985; Robert Joy, Deborah Ross, Mia Dillon, Roy Dotrice, Carolyn Seymour, Campbell Scott, and Rosemary Harris (photograph: Martha Swope).

In *Hay Fever*, the second act involves the arrival and the treatment of the weekend guests. It soon becomes apparent that the members of the Bliss family tend to treat their guests horribly, in addition to the lack of physical space for them in the house. It also rains the entire weekend, so they cannot avoid each other by going outside. On one level or another, all these guests are there to provide the individual members of the Bliss family with proof about their ability to attract the opposite sex, and clearly these guests are not liked particularly for themselves. Narcissists tend to use people for their own purposes, and we see this form of narcissism very clearly as the play progresses. Each of the family members becomes obsessed with another guest rather than the one he or she invited for the weekend, which adds to the irony and humor of the play.

The third act begins with each of the guests arriving onstage on Sunday morning with their luggage, eager to leave the Bliss house as soon as possible, and happy to be escaping with their lives. When it is reported, later in the act, to Judith Bliss that all the guests have left before the family awakened, her reaction is completely typical of the narcissistic personality. "How very rude!" she says. She sees herself as the victim of rudeness and in no way sees herself as in any way guilty of being a horrible hostess to her victimized guests.

But the play does have a happy ending (after all this is a Coward comedy), and each of the members of the Bliss family comes onstage and becomes engaged in his or her own artistic work — working on a novel, drawing, planning a play, etc. Clearly, Coward suggests, narcissistic types are essential in the arts, but murder on anyone around them. Though the Blisses are constantly bickering with each other in the final scene of the play, it is also apparent they have connected with each other in a familial way and support each others' artistic endeavors. They are producing art by the end of the play, and happily free at last of the guests they had invited earlier in the play.

Coward's next major success appeared in London in 1930, *Private Lives*, and it has remained his most popular play — staged more often that all his others. Even when Coward was out of popularity in the '60s, '70s, and '80s, *Private Lives* still appeared regularly on major stages in Britain and America. In this play we have the narcissistic couple. Noel Coward himself played the lead role, Elyot Chase, at its London premiere, with his favorite female partner, Gertrude Lawrence, playing the female lead role of Amanda. Laurence Olivier made his West End premiere in this play, as Coward's foil in the role of Victor Prynne. The same three appeared in the Broadway production in 1931, and both productions succeeded despite the Depression.

In this play, we see what happens when two narcissists marry. Before the play begins Elyot Chase had married Amanda; they had a tempestuous marriage which lasted several years, and then divorced. When *Private Lives* begins,

Elyot Chase is in a posh hotel on the French Riviera honeymooning with his second wife, Sybil. On the adjoining balcony, the audience discovers, is another honeymoon couple. There Amanda is also honeymooning with her second husband, Victor Prynne. The audience soon understands the comic situation and sees the two couples come onto the balcony overlooking the Mediterranean, and then going back to their rooms. The inevitable happens and Amanda comes on the balcony, only to discover her first husband Elyot on the other side of the balcony.

The awkwardness of the situation produces much comedy for the audience, and results in a shocking and amusing end for the first act: Elyot and Amanda run off together, leaving their respective new spouses alone to figure out what's happened. Elyot and Amanda's response seems completely narcissistic since they unceremoniously dump their new spouses on their honeymoons and run off together with their former spouses.

By the second act, and true to form, Elyot and Amanda seem madly in love, and not very guilty about how their treated their new spouses, and then

Private Lives, New York, 1983; Elizabeth Taylor and Richard Burton as Elyot and Amanda, the two narcissists of the play (photograph: Martha Swope).

Private Lives, **Broadway, 1948; Donald Cook as Elyot and Tallulah Bankhead as Amanda.**

have a horrendous fight. That they both dumped two new spouses on their honeymoons does not cause them much guilt. When Elyot brings this topic up, Amanda says, "Well, we left them a note. What more could they want." As they love each other, fight, and then reconcile with each other, the audience has the amusing perspective of watching two narcissistic people trying to live together. They are so obsessed with their own personalities that they can rarely see the effect of their self-absorption on the person they are living with. Also, true to the narcissistic type, neither can endure any kind of criticism, so that when one tries to point out the narcissism of the other, this produces the classic narcissistic rage. Any criticism is experienced as totally devastating and produces blinding rage, and then we see their hilarious battles. Coward seems also to be suggesting here how love and hate come together, though this becomes particularly dramatic when it is the narcissist who is in love.

By the end of the play, Elyot and Amanda come back together again, and their discarded mates, Victor and Sybil, are screaming at each other —

suggesting that they have fallen in love with each other. On the one hand the play suggests that love and hate are inevitably mixed, but the play also suggests that when this mixture occurs in narcissists it produces a special volatility. The play also suggests in a sly way that we are all essentially narcissistic and that love plays on all our needs as well as all our insecurities, producing the kind of love and hate which Freud describes as a result of the disappointment which love inevitably produces in the mind of the person in love. The love object can never become the fantasized perfect mate we all fantasize about, and that disappointment inevitably produces anger and even rage.

Coward's next major success, *Blithe Spirit*, appeared in 1941 and succeeded both in London and at its Broadway premiere. Coward's genius for comic situations is especially apparent in this play, where a man and his wife are unhappily invaded by the ghost of his first wife, who died seven years earlier. Charles and Ruth Condomine appear happily married in the first act, though we can immediately see some tensions in their relationship. Charles is a novelist who is working on a novel about spiritualism, and to get the right jargon, and also as a joke, he invites the local medium, Madame Arcati, to come and stage a séance. But the joke turns out to be on Charles since the séance produces the ghost of Charles's first wife, Elvira. While the medium, Madame Arcati, is delighted with her success in causing the appearance of a ghost, that ghost creates havoc in Charles's current marriage.

Elvira turns out to be the typical Coward narcissist, who wants to possess Charles totally, despite the fact that he has married a second wife, Ruth, after Elvira's death. With typical narcissistic grace, Elvira is plotting to kill Charles, so she can totally possess him again in the afterlife, just as she possessed and obsessed and maddened him while she was alive and they were married. Imagine her horror when she discovers that her plotting results in the death of Ruth, her rival and Charles's second wife, instead of the death of Charles. So the two women can spend an eternity fighting each other.

As the two ghostly wives battle it out, Charles leaves both of them and the house — to start a new life away from narcissistic women like Elvira. The play has a misogynist ending, suggesting that men are better off without selfish and self-obsessed women. Here it is the women who appear narcissistic rather than the male, Charles Condomine, who can achieve individual liberty at the end only by dumping both his wives, who are now feuding ghosts. But the overall effect of the play remains clearly comic since Coward, as he said repeatedly, had "a talent to amuse."

This play proved to be Coward's last major success for a long while since after World War II and the blitz, the English were tired of Coward's wealthy narcissists. Playwrights like John Osborne, Samuel Beckett, and Harold Pinter found greater favor in the postwar period. But Coward was not through yet as a playwright and did have some other successes.

After the war New York had still not tired of Coward's wealthy eccentrics. In 1946 his *Present Laughter* premiered in New York at the Plymouth Theater on Broadway and did rather well. In this play, Coward presents us with the narcissist par excellence: the actor Garry Essendine. This play had a very successful revival on Broadway in the 1990s with Frank Langella playing a very funny Garry Essendine. And in that production the actor was surrounded by a bevy of adoring "family"—not real family members but friends and employees of the actor who are there to nurture and admire the narcissistic actor. That Coward could spoof his own family arrangement and his own group of adoring employees and friends says much about his ability to own objective correlative—his own ability to distance himself enough from himself to see how the outside world must have seen this arrangement. Coward clearly had an ability to laugh at himself—part of his "talent to amuse," as he said of his abilities.

Actors are notorious narcissists, and Garry Essendine becomes the classic narcissist actor. There are hidden mirrors all over the set since the action is repeatedly interrupted as Garry checks his hair and overall appearance. He also lies about his age repeatedly and likes to be surrounded by admirers. Since he is a very successful actor, admiring actors, actresses, and budding playwrights are constantly turning up to seek his favors. The play was clearly based on Coward himself and the "family" around him who were his employees and helped him manage his wildly successful career. Coward began as a desperately poor actor in London and within five years had an international career that included acting, singing, writing plays, and even performing as a cabaret singer in Las Vegas and other cities around the world. He died in Jamaica after a wildly successful career.

Surrounded as he is by a former wife, a doting secretary, numerous female admirers, an agent, a lawyer, and numerous friends, Garry Essendine remains for most of the play surrounded by the kind of admiration that makes narcissists ecstatic. In this wonderfully comic play, Coward clearly enjoys spoofing the typical narcissistic actor, much to the delight of the audience. On some level, Coward may well have been spoofing himself, for as a hugely successful actor and playwright, he must surely have had a healthy share of narcissism himself. Yet Coward was consistently capable of enough self-analysis to be able to see objectively how much of the outside world saw him. His biographers report on his pounding his fists on his furniture in rage if something did not go the way he wanted.

In *Relative Values* of 1951 Coward looks at the narcissistic actress. While the play was not a major success at its premiere in London, it did run for several months. By then Coward was out of fashion, but the play now deserves a new look and a new production. The clever situation in this play, something Coward was such a master of, involves a Hollywood actress who is about to marry a British earl. When he brings her home to meet his family at the family estate, she is horrified to discover that her sister is a maid in the family. Coward creates wonderfully comic situations as the actress, Miranda Frayle, tries to keep the family from realizing that she is actually British rather than American. Her sister, the maid Moxie, is horrified at the prospect of having her detested and long-lost sister as her new boss.

What ensues in a clever examination of the narcissistic Hollywood actress and her determination to lie about her humble roots as she is introduced into upper-class British society. Coward clearly indicates something about the narcissistic personality's determination to maintain an illusion of an aristocratic background despite the realities of actual family life. Coward also indicates something about the rigidity of English society and its suspicion of foreigners, especially Americans, who do not fit easily into their preconceived notions of class.

While Coward was the most popular playwright in London in the late '20s, '30s, and '40s, after World War II he was increasingly booed on the London stage, and one after another of his plays flopped there — though some of these were successfully revived at the end of the 20th century. Mazzola and Mazzei report on the audience reaction after the premiere of Coward's play *Sirocco*: "By the time *Sirocco* opened Noel had already staged several flops; some were plays he'd written years before.... The final curtain at *Sirocco* brought catcalls and hisses from the audiences.... Noel made the mistake of going out for the usual author's ovation and was greeted by silence. 'We expected better,' someone called out. 'So did I,' Noel answered, maintaining his posture. He meant of course that he expected better from the audience.... This disaster put Noel's ego on the line. He was filled with self-doubt, depression, and a nagging worry that the press was right — maybe he was indeed a flash in the pan..." (103–104).

Clearly Coward's reaction was that of a typical narcissist — any criticism is accepted as total rejection and produces depression and self-doubt. Coward could not see criticism within the scope of his entire career and all the success he had had before this particular play flopped but instead saw criticism as totally devastating.

Coward was increasingly dismissed by the post–World War II generation as being a playwright of the wealthy. He was sensitive to that charge and tried to address this repeated criticism in his play *Waiting in the Wings*, which premiered in London in 1960. Here we have a household full of narcissists, although presented in dismal circumstances. This play is about a charity home for retired actresses who are too poor and too frail to live on their own. In this play, about the grinding and humiliating poverty of the failures in the acting profession — the people who did not become stars, but scraped a living and did not have enough to save for their old age — Coward confronts the uglier realities of a life in the theater. As the playwright Robert Anderson once said, "In the theater you can make a killing, but not a living." Coward was one of the few lucky ones who made many killings and became a very wealthy man, but that happens to about 1 percent of the people who are working in the theater.

As Coward presents his group of old actresses, they are as narcissistic as the stars, but without the success and the money that theatrical fame can bring. And as Coward presents it, *Waiting in the Wings* is a fascinating study of how these old narcissists learn to live with each other, and also learn how to face death. Several of the actresses die in the play, and these egocentric characters bond together and form a group to try to comfort and even entertain each other. What is waiting in the wings, of course, is death.

One of Coward's last successes as a playwright was surely *A Song at Twilight*, which opened in London in 1966 and later that same year in New York. Here Coward deals with the narcissistic author in the person of Sir Hugo Latymer. This play provides the only example in Coward's opus of many plays in which the subject of homosexuality comes up. Some have accused Coward of being duplicitous about his own homosexuality, but he would have said in his own defense that all the theater professionals around him knew about his sexuality, including his great co-star Gertrude Lawrence. Coward would have also reminded present-day readers that he could have been put in jail if he had been honest about his own sexuality before the British laws concerning homosexuality changed in the '60s.

In *A Song at Twilight* Coward has created yet another wonderfully theatrical situation: a famous and very pompous author has written his memoirs and created the illusion that he is heterosexual. In fact, during the play, he is married to her third, German wife Hilde. But Carlotta Gray, actress and former lover of Sir Hugo, enters early in the play to have dinner with him and without his wife. She is now a failed and aged actress who wants to write her own memoirs, and she wants to include his love letters to her since they had an affair. He pompously refuses to give permission for their publication, and she then responds that she has in her possession a group of love letters to a former male lover of his which prove that he is gay or at least bisexual. She offers to give him these gay love letters if he will give her permission to publish his letters to her.

At the time, the critics argued that Sir Hugo Latymer was actually based in the British novelist Somerset Maugham, who was married but a closeted gay man, though he eventually became honest to his friends about his sexuality. Coward clearly enjoys presenting us with the typically narcissistic successful author — pompous, authoritarian, treating others (especially his current wife) very badly, yet wanting to create a benign edifice of himself for the public to worship. But the clever actress Carlotta Gray outsmarts him by the end, and the audience gets to see some of the uglier consequences of narcissism as the author becomes more and more insufferable and pompous as the play progresses. This late play is surprisingly serious coming from a playwright famous for comedy rather than serious drama.

After Coward died, a group of his friends put together a play called *Star Quality*, which play Coward never wrote. He did write a wonderful story with that title, and that story was altered and became the play *Star Quality*. Here we have the typical narcissistic Coward situation. A group of producers and a director need a star with star quality for their new play. They get one, but true to Cowardly form, she is the classic Coward narcissist, although also an undoubted star who can mesmerize and fascinate an audience with ease. The play then shows how a savvy director has to handle the narcissistic star in order to get the show onstage, where it becomes a hit. Since Coward both acted and directed, in addition of course to writing plays, he knew first hand the special problems of handling narcissistic stars to get them to perform successfully and turn his own dream, his own play, into a theatrical success.

Clearly Coward knew first hand about the narcissistic personality, and he examined its various facets and manifestations in several of his own important plays, covering his entire career as a playwright — from the '20s to the '60s. And on a more basic level, Coward used his plays to examine himself with the insight and wit of a master entertainer. As he often said, he had a talent to amuse. But that talent included an ability to analyze a form of madness. While many narcissists end up alone and disliked, that did not happen to Noel Coward himself. He was able to distance himself enough from his own narcissism to endure some criticism — if tactfully expressed — and so develop permanent relationships with others. He had a circle of close friends and admirers, often gay men, who in effect became his family. One of the things that saved Coward from the isolation that narcissism can produce is that he himself knew of his own narcissism and tried to compensate and correct it so that he could relate successfully to other people.

But as his principal biographer Philip Hoare said of Coward: "His selfishness would approach megalomania, born of early success and an artificial life within the theatre. 'He was a vain man,' Rebecca West said. 'He talked constantly about himself, thought about himself, catalogued his achievements, evaluated them, presented to listeners such conclusions as were favourable, and expected, and waited for applause.' (Though she added, 'His sensitivity knew this and was shocked, and he regularly rough-housed his own vanity by considering himself in a ridiculous light. This he did for the good of his soul.') That Coward could not countenance opposition is well-attested, and a vicious instinct for revenge was apparent in his black list and its victims. Age did not assuage this ill-temper, and as the Twenties and Thirties gave way to a less certain future, these characteristics assumed greater importance" (Hoare 272–73).

It says much about his talents as a playwright that he could distance himself enough from his own narcissism to satirize it in his plays. He probably felt that actors had to be narcissists to survive in such a highly competitive and brutal business as the theater, but they made themselves unlikable and sometimes even ridiculous in the process. But not only artists are narcissists — even those without artistic talent can suffer from this personality disorder. Most narcissists, in fact, are not artists, but a high percentage of artists have the narcissistic personality and that in some ways enables them to produce art but in other ways makes them insufferable to other people. Not many people can stand being around narcissists, since they cannot relate to any needs but their own and cannot tolerate any criticism, which produces years of rage.

Coward also suggests something about the kind of narcissism which wealth can produce. He had very wealthy friends himself, including members of the royal family, and since he himself came from a poor background, he quickly discerned the kind of self-obsession which wealthy people can become addicted to. Once money is no object, they can easily see only themselves and their own needs. Another suggestion in Coward's plays is that in a way we are all self-obsessed — that the narcissists are extreme versions of us all. Maybe that self-obsession is a necessary survival skill, though clearly a survival skill which can be very off-putting to other people, and that very skill can also produce some wonderful comedy — at least when in the hands of a genius like Noel Coward.

Bibliography

Coward, Noel. *Autobiography* (consisting of *Present Indicative, Future Indefinite,* and the uncompleted *Past Conditional*). London: Methuen, 1986.
Day, Barry. *Coward on Film: The Cinema of Noël Coward*. Lanham, Md.: Scarecrow Press, 2005.

Hoare, Philip. *Noel Coward: A Biography.* London: Sinclair-Stevenson, 1995.
Morella, Joseph, and George Mazzei. *Genius and Lust: The Creative and Sexual Lives of Noel Coward and Cole Porter.* New York: Caroll and Graf, 1995.
Payn, Graham. *My Life with Noel Coward.* New York: Applause, 1994.
Payn, Graham, and Sheridan Morley, eds. *The Noel Coward Diaries.* London: Weidenfeld and Nicholson, 1982.

4

Samuel Beckett

Decadence and the Suicidal Impulse

As Richard Wagner lay dead in Venice in February of 1883, his influence continued especially strongly in literature all over Europe, even extending to Samuel Beckett. Today, Wagner is generally credited as one of the founders of the Decadent and Symbolist movements in European literature, which reached a high tide of popularity in the 1880s, 1890s, and around the turn of the century, although Wagner continued to exert his influence well into the middle of the twentieth century, and even afterwards. Wagnerian allusions and Wagnerian themes often occur in Decadent literature, especially the themes of death and suicide. A group of European writers at the time saw Wagner as the avant-garde artist who led by pointing to the inevitability of suicide, and they saw to it that his themes and literary techniques appeared often in their writings. The suicidal impulse became glorified in a school of literature which became known as the Decadents — they were called decadent, I believe, because some of them were homosexuals, and homosexuality was considered decadent by moralists at the end of the nineteenth century, and sometimes even now in the twenty-first century.

At the time Wagner died his operas had not entered the standard repertory of any English or American opera house. Already, in an effort to raise funds for Bayreuth, Wagner himself went to London in the spring of 1877, where he conducted a series of eight concerts. Although they failed to make much money for the Bayreuth enterprise, these concerts proved to be critically successful since they earned serious attention and widespread approval among the artistic avant-garde. While Wagner was in London he met George Eliot, her companion George Lewes, and Robert Browning, among other important writers. One of the first results of this attraction between intellectuals and artists and Wagner's operas was the appearance in 1881 of the first book on Wagner in English, Francis Hueffer's *Richard Wagner*. Hueffer, Ford

Madox Ford's father, had already left his native Germany, but he remained an ardent Wagnerian all his life and usually summered in Bayreuth, often attending performances there. In addition to writing the pioneering book on the composer in English, he started a periodical entitled, appropriately, *Die Meister*. The journal became popular among many avant-garde writers and musicians and it served to further the cause of Wagner's music throughout Europe and America. In May of 1882 Angelo Neumann staged the entire *Ring* in London, where it proved a popular success. These days the *Ring* cycle seems to be being staged all over the world — including Wales, California, the Amazon, China, and Japan.

Even English royalty helped the Wagnerian cause, as noted by Ernest Newman: "Neumann was very successful with this first production of the *Ring* in London. Thanks to an introduction from the German Crown Prince he managed to get the Prince of Wales (afterwards King Edward VII) to attend no fewer than eleven of the performances. The Prince had been so charmed by the swimming Rhine Maidens that at one performance of the *Rhinegold* he went behind the scenes and expressed a desire to see the apparatus at work; but when he discovered that the occupant of the car was not to be the pretty young Augusta Kraus but one of the male stage hands he turned away with an impatient 'What the devil!'" (Newman 673).

With the Prince of Wales's help, then, by 1882 London had seen on stage all the standard Wagnerian operas except for *Parsifal*, which Wagner wanted performed only at his new theater at Bayreuth. With performances available in London and advocates like Francis Hueffer, the operas were becoming popular in England by the end of the nineteenth century.

As the '90s became increasingly Wagnerian in their musical taste, this influence began to show itself in many of the arts in Britain, and in the increasing volume of critical appreciation of the German composer. In 1898 George Bernard Shaw wrote *The Perfect Wagnerite*, which summarized the complicated plot of the *Ring* and provided a Fabian socialist interpretation that remains today generally sound. Shaw saw the *Ring* as a parable about the corrupting power of money — which causes a loss of both love and life for many of the people who lust after it. Most critics since Shaw have used this basically Marxist interpretation, although changing some of its elements and eliminating most of Shaw's socialist doctrines. But Shaw never discusses the many suicides and the frequent suicidal behavior in the *Ring* cycle — the final opera ends with the Immolation Scene and the suicide of Brünnhilde, which brings peace and redemption to the rest of the world in addition to her.

During the Edwardian period in particular, Wagnerian themes appeared in the short stories and novels of some major British writers. Joseph Conrad's first novel, *Almayer's Folly* (1895), includes references to Wagnerian opera and ends with an immolation scene that imitates the German composer's work. Conrad's story "Freya of the Seven Isles" (1912) also includes allusions to *Tristan und Isolde* and ends with the death of both young lovers. In *Chance* (1913) Conrad uses patterns of imagery and characterization from Wagner's *Der fliegende Holländer*, and water imagery pervades this novel, as it does the opera, and that opera (like the *Ring*), ends in a suicide and redemption.

There are also similarities between Conrad's *Nostromo* and Wagner's *Ring*, and the connection is too close to be coincidental. It is significant that the San Tomé silver mine is first mentioned while Conrad is describing the young love and courtship of the Goulds in Italy. Early in her married life Emilia Gould becomes aware of an evil shadow darkening her happiness with her husband. The silver mine, ominously connected with death, poses a threat to the Goulds' new love — like the curse and rejection of love necessary for the golden ring to have its power in Wagner's tetralogy. Charles Gould believes that the silver mine had hounded his father to an early grave; that this death should occur while he is first in love parallels the curse in Wagner's *Ring*.

With *Victory* (1915) Conrad also used Wagnerian patterns to help create a suggestively operatic atmosphere, ending again with the death and suicide of the two lovers. Conrad mentioned his indebtedness to Wagner and Wagner's interest in suicide as the best alternative to some of life's very difficult situations, situations which appear in many of Conrad's tragic novels. Wagner's operas provided Conrad with many examples of the union of music and myth, and thereby helped him to give his own fiction what he called "the magic suggestiveness of music" — especially music from Wagnerian opera.

D. H. Lawrence's early novel *The Trespasser* (1912) has a major character called Siegmund who often quotes music from Wagnerian opera and who ends the novel by killing himself as a result of a love affair gone wrong. Lawrence's greater novel *Women in Love* (1916) includes even more Wagnerian allusions and ends with the suicide of one of the major characters, Gerald Crich — the suicide the result of a failed love affair. Lawrence clearly went through an early phase of what can be called Wagnerian decadence, and he used this influence in his writing. Early in his career Lawrence wrote to his friend Blanche Jennings: "I love music. I have been to two or three fine orchestral concerts here [London]. At one I heard Grieg's 'Peer Gynt' — it is very fascinating, if not profound. Surely you know Wagner's operas — *Tannhäuser* and *Lohengrin*. They will run a knowledge of music into your blood better than any criticism." Here too and in a very direct way Lawrence indicates his indebtedness to music and especially Wagnerian opera. Many of these earlier novels by Lawrence included love, love not reciprocated, and subsequent suicide, and he indicated that he absorbed many of these provocative themes from Wagnerian opera and its own uses of love and suicide.

Wagnerian patterns also exist in all of James Joyce's major works, and Joyce often combined his use of Wagner with his use of Giambattista Vico, having learned about Vico's cycles primarily through Wagnerian opera. While the mature Joyce was not very moved by Wagner's music, he always remained interested in the operas as mythic dramas. His fiction indicates an increasing use of Wagnerian patterns for a variety of artistic effects. In "A Painful Case" from *Dubliners* Joyce first used Wagnerian material, from *Tristan und Isolde*. The references to the opera in that story comment ironically on the sterility of Mr. Duffy and his cautious refusal of Mrs. Sinico's offer of love, and in that story alcohol becomes the magic potion which the lovers drink; the story also ends with her death. In *A Portrait of the Artist as a Young Man* Joyce uses the forest-bird motif from *Siegfried* and uses the musical motif thematically in the novel. Stephen's ashplant in that novel is a reference to Wagner's Wotan and the spear he carries and thereby dramatizes Stephen's pretentious desire for power and authority. Also, in *Portrait*, the fourth chapter ends with a vision of woman and water, which is the first of an important series of such allusions in Joyce's fiction.

In *Ulysses* the ashplant cane that Stephen carries has Wagnerian overtones, but they are used in a more complex way. In addition to references to Wotan's spear, as in *Portrait*, a new pattern of allusions to Siegmund's and Siegfried's sword Nothung also appears. They suggest Stephen's desire for a means of defense to assert his own generation and his own sexuality; the sword is a phallic symbol of his young manhood. The fact that the ashplant refers to both Wotan's spear and Siegfried's sword helps Joyce imply that the novel's generational conflict is cyclical rather than progressive — as in Vico. *Ulysses* also employs the symbolic combination of water and the female principle: in Stephen's vision of his mother as the sea, in the Rhinemaiden allusions in the "Sirens" chapter of the novel, and finally in the water imagery in Molly Bloom's final soliloquy. Joyce shared Wagner's redemptive view of woman; the symbolical connection of woman with the fertility of water exemplifies this. Also in *Ulysses*, a pattern of allusions to *Der fliegende Holländer* provides the novel with a counterpart of Homer's Odyssey myth. These allusions help Joyce to characterize Bloom's sympathy with the sufferings of the ordinary man, though his novel does not end with suicide, as does Wagner's opera.

Finally, in *Finnegans Wake*, the symbolic combination of water with the female principle and redemption figures prominently. Wagner's *Tristan und Isolde* provides a mythic body of allusions in *Wake* and helps Joyce to structure the novel and parody the Tristan myth. But in the process his characters, by their connection with the characters in the opera, have become more mythic. This is especially true of "Mildew Lisa," a name used for HCE's daughter. The Wagnerian pun involved is comic, a pun on the first line of the Liebestod ("Mild und Leise"), but it also reminds the reader of the cycle of love, death, and rebirth.

Finnegans Wake contains many other puns — on Wagner's life, titles, and theater — that cleverly parody Wagnerolotry. Joyce used Wagnerian patterns for many effects in his fiction, from mythic elevation to mythic parody, but the effects that recur most frequently are comic, varying in subtlety from irony to punning wordplay.

E. M. Forster loved Wagner's operas all his life. He was moved by performances of the complete operas as well as orchestral excerpts at concerts, and for even more performances went to the Wagner mecca at Bayreuth. What he especially enjoyed in Wagner's music was its specific definition and visual dimension. Forster liked knowing the literal and even verbal equivalents of the music he was hearing, and this of course is one of Wagner's fortes. As a result, Wagner figures significantly in Forster's essay "Not Listening to Music": "With Wagner I always knew where I was; he never let the fancy roam; he ordained that one phrase should recall the ring, another the sword, another the blameless fool and so on; he was as precise in his indications as an oriental dancer. Since he is a great poet, that did not matter." It is interesting here that Forster regarded Wagner's writing, at least his libretti, as highly as his music.

Wagner's leitmotivs are very useful not only for organizing music but also for giving the texts visual equivalents, and with opera, the text should be as important as the music. But Forster also recognized the literary possibility in this technique. In an interview with the *Paris Review*, he was asked, "Do you have any Wagnerian leitmotif system to help you keep so many themes going at the same time?" Forster responded, "Yes, in a way, and I am certainly interested in music and musical methods." We can see this in virtually all of Forster's novels, where Wagner and his operas are directly mentioned.

Howards End is the Forster novel which contains the most Wagnerian allusions, which help to communicate particular meanings and to establish a specifically Edwardian intellectual milieu. Early in the novel Margaret talks heatedly about the confused connections between the arts:

"But, of course, the real villain is Wagner. He has done more than any other man in the nineteenth century towards the muddling of the arts. I do feel that music is in a very serious state just now, though extraordinarily interesting. Every now and then in history there do come these terrible geniuses, like Wagner, who stir up all the wells of thought at once. For a moment it's splendid. Such as splash as never was. But afterwards — such a lot of mud; and the wells — as it were, they communicate with each other too easily now, and not one of them will run quite clean. That's what Wagner's done."

Margaret is perceptive here in recognizing Wagner's immense influence upon a succeeding generation of artists and thinkers.

Later in *Howards End*, one of the most important passages in the book appears and clearly states its major theme, using an image of a rainbow bridge derived from *Das Rheingold:* "Margaret greeted her lord with peculiar tenderness on the morrow. Mature as he was, she might yet be able to help him to the building of the rainbow bridge that should connect the prose in us with the passion. Without it we are meaningless fragments, half monks, half beasts: unconnected arches that have never joined into a man. With it love is born, and alights on the highest curve, glowing against the grey, sober against the fire. Happy the man who sees from either aspect the glory of these outspread wings."

As Forster says even more clearly later in *Howards End*: "Only connect! That was the whole of her sermon. Only connect the prose and the passion, and both will be exalted, and human love with be seen at its height. Live in fragments no longer. Only connect, and the beast and the monk, robbed of the isolation that is life to either, will die." Clearly here Forster intuited the bipolar quality of much of Wagnerian art and wanted to create a kind of novel which would move beyond polarity into a unified whole.

Wagner's operas also had a pronounced influence upon some of the major novels of Virginia Woolf. *The Voyage Out* (1915), *Jacob's Room* (1922), *The Waves* (1931), and *The Years* (1937) all owe something to Wagnerian opera. These works span most of Woolf's writing career, which implies a prolonged and probably changing influence, and the time gaps between the works also allow for some differences in her uses of the operas. She had a lasting fascination with the person of heroic potential, the influence of such a person upon the ordinary man, the suddenness of death, and the pervasive presence of the dead among the living. All these themes are archetypal rather than social or economic, and they lend themselves to mythic treatment.

Woolf's curiosity abut the artistic uses of myth naturally drew her to Wagner's mythic operas. Since Woolf often went to concerts and operas when she was in London, her lifelong involvement with music also attracted her to the composer, especially given the exalted opinion of his works and the frequency of their performance in London during her most formative years. The combination of myth and music, embodied so consummately in his operas, links two of her special interests. Woolf herself was bipolar and committed suicide in 1943 after repeated suicide attempts throughout her life; Wagner was probably also bipolar and mentions thoughts of suicide in his correspondence, and suicide of course often appears in his operas — especially *The Flying Dutchman, Tristan und Isolde,* and the *Ring* cycle.

In 1909 Virginia Woolf wrote a long article for the *London Times,* titled "Impressions of Bayreuth," describing the Bayreuth festival's season of 1909 for Londoners who were unable to get there. In the process of reporting her reactions to the performances, she demonstrates a profound knowledge of Wagnerian opera and Wagnerian production; this article was written by someone who knew the operas well. She was particularly fascinated by the Bayreuth production of *Parsifal* and says in her article:

> Somehow Wagner has conveyed the desire of the Knights for the Grail in such a way that the intense emotion of human beings is combined with the unearthly nature of the thing they seek. It tears us, as we hear it, as though its wings were sharply edged. Again, feelings of the kind that are equally diffused and felt for one object in common create an impression of largesse and ... of an overwhelming unity. The grail seems to burn through all superincumbences; the music is intimate in a sense that none other is; one is fired with emotion and yet possessed with tranquility at the same time, for the words are continued by the music so that we hardly notice the transition. It may be that those exalted emotions, which belong to the essence of our being, and are rarely expressed, are those that are best translated by music.

While her discussion of the opera's basic dichotomy of emotional appeals is highly perceptive, the desire to verbalize its effect implies an essentially literary response. Her final comment about music and literature sustains this impression of her as a music-lover with literary interests. Although she was fond of the other operas as well, "Impressions at Bayreuth" indicates that *Parsifal* had a special hold on her emotions, a hold that was reflected in references to the opera in several of her novels. Once of the things those Grail knights seem to be yearning for is death as a release from their suffering. Virginia Woolf, according to most of her biographers, suffered from bipolar illness. She may have sensed the bipolarity in many of Wagner's operas, and that may have been part of her attraction to his works, in addition to his repeated use of the theme of suicide.

In France, Wagner's influence was even more pervasive than in England according to Eugen Weber, despite Wagner's notorious Francophobia. As Weber writes: "Wagner's influence was limited by the anti–German reaction of 1870–71 and affected only narrow avant-garde circles for the next decade or two. After 1885, however, and especially in the 1890s, Wagner became the inspiration and touchstone of everything that was bold and new. The *Revue Wagnerienne,* devoted to his gospel, became one of the advance posts of decadence and symbolism" (Weber 144). In addition, many of the French

Symbolist poets like Valery, Mallarme, and Gautier wrote for this Wagnerian periodical, and they often used Wagnerian themes in their poetry.

Weber also comments on the increasing frequency of the performances
of Wagner's music in France:

> The introduction of ... Wagner himself to a broader public owed a great deal to
> two musical entrepreneurs of genius: Jules Pasdeloup and Jules-Edouard Juda
> Colonne. The former started his Sunday "popular concerts" in 1861. The later,
> once conductor for Pasdeloup, founded his own series in 1873. Here, for the first
> time, music lovers could actually listen to the great orchestral works so seldom
> heard by those who lived before the age of the phonograph. And though, in the
> wake of the Franco-Prussian War, Pasdeloup had promised to play no more Ger-
> man music, he soon broke his promise, as did Colonne. When Wagner died, in
> February 1883, *Le Figaro* noted in passing that fragments of his operas were "now
> accepted in France and played at the *concert Pasdeloup.*" After 1890 Wagner's
> works seem to have figured in every Sunday program [Weber 144–145].

Along with the music of Wagner came many of the ideas contained in
his operas — especially the attraction to suicide, which recurs in the operas
and which influenced the intellectual movement that eventually came to be
known as Decadence. As an example of such Decadence of the Wagnerian
sort, *Axel,* a play by Villiers de l'Isle Adam, gained a special notoriety. Here,
the yearning for death is especially prominent among the main characters. As
to normal life, says one of the characters in the play, "our servants will see to
that for us." Throughout this play the author uses his characters, especially
his main character, to give voice to a cultural yearning for death and suicide —
a yearning almost as powerful as that voiced by Wagner's Tristan.

Eugen Weber also discusses Wagnerian influences in the French novel *A
Rebours:*

> One of the most forceful expressions of this point of view sprang, fully armed,
> from the pen of a converted Naturalist as early as 1884. Joris-Karl Huysmans,
> when he wrote *A Rebours,* was a high civil servant, deputy head of that branch of
> the Surete which kept an eye on anarchist and other subversive activities. The
> book's conclusion was not that everything was decaying; it was already hopelessly
> rotten. The aristocracy had been despoiled and cast aside, the clergy was at a low
> ebb, the bourgeoisie was vile, the people crushed, the crowd turbid and servile,
> the arts silly at best. "Collapse society: die, old world!" Des Esseintes cries as the
> book ends and the tide of human mediocrity surges to the heavens. The disgust
> with humanity, already striking in the writings of the Naturalists, erupts among
> the aesthetes of the fin de siecle [Weber 148].

The world-weary despair and longing for death that characterize much
of fin de siècle literature, especially Villiers and Huysmans, powerfully reflect
the depression and suicidal ideation which we have found so frequently in
Wagnerian opera. Just as Tristan and Isolde conclude at the end of Wagner's

opera that they both will be better off dead, so too these later writers echo this Wagnerian theme, which they revive and amplify to create what became known as the Decadent period in European literature. Villiers himself visited Wagner several times in his home in Tribschen in Switzerland, in Munich, and in Bayreuth with his friend Judith Gautier (daughter of the poet Theophile Gautier) and was clearly very influenced by the Wagnerian operas, especially the *Ring*.

In addition to France and Britain, Italy became obsessed with Decadence and the Decadent writers as well. Gabriel D'Annunzio clearly reflected the death-obsessed movement of Decadence in his *Il Trionfo della Morte*, where death is seen as the ultimate triumph and where life is seen as futile and stupid. D'Annunzio claimed to be one of Wagner's pallbearers in Venice, where the composer died in 1883, and in his writings the Italian poet made personal use of many Wagnerian themes, particularly suicide and death, which must be regarded as recurrent Wagnerian obsessions. For example, D'Annunzio often suggests in his work that the human act of playing with death may well be the principal source of enjoyment in life.

In Germany the leading Decadent writer became Thomas Mann, who wrote about Wagner and Wagnerian opera repeatedly, especially in his famous essay *The Suffering and Greatness of Richard Wagner*, where he confesses his debt to the opera composer. Several Wagnerian themes appear throughout Mann's writings, but especially the themes of futility, frustration, and death. Other critics have noted the connection between *Tristan und Isolde* and Thomas Mann's *Death in Venice*, which is a homosexual variant of the Liebestod theme, with the famous writer Gustav von Aschenbach going to Venice and becoming obsessed with Tadzio, a young boy from Poland. Since Wagner died in Venice, Mann's title is clearly a Wagnerian allusion; and in his novel we have an artistic work about obsessive love and its result, the suicidal death of Gustav at the end of the story. Though he is repeatedly warned about the presence of the plague in Venice, Gustav refuses to leave his beloved Tadzio, though ironically he never speaks a word to him. The final pages of the novel reflect the final fantasy vision of Aschenbach as he imagines the beloved Tadzio in the water and beckoning to him — just as Isolde's Liebestod ends with her vision of Tristan in the water, beckoning to her. Aschenbach's behavior strikes most readers as suicidal since he has been warned about the plague in Venice but refuses to leave and so dies while watching his beloved Tadzio wave to him from the water.

Mann also wrote a famous story called "The Blood of the Walsungs," which makes use of the incestuous Wagnerian Walsung brother and sister, Siegmund and Sieglinde. By the end of Mann's story, the sibling relationship becomes incestuous as well. Again, as if to underscore Wagner's perceptive portrayal, Mann's story "Tristan" provides a modern, ironic love story which uses allusions to Wagner's *Tristan und Isolde* for purposes of contrast with a modern absence of a loving relationship.

The last of the great Decadent writers was undoubtedly Samuel Beckett, whose Nobel Prize for Literature in 1962 capped a distinguished career. His writings extend the main Decadent themes into mid-century, for in his plays as well as his novels ideas of death and especially suicide play an important role, the result of a view of life that remains essentially bleak and hopeless. While Beckett never alludes to Wagnerian opera directly, his use of Wagnerian obsessions such as death, suicide, dream-visions, and hopelessness clearly reflect the depressive element in Wagnerian opera. He attended Wagnerian performances while he was living in Paris with his mentor James Joyce, but Beckett himself never became a great lover of opera, though he absorbed Wagnerian themes through Joyce.

Beckett began as a novelist, and his most famous novel, *Malone Dies*, appeared in 1951. The novel begins with the following sentence: "I shall soon be quite dead at last in spite of all." The novel ends with the following sentence: "Where I am, I don't know, I'll never know, in the silence you don't know, you must go on. I can't go on. I'll go on." Clearly the novel begins and ends with obsessive thoughts about death, and just as clearly the novel implies that the truly noble commit suicide, thereby glorifying suicide as both logical and brave.

Beckett presents us with the grim realities of post–World War II Europe, having endured the ugly realities of the Jewish Holocaust plus the deaths of about sixty million people — 20 million in Russia alone — as a result of this horrible war. The war ended with two atomic bomb explosions on Hiroshima and Nagasaki in 1945, causing millions of deaths as well. The last '40s and early '50s became haunted with the image of those two ugly mushroom clouds, which both hastened the end of World War II and created the nightmarish image of the end of the world in a mushroom cloud of final destruction caused by the Cold War between the Soviet Union and the West. Of course, Wagner's *Ring* cycle ends with the total destruction of the world after Brünnhilde's self-immolation. Now that both the United States and the Soviet Union had atomic bombs and hated each other, how long could the world survive such a dual threat? Given such grim realities and ugly fears, suicide — Beckett suggests — is both logical and maybe even inevitable. Knowlson in his biography of Beckett also pointed out that in the '30s in London Beckett underwent Freudian psychoanalysis and treatment for anxiety and depression — three times a week for quite a while. Undoubtedly depression and the suicidal thoughts which go with depression were part of the problem and under treatment — a treatment which worked enough to enable him not to kill himself but instead to lead a productive and even heroic life. He worked for the Free France underground during World War II, trying to get the Nazis out of France, and he won the Nobel Prize after a long and distinguished literary career. Those successes were undoubtedly facilitated by his two years of Freudian analysis (1933–35) with Dr. Wilfred Ruprecht Bion at the Tavistock Clinic in London (Knowlson 169). Beckett's main reasons for seeking treatment were depression, anxiety, and alcoholism, and he commented later in life that Dr. Bion helped him.

Beckett's most famous play, *Waiting for Godot* (written in 1952 and first staged in 1953 to great success in Paris as *En Attendant Godot*; it was first staged in English in London in 1955), for example, presents us with an onstage image of two old bums, two old comedians, who are waiting for a Godot who never arrives. They are killing time until time kills them, waiting for Godot, who keeps sending messengers who promise his eventual arrival. "Godot" sounds like a variant of God, and indeed there are numerous religious references in the play. Yet while Godot can be God, he can also be a symbol of something people always want but will never find — demonstrated by the futile

Waiting for Godot, New York, 1956; Kurt Kasznar as Pozzo, E. G. Marshal as Vladimir, Alvin Epstein as Lucky, and Burt Lahr as Estragon.

waiting and frustration throughout the play. One of the few bright spots in Vladimir and Estragon's lives is the thought of suicide. They sometimes become excited about the thought of suicide because they hope death by hanging will give them an erection and an orgasm, things very unusual in their impotent existence of futile waiting. To us, their fascination with death and suicide, and their yearning for some fulfillment, some god, who will never arrive, seems very similar to the fate of Tristan and Isolde in Wagner's opera. In both Wagner's opera and Beckett's play suicide is eroticized as a sexy alternative to the grim realities of life. Just as Tristan attempts suicide at the end of each of the opera's three acts — achieving his suicide at the end of the opera — Beckett's Vladimir and Estragon seem to yearn for the courage to commit suicide as a release from their sterile and pointless and frustrating waiting throughout Beckett's play. The play also suggests that the two men may well be gay since they talk about going on a honeymoon when they were younger. Images of impotence and futility pervade the play's themes and basic situation. The play clearly suggests that suicide is the rational choice in such a life as Beckett's main characters lead, and that to continue living is absurd — a theme from the Decadent literature of fifty years earlier. But Beckett put a modernist, absurdist twist on the theme,

Waiting for Godot, original production, Paris, 1953; Pierre Latour as Estragon, Jean Martin as Lucky, Lucien Raimbourg as Vladimir, and Roger Blin as Pozzo.

and a movement called Theater of the Absurd was born, with much help from Luigi Pirandello's plays.

These same images occurs in Beckett's *Krapp's Last Tape*, which was first staged in 1958. Here we have a play which seems like a non-play — with only one character and very little actual dialogue for that character. The very name of the character, Krapp, reminds most audience members of "crap," the slang word for excrement — named from the inventor of the flushing toilet, the Victorian inventor John C. Crapp. Beckett's Krapp spends most of the duration of the play listening to old tape recordings he made at five year intervals throughout his life, and what those tape recordings report are a series of failed love affairs and failed attempts to stop his self-destructive behavior like excessive drinking. Ultimately the audience is presented with a vision of total failure — Krapp as completely isolated and an alcoholic who is near death. The inevitable implication remains that given the realities of Krapp's life and future, he would probably be better off committing suicide, which he might well do in the future the play suggests. Given the problems of alcoholism and failed relationships in the play, Krapp's continued existence seems absurd and the play suggests that he might be better to commit suicide, but here as in *Waiting for Godot*, the main character chooses to continue to live rather than to die — which may be the result of the psychotherapy which Beckett went through in London in the '30s.

Krapp's Last Tape was undoubtedly a result of Beckett's own fears of his own failure. Krapp is a failed writer who has written books which sold few copies, and he is also a failed lover since he has never been able to sustain a relationship with a woman for very long. By the end of the play he keeps trying to deny the obvious regret he must be feeling for the failure of everything he ever attempted to do with his life. The play clearly suggests that given his total failure, Krapp's most logical option is clearly suicide.

In this later work, however, suicide and death, recurrent themes in the plays of Beckett, become a final endorsement, the last and perhaps most brilliant flowering of the Decadent movement in literature, and of the larger artistic movement which clearly began with Wagnerian opera. To die, even to commit suicide, thus becomes the final act of both desperation and hope. For Beckett as much as for Wagner, suicide stands as the ultimate escape and a source of comfort for a long-suffering humanity. Suicide is even eroticized in some of Beckett's writing, especially *Waiting for Godot*. Though Beckett wrote repeatedly about death and the attraction of suicide for both himself and much of humanity, his own life was much more successful and his writings achieved not only popularity but even a Nobel Prize for Literature. Beckett himself succeeded as a writer, though his main themes were failure, death, and suicide.

Bibliography

Bair, Deirdre. *Samuel Beckett: A Biography.* New York: Harcourt Brace, 1978.
Brater, Enoch. *Beyond Minimalism: Beckett's Late Style in the Theater.* New York: Oxford University Press, 1987.
Cronin, Anthony. *Samuel Beckett: The Last Modernist.* London: HarperCollins, 1995.
Davis, Tracy. *George Bernard Shaw and the Socialist Theatre.* Westport, Conn.:
DiGaetani, John Louis. *Richard Wagner and the Modern British Novel.* Rutherford, N.J.: Fairleigh Dickinson University Press, 1978.
_____. *Wagner and Suicide.* Jefferson, N.C.: McFarland, 2003.
Fletcher, John. *Beckett: A Study of His Plays.* New York: Hill and Wang, 1972.
Gautier, Judith. *Wagner at Home.* Translated by Effie Dunreith Massie. London: John Lane, 1911.
Homan, Sidney. *Beckett's Theaters: Interpretations for Performance.* Madison, N.J.: Associated University Presses, 1984.
Knowlson, James. *Damned to Fame: The Life of Samuel Beckett.* New York: Simon and Schuster, 1996.
Newman, Ernest. *The Life of Richard Wagner.* 4 vols. Cambridge: Cambridge University Press, 1976.
Oppenheim, Lois, and Marius Buning. *Beckett On and On.* Madison, N.J.: Fairleigh Dickinson University Press, 1996.
Weber, Eugen. *France Fin de Siecle.* Cambridge, Mass.: Harvard University Press, 1986.
Woolf, Virginia. "Impressions at Bayreuth." *London Times,* 1909; rpt. in *Opera News,* 41 (August 1976), pp. 22–23.

5

Tennessee Williams
Sibling Rivalry

Madness became one of the central issues in much of the theater of Tennessee Williams. The most graphic example certainly remains the horrible closing scene of *A Streetcar Named Desire,* when Blanche DuBois is pinned on the ground and then taken off to a state mental hospital. Alcoholism appears in *The Night of the Iguana,* in addition to *Streetcar,* and cannibalism becomes a theme in *Suddenly Last Summer.* The character of Laura in *The Glass Menagerie* clearly has some sort of mental or physical problem which isolates her from other people her age. Brick's alcoholism and possible homosexuality dominate *Cat on a Hot Tin Roof. Eccentricities of a Nightingale* as well as *Summer and Smoke* concern people whose emotional problems lead to isolation in society if not insanity. Thus both emotional problems and their most extreme form, madness, recur in many of Williams's plays.

Even Williams's famous novel *The Roman Spring of Mrs. Stone* is a portrayal of a woman who is gradually going insane. The biography of Williams by Donald Spoto indicates as well that madness and forced incarceration in an insane asylum were Williams's two worst fears throughout his life. Of course, these are popular concerns in the general population as well. Most people fear that they will face some horrible crisis in life which will demand more than they can endure, and they too will become insane. Madness, then, a major theme in Williams's plays as well as his life, naturally piques our interest since we too fear this horrible consequence in our own life. Some critics have seen Williams's portrayals of insanity as part of the American literary tradition of Southern grotesque (Mayberry 360).

But several psychologists and psychiatrists from Freud on down to more recent writers have indicated that sibling rivalry can precipitate intense emotional conflicts and finally lead, in its most extreme form, to emotional collapses. Contemporary writers and psychologists like Fishel, Kendrick, Dunn,

Ames, Haber, and Kiell have written extensively on the emotional conflicts and trauma which can result from the most intense forms of sibling rivalry. Emotional problems like inferiority complexes or paranoia and even psychosis can result from the more extreme forms of sibling rivalry. Experts also attest to the fact that sibling rivalry is not merely a phase that children go through but a pervasive reality in many adult lives as well, with often traumatic consequences for some lives. This theme in Williams's plays has received no critical attention that I can find, though the biographers of Williams do comment on sibling relationships and sibling rivalry as dominant concerns in his own life. The play of Williams which most directly dramatizes sibling rivalry is certainly *A Streetcar Named Desire*. While it seems unfair to assume that a writer's personal problems are always reflected in his own work, this autobiographical fallacy can apply in some ways to *Streetcar*, especially when seen in terms of sibling rivalry.

The traditional view of the conflict between Blanche DuBois and Stanley Kowalski in *A Streetcar Named Desire* is that of the sweet, delicate woman and the brutal man. The climactic, penultimate scene in the play is generally performed as a rape scene, in which Blanche becomes the helpless victim of Stanley's brutal sexuality and aggression. The film version of the play, directed by Elia Kazan, underscored this traumatic experience for Blanche by having her look into a shattered mirror during the scene. In the film, the ending of the play was changed; Stella, rather than being in Stanley's arms at the end (as in the play), is shown leaving Stanley and moving in with a neighbor. This change, protested without success by both Williams and Kazan, testified to the power of American film censorship during the 1950s.

Among audiences, responses have varied. Some have even seen Blanche as a symbol of the older American aristocracy, and Stanley as a symbol representative of the new immigrants who attempt to marry into and to destroy the older power structure of America to assert a new political power representing the new immigrants. If rape becomes necessary to remind the old aristocracy that they are no longer in control, then rape will be used. But Williams's version of his characters suggests greater depth, realism, and far more complex causes and motives. One principal reason for the desire of so many actors and actresses to play the major roles in *Streetcar* derives from the author's subtlety. That subtlety pervades his characterizations, just as it complicates the definition of relationships among the three main characters (Blanche, Stella, and Stanley). Here, an important complication can be identified as sibling rivalry, though this aspect of the play has not been investigated. Yet, at the core of the play remains the relationship among one man and two women: Stanley, Stella (his wife), and Blanche (his sister-in-law). To begin to understand these connections, we must look at the relationship between the two sisters.

In Williams's own life, also, the relationship of siblings remained an important factor. Donald Spoto, in his excellent biography, indicates that Williams's sibling tie to his sister Rose remained the most enduring relationship in his life (Spoto 189–191). Most Williams critics consider this biography the definitive one. Williams even had his sister moved to a private mental hospital in Ossining, New York, so that she could be near his home in New York City. Once she was in Ossining, he visited her frequently, often bringing his friends. Sometimes he took Rose to Manhattan for shopping trips and meals at fashionable restaurants (Spoto 240). Rose Williams had to be in a mental hospital because of a lobotomy performed on her, on the advice of doctors in St. Louis and with the permission of her parents. Rose had had several mental collapses, and the doctors suggested to Edwina Williams, the playwright's mother, that a lobotomy would be able to cure Rose. The results of the operation were tragic for they left Rose with the mind of a child and in need of constant supervision and custodial care. The playwright never forgave his mother for the lobotomy on Rose, and he always feared that this procedure would one day be performed on him as well (Spoto 65–68).

In another biography, Dotson Rader endorses Spoto's emphasis on this very important relationship in Williams's life — to the point of reporting that, in his drunken stupors, Williams actually called himself Miss Rose and dressed himself in her clothes. The identification, Rader shows, was important to Williams, who felt (at least at times) that both Rose and he were essentially insane, and cut off from successful intimacy with other people (Rader 228–232). But apparently Williams also felt that he and Rose had in some way been joined throughout their lives. Of his plays, *Two Character Play* and *Out Cry* involve incest between brother and sister, indicating perhaps Williams's own sometimes incestuous feelings for his beloved sister.

Both Spoto and Rader also report that Tennessee Williams had an altar to his sister Rose in his house in Key West (Spoto 365; Rader 231). There he kept mementos and pictures of his sister along with religious objects. Both biographers also report Williams's lifelong fear of becoming insane, of having a mental collapse which would result in his lobotomy and permanent incarceration. Williams often feared that his sister's fate, life in a mental hospital, would eventually become his own. Significantly, this is Blanche DuBois's fate at the end of *A Streetcar Named Desire*, when she is forcibly committed to a state mental asylum, just as his sister Rose was forcibly committed to a state mental asylum by their parents. Williams felt that insanity ran in his family: his mother became insane by the end of her life, his father was an alcoholic, and his sister Rose would live in a mental hospital until she died. But Williams had another sibling as well, his brother Dakin, and he rarely mentioned him in his conversations with friends.

Significantly, sibling rivalry played a part in Tennessee Williams's relationship with his only other sibling, his brother. In 1983 Dakin Williams wrote *Tennessee Williams: An Intimate Biography*, and that book describes a mental fantasy experienced by the playwright during one of his hospitalizations: Tennessee "had vivid dreams or hallucinations including one rather Freudian one in which, shortly after the birth of Dakin, he [Tennessee] watched him [Dakin] sucking the breast of his mother in a St. Louis hospital. He [Tennessee] thought it represented a 'never-before-spoken sibling rivalry.' Perhaps never spoken before, but one that always existed strongly, in both directions, and still does." (Williams and Mead 294). When this passage was written, both men were well past middle age; but his commentary shows that Dakin Williams believed that sibling rivalry had played a major part in his relationship with his older brother. In fact, that relationship became *very* unpleasant after Dakin (in 1969) signed the papers necessary to have Tennessee Williams forcibly held in Barnes Hospital in St. Louis for detoxification from drugs and alcohol. Afterwards, the playwright became furious, and as he told an interviewer, actually wrote Dakin out of his will and would have nothing more to do with him (Spoto 316–317). Eventually, the relationship improved a bit, but the Williams brothers remained very wary of each other. Many of his friends saw Tennessee's attitude as largely mistaken; they told the playwright that he should be grateful to his brother, that the forced hospital stay had saved Tennessee's life, and even that Dakin did only what well trained doctors urged him to do. But Tennessee Williams never forgave his brother — perhaps because of sibling rivalry, in addition to his lifelong dread of forced confinement. Williams perhaps used Dakin's forced confinement as a pretext to avoid dealing with his only brother.

Not surprisingly, since sibling relationships remained important in his own life, they appear prominently in many Williams plays. Tennessee's first success in the theater, *The Glass Menagerie*, involves the relationship of a brother and sister. Here, Tom's efforts to help his sister Laura by bringing home an eligible young man for her to meet, and especially his first and last monologues in the play, indicate something of the depth of his feelings for his sister. Of course, Tennessee Williams's real first name was Tom — and by that name he was called by members of his own family. All this tightens the biographical connection between this play and its author's own intense bond with his sister. *The Glass Menagerie* does not stand alone in this regard.

Cat on a Hot Tin Roof also involves a relationship among siblings, and here sibling rivalry becomes much more apparent and centrally important to the play. The brothers Brick and Gooper are competing in their efforts to get the love (and inheritance) of their father, Big Daddy. The final scene of the play, showing Brick's sexual reconciliation with his wife Maggie, suggests that one of his motives for this reconciliation is to impregnate her, thereby making his father happy and ensuring a larger share of the family inheritance for himself. Sibling rivalry operates on another level in the play in the intense hatred portrayed in the play between Maggie and her sister-in-law Mae. Both women are clearly competing within the family for the primary affection of Big Daddy, the head of the family and dispenser of all its wealth. Both Gooper and Mae like to contrast their own fertility (with three children) with the barren marriage of Brick and Maggie. But the play which uses sibling rivalry most dramatically and most forcefully remains *Streetcar*.

In *A Streetcar Named Desire* the sisters Blanche and Stella interact; given their relationship as sisters, some sibling rivalry seems to be natural. For some insight, let us look at their relationship as it develops in the play. Blanche is, of course, the older sister, even though she pointedly tells Mitch during the play that Stella is her older sister. That lie reveals something about the complexity of the sisters' bond, especially about the rivalry it contains. First, the most immediate and obvious facts about the two women: Blanche is older than Stella, yet Stella seems to be more successful in several ways. Stella is married, Blanche is a widow. Stella seems to have a very active and healthy sexual life with her husband; Blanche's deceased husband was a homosexual (at least according to Blanche). Stella, in addition to a husband, has a home, while Blanche is homeless and has been forced to ask her younger sister for shelter. Finally, Stella is happily married for most of the play; indeed, she is pregnant, while Blanche shows no such visible signs of femininity (Cardullo 4–5). Given these facts, Stella looks like the much more successful woman — in traditional rather than non-traditional terms. This is not surprising since the play was first staged in New York City in 1947, long before the modern women's liberation movement. Given the facts about the characters as presented by Tennessee Williams, then, their relationship is fraught with potential for sibling rivalry.

Now looking at how these characters interact during the play, dramatic evidence of sibling rivalry between the two women soon becomes apparent. In the first scene of the play, after Blanche's long trip, Blanche and Stella immediately embrace, but then things quickly become tense. First, Blanche's comment about Stella's apartment begins to sour the reunion. Blanche says: "What are you doing in a place like this? ... I'm not going to be hypocritical, I'm going to be honestly critical about it. Never, never, never in my worst dreams could I picture.... Only Mr. Edgar Allan Poe could do justice to it." Here, certainly, Blanche is treading on very sensitive ground. An attack on the appearance of someone's home is not appropriate behavior for a guest, but this display of bad manners does serve to dramatize Blanche's competitive relationship with her sister. Stella may have her own home, but Blanche feels compelled to dismiss it as a hovel.

To change the subject, Stella tells Blanche how good she looks, which Blanche obviously enjoys, yet her response to this compliment deserves attention. Blanche says to Stella, "You've put on some weights, yes you're just as plump as a little partridge.... And it's so becoming to you.... Yes it is, it is or I wouldn't say it! You just have to watch around the hips a little." There is a double-edged compliment if ever there was one. Blanche begins by calling her sister fat, but then says the fat looks good on her (except, of course, for the hips). Later Blanche boasts to Mitch that she is still as thin as when she graduated from high school—which reveals that her compliment to Stella about her gained weight could not have been sincere (as Stella undoubtedly sensed). Even in their first meeting, then, there is evidence of sibling rivalry in the connection between the two sisters—primarily on the part of Blanche, the alcoholic older sister who, on moral grounds, has been fired from her job as a teacher. Blanche, unlike Stella, who is happily married and very content to be Stanley's wife, is without home, without mate, without job, and without happiness.

Their rivalry may explain Blanche's ugly accusations to her sister later in the scene. When Blanche tells her sister that the family home, Belle Reve, is gone, Stella innocently asks, "But how did it go? What happened?" Those innocent questions Blanche immediately turns into an accusation, as she begins a long speech: "You're a fine one to sit there accusing me!" And, later, she ends with: "Yes, accuse me: Sit there and stare at me, thinking I let the place go.... I let the place go? Where were you? In bed with your Polack." In its entirety, this nasty speech reduces Stella to tears, serves to attack Stella's husband, and also provides the cue for Stanley himself to appear. Even before she has met Stanley, then, Blanche can dismiss him as an oaf, a "Polack."

The second scene of the play, occurring at six o'clock the next evening, intensifies the pattern of sibling rivalry between the women. Blanche is, of course, a guest in Stella and Stanley's very small apartment; in fact, only a thin curtain separates Stanley and Stella's bedroom from Blanche's quarters. Even though Blanche has been in the house no longer than a day, she has managed to turn her sister into a servant. Beneath her gushing over "my dear little baby sister," the play indicates a malicious intent on Blanche's part to attack her sister's self-esteem. This Blanche does in two ways during this scene, and both methods will be continued throughout the remainder of the play. First, she tries to turn her sister into a servant by making a series of requests for personal service; Stella is asked to bring Blanche's clothes while she's in the bath, later to bring Blanche a Coke from the corner drug store, etc. Throughout the play, Blanche consistently tries to place and then keep her sister in the degraded position of personal maid.

Again, as a second way of belittling Stella, Blanche for much of this scene acts out an extended flirtation with Stella's husband, Stanley. Blanche coyly tells Stanley: "Excuse me, while I put on my pretty new dress." Next, she asks him to button up the back of her dress, and calls for a drag of his cigarette. Instead, Stanley offers her a cigarette of her own, but he has noticed Blanche's flirtatious behavior. So he tells her: "If I didn't know that you was my wife's sister, I'd get ideas about you!" When Blanche says, "Such as what?," Stanley quickly responds: "Don't play dumb. You know what." Blanche may appear to be playing dumb with Stanley, but her behavior indicates that she knows exactly what she is doing — in fact, she is subtly telling him that she is more desirable and attractive as a woman than her sister, and also that Blanche is sexually available to him.

As the second scene of the play ends, Blanche and Stella are leaving the apartment, so that Stanley can use it for his all-male poker party. As the sisters depart, Blanche comments to Stella about how she handled Stanley: "I laughed and treated it all as a joke. I called him a little boy and laughed and flirted. Yes, I was flirting with your husband." Significantly, Blanche admits to herself as well as to her sister that she was flirting with Stanley.

Here, the question arises: Why would Blanche flirt with

A Streetcar Named Desire, 1992; Alec Baldwin as Stanley with a bottle of beer (photograph: Brigitte Lacombe).

Stanley, her brother-in-law, which she continues to do through the rest of the play? Is this a way of defending herself? If so, it is hardly a useful method of defense against Stanley, since her flirting implies that she desires Stanley and is available to him. Or is this merely Blanche's way of encouraging those men she finds desirable? Yet she often says in the play to her sister that Stanley seems not desirable at all; rather, he is an ape. Again, isn't it malicious of her to flirt with her sister's husband? The only possible explanation is Blanche's intense sense of rivalry and competition with her sister. What better way to best her sister than by coming into her house, seducing her husband under her sister's own nose, and reducing Stella to the status of personal maid and female cuckold?

The play provides more evidence of this malice in Blanche's repeated attacks on Stanley in conversations with her sister. Stella is obviously very much in love with Stanley, and she seems happily married; but Blanche repeatedly attacks Stanley to her sister and urges her to end the marriage. In the fourth scene of the play, as the two sisters are talking, Blanche suddenly tells Stella: "You're married to a madman." And a few moments later, Blanche continues: "You're not old! You can get out." Stella immediately responds: "I'm not in anything I want to get out of." Yet despite Stella's repeated assertions that she is happily married to Stanley, Blanche continues to attack him and to encourage her sister to leave him. It is certainly significant that Blanche calls Stanley a "madman," implying that she thinks he is insane. What does she mean by this? What evidence does she have? She seems to feel that he is a brutal destroyer who is trying to destroy her, and in that sense she sees him as insane. Of course, this is not how Stanley sees his own motivation in terms of his reaction to Blanche.

Finally, these repeated attacks on Stanley culminate in Blanche's long speech about him at the end of the fourth scene: "He acts like an animal, has an animal's habits! Eats like one, moves like one, talks like on! There's even something — sub-human — something not quite to the stage of humanity yet! Yes, something — ape-like about him, like one of those pictures I've seen in — anthropological studies! Thousands and thousands of years have passed him right by, and there he is — Stanley Kowalski — survivor of the stone age! Bearing the raw meat home from the kill in the jungle! And you —YOU here — waiting for him! Maybe he'll strike you or maybe grunt and kiss you! That is, if kisses have been discovered yet!... In this dark march toward whatever it is we're approaching, DON'T—DON'T HANG BACK WITH THE BRUTES." Blanche not only calls Stanley an ape, she also implies that her sister is a fool to be married to him. Though Stella is married, the ever-competitive Blanche simply dismisses Stella's husband as subhuman and insane.

A Streetcar Named Desire, 1992; Alec Baldwin as Stanley and Jessica Lange as Blanche Dubois (photograph: Brigitte Lacombe).

What Blanche does not know during this speech is that Stanley is over-hearing it. The experience leads Stanley to be convinced of what he has long suspected: that his sweet-seeming, high-class sister-in-law is there — as a guest in his home — trying to destroy his marriage. Because his wife does not have the heart to ask Blanche to leave, he feels that he must get her out of his house before she destroys the most important thing in his life, his marriage to Stella. As their famous reconciliation scene in the third scene of the play makes clear, Stanley desperately needs his wife for without her love he is a whimpering, sobbing child. Stella is the very lynchpin of his existence; their crucial rela-tionship is exactly what Blanche is trying to destroy.

Later, in the tenth scene of the play, the famous "sexual" confrontation between Stanley and Blanche occurs. Significantly, while this scene is played out, Stella remains in the hospital, having her and Stanley's baby. That bio-logical fact must be very much on Blanche's mind, as she indicates with the first question she asks after Stanley enters. At a time when Stella is most suc-cessfully a woman (in traditional terms, at least), having the child of the man she loves, Blanche continues to flirt with Stella's husband. Now, Blanche wants to cuckold her sister, as she becomes a victim of her intense feelings of sib-ling rivalry with Stella. Of course, the scene can be played in various ways, depending on the actors' approach and the director's interpretation, as either Stanley's final response to all of Blanche's flirting or Blanche's final victory over her sister — or both. But by the end of the scene Blanche does not fight Stanley's sexual aggression but instead becomes limp and passive. That she makes no attempt whatsoever to fight Stanley off is itself a telling indication of her real motivation.

In any case, some sort of sexual assault has occurred and clearly Blanche is a victim of Stanley's brutal attack. Stanley is attacking what appears to him as the person who is trying to destroy the most important thing in his life, his marriage, but he still has no right to use violence.

But Blanche is anything but passive in her attempts to attract Stanley's co-worker Mitch. She indicates to her sister that she is attracted to Mitch because he seems much more refined than Stella's husband, Stanley. And in her scenes with Mitch we see Blanche playing games and being duplicitous — she lies about her age, tells Mitch that Stella is the older sister, and creates an air of the genteel Southern belle — upper class and virginal. Stanley rather brutally tells Mitch the results of Stanley's research into his sister-in-law's sexual past, but from Stanley's point of view he has to protect a good friend from the lies and snares of his lying sister-in-law. Mitch's final rejection of Blanche may be more important than the sexual scene with Stanley in explain-ing Blanche's final emotional collapse. Blanche interprets Mitch's rejection of her as the victory of her sister since her sister's unpretentious honesty attracts more men (or at least Stanley) than all Blanche's jewelry, summer furs, and dishonest wiles. Stella has an earthy authenticity, while Blanche is a game-player who rarely reveals the truth about herself, least of all the competitive part of her personality. Instead, Blanche presents herself as the sweet, delicate, genteel, artistic belle. While Blanche would never admit to any feelings of hostility or rivalry with her sister, they certainly occur in the play. But Stella, the non-neurotic sibling, seems clearly uninterested in any competition with her sister. Her responses to her sister remain consistently supportive of her, despite the increasing anger of her husband about Blanche's obtrusive presence in their very small apartment.

As Tennessee Williams subtly indicates in the play, Blanche's competition with her sister, coupled with her alcoholism, her sexual attraction to young boys, and her consequent loss of her job are all contributory factors in her final breakdown and madness. By the end of the play, Blanche has been destroyed. She clings to the arms of the doctor who is taking her to a state mental hospital, and she remains dependent on the kindness of strangers. In part at least, her sorry state results from an intense feeling of competition with a sibling member of her immediate family. And Blanche's famous final line, "I have always depended on the kindness of strangers," is a not very subtle criticism of her sister, who is onstage to hear the line. Blanche is stating that she has to depend on the kindness of strangers because of the betrayal of members of her own family, specifically her sister.

Depending on the production and how the actors and actresses play their roles, sibling rivalry can be either more or less apparent in *A Streetcar Named Desire*. But in either case, Tennessee Williams has made that theme central to the play as a whole. Insanity has many causes — certainly no single one — but among the contributing factors in Blanche's emotional collapse and her need for institutionalization, her intense feelings of rivalry with her sister must be discerned. Instead of being able to feel gratitude towards her sister and brother-in-law for taking her into their lives and very small apartment, instead of trying to find a new life for herself, instead of looking for a job, Blanche insists on pursuing an unrealistic fantasy life with either the gullible Mitch or her alleged former suitor, the Texas oil millionaire Shep Huntleigh. Unlike her sister Stella who has her Stanley Kowalski, Blanche lives on illusions — her illusion of better opportunities offered her. While Stella has settled for Stanley, Blanche makes clear to her sister that her standards for men are much higher.

Earlier, sisterly rivalries appeared in much great drama, going back to the Greek tragic playwrights. Sophocles's *Electra* in part concerns the vast differences between the rigid, vengeful Electra and her more realistic and forgiving sister Chrysothemis. The three daughters of Shakespeare's King Lear show hatred for each other early in the play, and Goneril and Regan later become rivals for the love of the same man, Edmund. More recently, the loving but intense rivalry between sisters in Alan Ayckbourn's *Sisterly Feelings* has continued the dramatic tradition of siblings who can sometimes be a source of strength and encouragement for each other but, at other times, symbols of intense competition and rivalry. Sam Shepard's *True West* dramatizes the complex relationship between brothers who both love and hate each other. In Williams's *A Streetcar Named Desire* this very rivalry drives Blanche Dubois into a psychological breakdown.Perhaps she has to depend on the kindness of strangers because she has driven her family away. In her case, sibling rivalry has lead to insanity. While this theme also appears in *Cat on a Hot Tin Roof* and *The Glass Menagerie*, it finds its most intense and dramatic portrayal in the complex and difficult relationship of Stella and Blanche.

Bibliography

Ames, Louise and Carol Haber. *He Hit Me First: When Brothers and Sisters Fight.* New York: Dembner Books, 1982.

Blackwell, Louise. "Tennessee Williams and the Predicament of Women." *South Atlantic Bulletin,* March 1970, 9–14.

Cardullo, Bert. "The Role of the Baby in *A Streetcar Named Desire.*" *Notes on Contemporary Literature,* March 1984, 14–24.

Dunn, Judy. *Sisters and Brothers.* Cambridge, Mass.: Harvard University Press, 1985.

Dunn, Judy, and Carol Kendrick. *Siblings: Love, Envy and Understanding.* Cambridge, Mass.: Harvard University Press, 1982.

Fishel, Elizabeth. *Sisters: Love and Rivalry Inside the Family and Beyond.* New York: Morrow, 1979.

Kiel, Norman, ed. *Blood Brothers: Siblings as Writers.* New York: International Universities Press, 1983.

Mayberry, Susan Neal. "A Study of Illusion and the Grotesque in Tennessee Williams' *Cat on a Hot Tin Roof.*" *Southern Studies,* Winter 1983, 359–65.

Melman, Lindy. "A Captive Maid: Blanche DuBois in *A Streetcar Named Desire.*" *Dutch Quarterly Review of Anglo-American Letters,* 1986, 125–144.

Nelson, Benjamin. *Tennessee Williams: The Man and His Work.* New York: Ivan Obolensky, 1962.

Rader, Dotson. *Tennessee: Cry of the Heart.* Garden City, N.Y.: Doubleday, 1985.

Spoto, Donald. *The Kindness of Strangers: The Life of Tennessee Williams.* New York: Ballantine, 1985.

Tharpe, Jac, ed. *Tennessee Williams: 13 Essays.* Jackson: University Press of Mississippi, 1980.

Tischler, Nancy M. *Tennessee Williams: Rebellious Puritan.* New York: Citadel Press, 1965.

Williams, Dakin, and Shepherd Mead. *Tennessee Williams: An Intimate Biography.* New York: Arbor House, 1983.

Williams, Edwina, and Lucy Freeman. *Remember Me to Tom.* New York: G.P. Putnam's
    Sons, 1973.
Williams, Tennessee. *A Streetcar Named Desire.* New York: New American Library, 1947.
Yacowar, Maurice. *Tennessee Williams and Film.* New York: Frederick Ungar, 1977.

6

Eugene O'Neill, Edward Albee, Simon Gray, Brian Friel, Martin McDonagh

Alcoholism

As one thinks about this sad topic, alcoholism (or addiction problems in general), one cannot help noticing the strong connection between alcoholism and writers in American literature. Among the names that immediately come to mind are William Faulkner, Ernest Hemingway, F. Scott Fitzgerald, Eugene O'Neill, Hart Crane, John Cheever, Truman Capote, and Tennessee Williams. John Unterecker's biography of Hart Crane describes night after night of drunkenness on Crane's part — as the biographer keeps insisting that Crane was not really an alcoholic! One often gets the feeling in American literature that only the second-raters were sober. But in British literature as well, writers like Evelyn Waugh, James Joyce, and others have written about these problems. One sees the tragedy of alcohol addiction particularly clearly in the family of James Joyce since his father was an alcoholic, Joyce had his own drinking problem, and his son Giorgio was a binge drinker with a resultant early death. While Giorgio did not seem to inherit his father's literary genius, he did inherit his drinking problems. Joyce's poor daughter Lucia died in a mental asylum due to her schizophrenia. But such problems also occur from generation to generation without the saving grace of literary genius, alas.

Among American playwrights we see this problem most acutely in the family and literary career of the great American playwright Eugene O'Neill. Both the Sheaffer and Gelb biographies of Eugene O'Neill mention his repeated bouts of alcoholism, though his last wife, Carlotta, managed to keep him sober for much of the last twenty years of his life. But before that and through his three earlier marriages, we can read over and over again about the alcoholism that plagued his life and incapacitated him as both a husband and a father. One of his sons committed suicide, and one cannot help concluding that O'Neill's neglect of his children was a result of his addiction problems. This becomes glaringly ironic since O'Neill repeatedly bewailed his own neglect by his parents, James and Ella O'Neill, themselves addicts who failed to provide either Eugene or his brother Jamie with the kind of stable home life which any child needs. When the playwright himself became a father, he neglected his children even more brutally than his own father did.

And in recent English literature, the record is hardly much better. Among the obvious alcoholics are James Joyce, Evelyn Waugh, Dylan Thomas, and W. H. Auden. But certainly there are others as well, and among Irish writers, the problem has become a cliché—viewed sometimes comically, sometimes tragically. Both Brendan Behan and Martin McDonagh have treated comically rather than tragically the Irish problem with alcoholism, though Sean O'Casey's earlier play, *Juno and the Paycock* (1924), emphasizes the tragic aspect in its sad ending.

Eugene O'Neill's brother Jamie died from alcoholism, and the author himself had several bouts with alcoholism. In fact, his biographers state that he was expelled from Princeton University because of his excessive drinking. The theme occurs often in his plays, most obviously in *The Ice Man Cometh* (1946), which is set in a bar. The main character, Hickey, is obviously an alcoholic. He describes his murder of his wife as something she really wanted and the best thing for her. The connection between profound depression and alcoholism is clearly indicated in that play, and O'Neill battled both of these tendencies for his whole life—according to most of his biographers, especially the Gelbs. O'Neill's own repeated battles with alcoholism are clearly illustrated by all his earlier biographers—in fact they also report that he even attempted suicide during one of his drinking binges in Manhattan, luckily surviving this suicide attempt to become one of America's most important playwrights.

Much drinking also occurs in *Long Day's Journey into Night* (1941). All the male characters do a lot of drinking in the play, especially the father. And we soon find out that the mother has another addiction problem, morphine, which was the sad reality for O'Neill's mother Ella. Addiction problems seem to be the tragedy of the entire family in *Long Day's Journey into Night*, as the very title of the play indicates. Addiction problems can turn our own journey from day to night into a very long journey indeed, in which we are made incapable of providing ourselves or others with the love and nurturing which all human beings need, particularly children. By the end of this play, none of the characters — not even the servants — seems sober any more. Certainly one of the main reasons Ella was not a very good mother to her children was her own addiction problem. O'Neill's own battles with the bottle continued for much of his life — he almost died in a bar in Manhattan when he was a young man, due to his drinking. Drinking and addiction problems became the curse of the O'Neill family, and indeed Eugene O'Neill's brother Jamie died in his 40s as a result of his suicidal drinking binges.

Edward Albee is another playwright who successfully dramatizes drinking problems. His most famous play, *Who's Afraid of Virginia Woolf* (1962), seems centrally concerned with drinking. The four characters spend most of the play drinking and are clearly drunk by the end of the first act. The main characters in his play, both George and Martha, strike most audience members as very serious drinkers and probably alcoholics — and it was played this way in the very famous film version with Elizabeth Taylor and Richard Burton, actors who themselves have also had serious bouts of alcoholism. After this play, *A Delicate Balance* (1966) also includes much drinking and a female character whom the other characters clearly think is an alcoholic. In both these plays, onstage drinking occurs in every act, and by the end most of the plays' final acts, characters seem drunk and incapacitated because of their excessive

Who's Afraid of Virginia Woolf?, 1962; Arthur Hill and Ute Hagen both drinking (photograph: Jos Abeles Studio).

Top: Who's Afraid of Virginia Woolf?, 1962; Melinda Dillon and Arthur Hill. *Bottom: Who's Afraid of Virginia Woolf?*, 1966; George Segal, Richard Burton, Sandy Dennis, and Elizabeth Taylor — drunk or hung-over.

Who's Afraid of Virginia Woolf?, 1966; Elizabeth Taylor, Richard Burton — both drinking.

drinking. George and Martha in *Who's Afraid of Virginia Woolf* seem to have achieved some kind of a peaceful reconciliation by the end of the play, but only after both face horrendous drunkenness and horrifying hangovers as a result of all that drinking.

In Tennessee Williams's plays, as well, drinking and drinking excessively become major themes. Blanche in *A Streetcar Named Desire* is drinking for most of the play and Stanley refers to her as a lush several times. One of her problems seems to be excessive drinking. Brick in *Cat on a Hot Tin Roof* also spends most of the play drinking, and the audience inevitably begins to suspect that he too is an alcoholic. His father warns him that he is throwing his life right down a gutter if he becomes an alcoholic, but his constant drinking onstage suggests to the audience that this has in fact already occurred, which also helps to explain his souring relationship with his wife Maggie. The play also suggests the possibility of Brick's homosexuality, but alcoholism seems to be the main problem.

Tennessee Williams himself was an alcoholic and had to be hospitalized by his brother Dakin because of his excessive drinking. While the action made

Williams furious, his friends concluded that Dakin's actions saved his life since the playwright was on the point of drinking himself to death. But Williams rarely talked to his brother Dakin as a result of his causing his playwright brother to be hospitalized for alcoholism. Most of Tennessee Williams's friends urged the playwright to forgive his brother, since he did a very good thing for the writer. Williams could never forgive Dakin despite the fact that the playwright had almost drunk himself to death before he was forcibly hospitalized.

This problem is not only one among American and Irish playwrights, since alcoholism is clearly a major theme in Simon Gray's plays. Arguably his best play, *Butley* (1971), includes a lot of talking, but it includes the professor taking bottles of booze out of his teacher's desk and often drinking onstage. Clearly the playwright is suggesting that his main character is an alcoholic and that his alcoholism might be the reason for the breakup of his most important relationships — with both his wife and his male lover. By the end of the play Ben Butley is once again reaching for a bottle of Scotch, hidden in his teacher's desk in his faculty office — clearly suggesting that this problem is not going to go away and that the next tragedy might be his being fired from his teaching job due to alcoholism.

In Simon Gray's *Otherwise Engaged* (1975), drinking is also a major problem since the characters spend most of the play talking and drinking. The audience inevitably begins to suspect that alcoholism is one of the main character's major problems. These characters are constantly drinking during the play, and one cannot help suspecting that alcoholism is an issue in their lives.

Harold Pinter's plays also dramatize this problem since many of his characters are serious drinkers. In *Betrayal* (1978) the characters sometimes complain of being hung-over and they are constantly drinking — the suspicion is inevitably planted in the audience's mind that they may be alcoholics. They cannot conceive of talking or socializing without drinking to excess. All three of the main characters in this play — Emma, Robert, and Jerry — drink and sometimes seem drunk or impaired or hung-over.

Of course, the Irish have a legendary problem with drink and an appallingly high rate of alcoholism — both in other countries and in their homeland. Alcoholism is certainly a major theme in the plays of Brian Friel. Repeatedly in his theatre the alcoholic character appears, and the consequences of his alcoholism become profound and unfortunate as the play progresses. This theme suggests to me that Friel is not an alcoholic since his plays clearly display the horrors of the disease. Let us hope, in any case, that Friel does not suffer from the Irish disease — and it can also be called the English disease and the American disease.

Looking at Brian Friel's plays, one of his first international successes was *Philadelphia, Here I Come!* (1965 premiere in Dublin), which certainly includes alcoholism. Before the main character leaves Ireland for new opportunities in Philadelphia, he visits his old English teacher, Master Boyle, and reports that he found him desperate for a drink. He is notorious in Ballybeg as a confirmed alcoholic. How sad for the main character, Gar O'Donnell. He wanted to make one last contact with his favorite teacher, but he soon surmised that he was dealing with a drunkard. On the other hand, Boyle is capable of telling Gar that he will miss him, while his father cannot bear to say that to him. Failed father figures, a major theme in the fiction of James Joyce, became a famous theme in the theatre of Brian Friel. Many of the father figures of Brian Friel's plays also fail both as fathers and in their careers because of their alcoholism.

Another Friel play, *The Freedom of the City* (1973), certainly Friel's most obviously political play, involves the re-creation of an actual historical event, the killing of three Irish people during a demonstration in Londonderry. Here one of the three alleged revolutionaries gets very drunk onstage, which serves to weaken his pretensions to political revolution. The play involves the events of February 10, 1970, in Londonderry, Northern Ireland. During rioting in the city, a group of three demonstrators, trying to avoid all the tear gas, run into the top room of an old building, only to discover that it is the headquarters of the city government, and they are in the lord mayor's opulent office. They help themselves to the comforts of the place, including a well-stocked bar. One of the three characters, Skinner, is quite drunk by the end of the play. Another recurrent character who comments on the action, the Balladeer, is described in the stage directions as "a maudlin drunk." But the play ends tragically when the three characters—whom we come to see as comic and human figures trying to survive poverty rather than fanatical political revolutionaries—in trying to get out of the building, are all shot dead by the police.

In Friel's later play, *Living Quarters* (1977), his investigation of alcoholism appears again. This play was Friel's only attempt to create Greek tragedy on classical, Aristotelian principles. In fact, on the title page, Friel placed the phrase "After *Hippolytus*." That is of course the title of Euripides's famous play about Theseus, his wife Phaedra, and her love for her stepson Hippolytus. While in that play Hippolytus is destroyed at the end, in Friel's play it is the Theseus-figure who is destroyed. Friel follows the three unities of time, place, and action, and for his tragic hero he has an Irish general named Frank Butler who has just been honored for his work for the United Nations. By the end of the play, and to his horror, he discovers that his son

***Philadelphia, Here I Come!*, original Broadway production, 1966; Patrick Bedford and Donal Donnelly.**

Ben by his first marriage is having an affair with his new young wife Anna. Frank becomes desperate at the news and goes to consult Father Tom Carty, who is the chaplain to his military camp, in addition to being an old friend of the family. To his horror, and ours, the priest is drunk and totally unable to help him with his problems. In the very next scene, the general commits suicide. Here the failure in his duties of an alcoholic priest results in the death of a decorated general. Frank Butler, Friel's heroic Theseus-figure, does not get the desperate help he needs from his chaplain because that chaplain is yet another Friel alcoholic. And the effects of that alcoholism prove tragic to the people around the alcoholic. That the drunk is also a Catholic priest certainly adds to the sadness and irony of the situation.

    Aristocrats (1979), Friel's version of a Chekhov comic tragedy, *The Cherry Orchard,* also includes the problems of drink. Two of the grown children in the family, Willie and Alice, are obviously alcoholics and they (though adults) are unable to stop the decline of the family. Several of the other O'Donnell children seem like borderline alcoholics as well. As the newly arrived Eamon says: "Less than twenty-four hours away from temperate London and already we're reverting to drunken Paddies. Must be the environment, mustn't it?" By the end of the play, as in *The Cherry Orchard*, a family has both lost its ancestral house and been destroyed, and alcoholism is obviously one of the main reasons for the destruction of this family. Like the destruction of the Butler family at the end of *Living Quarters,* the once wealthy and prominent O'Donnell family loses its estate, Ballybeg Hall, and its family cohesion in part because of the alcoholism of several of the judge's children. They drink away the patrimony and prestige he has given them, symbolized by Ballybeg Hall. With the death of the old judge, none of his adult children is capable of maintaining the house and its surrounding estate. Instead, all is lost, as in the end of *The Cherry Orchard*, when another incompetent Russian family fritters away its patrimony. The fall of a great and prominent family has become a recurrent theme in the theatre of Brian Friel — rather like the fall of the house of Atreus in Greek tragedy.

Faith Healer (which premiered in New York in 1979) has remained one of Friel's most often performed plays — primarily because it only requires three actors and has a fascinating central character, the faith healer Francis Hardy. As Hardy says about his faith healing powers early in the play: "But faith in what? in me?— in the possibility?— faith in faith? And is the power diminishing? You're beginning to masquerade, aren't you? You're coming a husk, aren't you? And so it went on and on and on. Silly, wasn't it? Considering that nine times out of ten nothing at all happened. But they persisted right to the end, those nagging, tormenting, maddening questions that rotted my life. When I refused to confront them, they ambushed me. And when they threatened to submerge me, I silenced them with whiskey. That was efficient for a while. It got me through the job night after night." The theme of Hardy's dwindling powers over his audience, caused in part by his alcoholism, which gets worse and worse as the play progresses, forms the central core of this interesting play. But his effects on his audience, plus his effects on the woman he lives with and on his manager, all colored by his constant drinking, culminate in his murder at the end of the play. Ironically enough, he seems to have been murdered by a gang of drunks. Grace, the woman who lives with him and follows him on his faith healing tours, ultimately commits suicide while in Ballybeg, Ireland. And the faith healer's agent, Teddy, is constantly sipping bottles of beer for much of his time on stage. Ballybeg is Friel's generic small Irish town, and he uses the name repeatedly in his plays, though the name is made-up and the town does not really exist.

Faith Healer revolves around the alcoholism of the central character, and that alcoholism is in part responsible both for his death and the death of the woman he loves. Friel uses the format of the monologue for this play; the play is composed of four very long monologues by the three central characters. The main character of Frank gets two monologues which open and close the play. Frank's insecurities about the existence of his faith healing powers suggest most artists' insecurities about their own artistic powers. Are they real? Are they fake? Will the powers last? These are central concerns in this play, which always connects artistic powers with faith healing powers — and by implication, connects art with religion. Both art and religion, Friel suggests, have the power to heal suffering humanity. Friel uses the monologue technique later in his career in his play *Molly Sweeney*, also with three characters.

Soon after *Faith Healer* was staged, Brian Friel wrote *Translations*, which was first staged by the Field Day Theatre Company in the Guildhall in Derry on September 23, 1980. Some critics have argued that this is the best play he has written so far, and it is certainly his most ambitious. The play has also succeeded in London and New York, appearing three times on Broadway. It involves the hedge school movement in Ireland right before the potato famine, an indigenous movement of the Irish to educate their own people. One of the most clever aspects of this play is its juggling of four languages, though the play itself is of course written mainly in English. Most of the characters are supposed to be speaking the native Irish language, and also studying Greek and Latin in their hedge school, but the English enter speaking only their own language. So Latin, Greek, Irish, and English are all supposedly being spoken in the play — though in reality it's mainly in English with some Greek and Latin quotes. Friel has accomplished here a linguistic tour de force. The English come into the play saying they are there to create a map of Ireland to help the Irish people, though some of the Irish characters are immediately suspicious of them. That suspicion becomes fully realized when, at the end of the play, the English use the pretext of a missing soldier to steal all the land from the Irish and force them into refugee camps so that Scottish and English settlers can occupy the stolen land. The English commander, Captain Lancey, accuses the Irish of being terrorists to justify stealing all their property.

If ever that town, Friel's archetypical Ballybeg, needed a shrewd leader to defend Irish interests, it is during this English invasion. And the potato famine would occur soon after this invasion and its resultant ethnic cleansing. Alas, the main authority figure in the play remains Hugh, the person in charge of the hedge school. When he enters in the first act, he is described in the following stage directions: "A large man, with residual dignity, shabbily dressed, carrying a stick. He has, as always, a large quantity of drink taken, but he is by no means drunk." His drinking problem becomes immediately apparent here, and one of the running jokes in the play becomes the efforts of the other characters to keep Hugh away from bottles of whiskey. In the crucial final act, when the English push all the Irish in the town into refugee camps so that their land can be given to Scottish and English settlers, Hugh is totally drunk and completely unable to defend his school and his people. Like the drunken father figures in some of Friel's earlier plays, Hugh becomes yet another example of an Irish leader incapacitated by alcoholism in a time of crisis.

One of Friel's major successes, *Dancing at Lughnasa*, which was first staged in Dublin in 1990, and which appeared in 1998 as a movie with Meryl Streep, includes another sick father figure, Father Jack. While the text is not explicit on this character, since the whole play is a memory play from a child's point of view, the often mysterious behavior and sudden death of Father Jack, a priest and former missionary in Africa, suggests that he too was an alcoholic. The little boy, Michael, whose memory is the basis of the play, was abandoned by two fathers. His real father, Gerry, who never married his mother Chris, was also an alcoholic. When I saw the play done in both London and New York, Gerry often seemed drunk when he appeared. Ultimately, he abandoned his lover Chris and his son Michael. Michael's uncle, Father Jack, also died suddenly and seemed to be an alcoholic as well. He is also a partially comic figure; as a young priest he had gone to Africa to convert the natives, but we soon discover that the natives had converted him instead. He has become a devout believer in their pagan religion and abandoned his Catholicism. While his five sisters want him to say the Catholic Mass, he seems much more interested in the African religious rituals, for these are what he keeps talking about, and he never does say Mass. His sudden appearances, disappearances, and his sudden death suggest that he was probably a closeted alcoholic. He is yet another one of Friel's failed father figures, most of them alcoholics.

The human need for a father figure often becomes pathetically thwarted in Friel's plays because of paternal alcoholism. Over and over again a son or daughter's need for a father figure becomes a desperate and doomed search for guidance in the face of the authority figure's alcoholism and inability to perform duties, and the needs of the young person are doomed not to be met by the father figure.

One of Friel's more recent successes, *Molly Sweeney*, was first staged in Dublin in 1994, and was staged at the Roundabout Theater in New York the following year to very favorable reviews and had a very long run. Here Friel presents the problems of vision and blindness, based on his central character, Molly Sweeney, a contented and self-sufficient blind woman who is destroyed

Top: *Translations*, original Broadway production, 1981; Jarlath Conroy as Manus, Barnard Hughes as Hugh, and Stephen Burleigh as Owen (photograph: Gerry Goldstein). *Bottom*: *Translations*, 1995 Broadway production; Donal Donnelly as Jimmy Jack, David Herlihy as Doalty, Amelia Campbell as Sarah, Rufus Sewell as Owen, Dana Delaney as Maire, and Brian Dennehy as Hugh.

when her vision is partially restored after a long and delicate operation. The person who does the surgery is Dr. Rice, the local ophthalmologist, who is also clearly an alcoholic. While his motivations, and those of Molly's husband Frank, at first appear altruistic, we soon see the complexities of the situation. Dr. Rice, whose career and personal life have been so damaged by his alcoholism, tries to cure Molly Sweeney's blindness in part to save his damaged career. Molly's husband, Frank Sweeney, sees the miraculous operation as a way to get the publicity which he so obviously desires. Poor Molly, at the beginning of the play a confident and self-sufficient blind woman, has to be institutionalized by the end because her new sight has caused a complete emotional collapse. Friel again uses the long monologue technique for this three character play — as in *Faith Healer*. Friel also uses a terrible irony: when Molly was blind she was content but when her vision was restored she became incapacitated. Her husband and her doctor have destroyed her, thanks to their own private motives, which have nothing to do with her well-being and desires.

The alcoholism of the famous eye surgeon becomes apparent and indeed his whole career has clearly been damaged by his drinking problem. This has tragic consequences for both the eye doctor and for Molly Sweeney. Ophthalmology becomes a metaphor and symbol for the ability to see clearly in Friel's play, and the inability to see clearly becomes an incapacitating way of going through life, which is full of complicated needs which can never be rightfully fulfilled by an alcoholic. But this is clearly not just an Irish problem, given the high rates of alcoholism in other countries like Britain and America. One of the leading causes of failing out of college can be blamed on the excessive drinking and indeed alcoholism of many college students. Every year in the United States, about a thousand students drink themselves to death — a tragic loss of life in terms of the avoidability of such human losses.

While alcoholism was often part of the comedy of the stage–Irishman in many popular English comedies in the 19th century, early in this century many Irish playwrights came to resent this view of the Irish. But Irish playwrights themselves soon addressed the problems of alcoholism and its effects on the destruction of home life. Sean O'Casey's *Juno and the Paycock*, first staged in 1924, presents the main character, Captain Jack Boyle, and his friend, Joxer Daly, as drinking buddies and fellow alcoholics who are incapable of handling the responsibilities of family life; those responsibilities in fact fall onto the shoulders of the women of the family. By the final scene of the play the two men, Captain Boyle and Joxer, are dead drunk and staggering around the stage as the curtain falls. Throughout the play the audience hears the other characters complain about these two constantly running off to pubs to drink, but they remain essentially comic figures until the very end, when we finally see them as the hopeless drunks they really are. In our own time, Brian Friel has courageously addressed in his theatre all the horrors of alcoholism, since they are part of Irish culture and society, and part of our own society as well. But writers can write about alcoholism without themselves becoming alcoholics. While it is wonderful that so many great writers have written about this tragic social problem, it is also tragic that so many writers have themselves been alcoholics. Is that a requirement for writers? Are only the second-raters sober? I hope not! Among the sober writers I can list are Oscar Wilde, Bernard Shaw, Joseph Conrad, E. M. Forster, Wallace Stevens, D. H. Lawrence, Virginia Woolf, Doris Lessing, Tom Stoppard, and David Hare. Clearly one does not have to be a drunk to be a great writer. In addition, one does not have to be a drunk to understand and present onstage the damaging effects of alcoholism both on alcoholics and on the people around them. And certainly Brian Friel and others have written great plays which suggest, in part, what alcoholism does to people and the tragic damage it causes.

More recently, another Anglo-Irish playwright, Martin McDonagh, also uses the sad theme of alcoholism in Ireland. Some of his Irish critics argue that he is playing to the anti–Irish stereotypes to please his British and American audiences, though his plays have succeeded in Ireland as well. But in *The Cripple of Inishmaan* we have several alcoholic characters who are quite cheerful and entertaining. Serious, excessive drinking remains the curse of the Irish in some of Martin McDonagh's plays, but American and English playwrights have presented that curse as a major problem of every society.

One of McDonagh's most recent plays, *The Lieutenant of Inishmore,* includes the character of Donny, an alcoholic father, who waves a half-empty bottle of whiskey during many of his scenes and is visibly drunk. This comic, grotesque, violent, and bloody play presents a comedy using the British anti–Irish stereotypes, the Irish as alcoholic and bloody and the IRA and its splinter groups as personifications of this anti–Irish stereotype. As one character says while he is sawing a body in half, "Oh, will the bloodshed never end!" The audience laughs at the comedy of the situation and how clichéd the line is — implying that no, the bloodshed will never end. Alcoholism seems to be a central issue here as bottles of booze remain constantly on stage as the characters drink to motivate their bloody and bizarre behavior. Perhaps making a joke about this tragedy becomes a survival mechanism — and a means of entertaining an audience.

Addiction problems, especially addition to alcohol, remain central to both British and American cultures and that their theatre reflects these problems is hardly surprising. That British, English, Irish, and American playwrights depict characters constantly drinking and often drinking to excess clearly reflect addiction problems in their respective cultures. And the consequences of those addiction problems become dramatized in the failed marriages, failed relationships, violence, and ruined lives which result.

Too often American and British movies and plays present getting drunk as cute and a rite of passage for college students; instead, the sober ones are often presented as nerds while the drinkers are presented as the really cool ones. Indeed, in many American movies virtually all the characters are constantly smoking—no doubt a result of the product placement campaigns of the films' producers—so that the stars are always drinking and smoking. The image for the viewer is that the really cool people, the stars, spend all their time drinking and smoking. If viewers then absorb these subconscious messages in the movies, and as a result themselves become addicted to alcohol and tobacco, movie directors and producers do not seem to care much about the consequences once they have received their money. But sometimes both plays and playwrights portray the tragic consequences of these addiction problems. Serious drinkers and smokers die fairly early, so the manufacturers of these substances clearly need to replace constantly their customers since the older customers are dying at an alarming rate. Subconscious advertisements for products like tobacco and alcohol appear in many films, and that can hardly be an accident but instead the result of money changing hands.

While playwrights can portray these problems, many Hollywood movies perpetuate the problem by continuing to glamorize drinking and smoking as signs of wealth and status in the society. These subconscious product and addiction endorsements have tragic consequences for many of the viewers of these movies.

One can find a classic example of this kind of advertising in the American film *Titanic*, which was wildly popular and made millions of dollars in revenue. Millions of dollars were also spent on advertising this film, and the money most probably came from the tobacco lobby since the young lovers in the movie, played by Leonardo DiCaprio and Kate Winslet, are constantly smoking—in fact the heroine proves her liberation from her calculating mother by smoking. This is exactly the message which the tobacco lobby wants to get out to young people to sell their addictive products to them.

People who smoke tend to drink, and that problem has often appeared in the theatre of Brian Friel, Edward Albee, Simon Gray, Harold Pinter, and Martin McDonagh. Clearly the neuroses of alcohol addiction, and other kinds of addictions, appear in many famous contemporary plays. And many of these very playwrights had to struggle with their own addiction problems and used their plays to dramatize these personal struggles.

Addiction problems, especially the addiction to alcohol, cost both Britain and America countless millions in lost revenue through absenteeism, lost lives, and thwarted careers. Many psychiatrists and other counselors see many needy patients as a result of this and other addictions, and some of our most important contemporary playwrights have used their own personal addiction struggles as the basis for some very exciting plays.

Bibliography

DiGaetani, John Louis *A Search for a Postmodern Theater: Interviews with Contemporary Playwrights.* Westport, Conn.: Greenwood Press, 1991.

Floyd, Virginia. *The Plays of Eugene O'Neill: A New Assessment.* New York: Frederick Ungar, 1985.

Gassner, John. *Eugene O'Neill.* Minneapolis: University of Minnesota Press, 1965.

Gelb, Arthur and Barbara. *O'Neill: Life with Monte Cristo.* New York: Applause, 2000.

Sheaffer, Louis. *O'Neill: Son and Artist.* Boston: Little, Brown, and Co., 1973.

Sternlicht, Sanford. *A Reader's Guide to Modern American Drama.* Syracuse, N.Y.: Syracuse University Press, 2002.

_____. *A Reader's Guide to Modern British Drama.* Syracuse: Syracuse University Press, 2004.

7

Harold Pinter
Sadomasochism

Patterns of sadistic and masochistic behavior occur often in the plays of Harold Pinter, particularly very subtle aggressive and passive-aggressive behaviors. This chapter will show where these behaviors occur, primarily in Pinter's *The Caretaker, The Homecoming, and Betrayal* —arguably his three greatest plays, certainly the plays which have been staged most frequently in both England and America. But this chapter will also look at some of his other plays as well, in an attempt to explain the nature of his appeal as a dramatist. Since winning the Nobel Prize for Literature in 2005, his plays have attracted even more attention internationally and been staged more frequently on the world's stages to ever larger audiences.

Pinter silences have become a staple of the modern theater — indeed for a while *The New Yorker* magazine did a series of jokes about the famous Pinter pauses. But what do they mean? Pinter himself has said in interviews that he regrets that he ever put those pauses in his scripts since they have become such a cliché and even a joke.

All three of these plays trace a pattern of sadism in Pinter's characters which seems to indicate his cynical view of human nature, human behavior, and human relationships. Pinter's famous uses of silences and pauses often indicate the sadistic intent of his characters, an intent which has been rarely presented on the contemporary stage. Those famous Pinteresque silences and pauses are usually one character's attempt to make another character very uncomfortable. Often the silences occur after a question. When one character asks a question and the other delays a response, that can be a way to torture the other person — the classic passive-aggressive behavior of using a passive action (silence, pause) for an aggressive intent (to make another person suffer). An even more frequent example of passive-aggressive behavior is the person who is always late — being chronically and repeatedly late is a classic example of passive-aggressive.

Such behavior can also have a sexual component, as we will see in our discussion of these three popular Pinter plays. Pinter's investigation of this element in human behavior and the theme of human cruelty remain his most original contributions to the contemporary stage. Several of these plays have also been filmed to great effect — especially *Betrayal* with Jeremy Irons, Ben Kingsley, and Patricia Hodge and Peter Hall's famous film version of *The Homecoming*, though this latter is clearly a filmed version of a staged play rather than an independently made film.

In *The Caretaker*, which was first staged in London in 1960 but was soon staged all over the world, we are presented with an old, homeless man — Davies — who seems desperate for housing. But we are also presented with an apparently mentally handicapped young man, Ashton, who invites him into his dilapidated house. His crueler brother, Mick, seems to enjoy torturing the old man by repeatedly asking who he is, what he is doing in his house, and tossing the old man's possessions around the room. There are many power plays in the play — an intended pun — but the questions remain: Who is using whom? Who is the crueler character? The old man Davies seems to be an old reprobate who appears kindly but clearly wants to use the young man for a free roof over his head. And what of the two young men? Are they looking for a father figure, or are they looking for someone to torture? Is there a homoerotic element in the young men's interest in the destitute old man? While the older brother Ashton seems passive and more kindly and more emotionally needy, the younger brother Mick seems meaner but is perhaps even more needy. Perhaps Pinter is suggesting that sadomasochistic behavior indicates both a real personal need plus anger at having such a need — often caused by a previously unsuccessful relationship with a rejecting partner or rejecting parent.

While the ending presents the old man Davies as desperate at being pushed out of the house by the two young men who own it, one is left wondering who is using whom, and who is torturing whom. Such a complex view of power relationships among people is a highly original theatrical device and insight used by Pinter. One can't help wondering if his view of humanity and human relationships is overly cynical or absolutely realistic.

Often the title in a Pinter play has multiple meanings. Who is the caretaker in *The Caretaker*? Is Davies looking for a caretaker to take care of him and keep him off the streets, where he has been living? Is Mick taking care of his brother Ashton because he is mentally handicapped? Is Ashton taking care of his brother Mick because he is violent and angry? Are all three men in the play looking for a caretaker because all three need someone to take care of them? All three men are also without women, the classic caretakers of society; do all three men need some woman to take care of them? The title remains highly suggestive and can mean many things.

In *The Homecoming*, first staged in 1965, the title itself indicates a central concern with family life. The title itself also seems like the title of a kitschy Norman Rockwell painting — with the long-lost wandering or even prodigal son returning to his loving family. Here too we have a long-lost son, Teddy, returning to London with his wife Ruth to introduce her to his family — a father, an uncle, and two brothers. He has been living as a college professor in America, and he and Ruth have three sons. But his father Max and two younger brothers, Lenny and Joey, steal his wife and turn her into their own mistress plus a prostitute — something she fully agrees to.

But who is the real victim here? Who is the aggressor? Teddy has married and fathered three sons after moving to a college town somewhere in America, but he has never told his family about all these changes in his life. The family have neither seen nor heard from him in years. This is classic passive-aggressive behavior, since his silence about his marriage and family has the effect of denying his family knowledge they would expect. Such

The Homecoming, original Broadway production, 1967; John Norrington as Sam, Paul Rogers as Max, Terence Rigby as Joey, Ian Holm as Lenny, and Michael Craig as Teddy.

The Homecoming, New York, 1978; Danny Sowell as Joey, John Harkins as Teddy, Patricia Roe as Ruth, Lloyd Battista as Sam, William Roerick as Max, and Denis Holmes as Lenny (photograph: Friedman-Abeles).

behavior generates real anger in this family, and they get even by trying to seduce his wife. So we have an ugly view of family life: a father and two sons seducing the wife of the other son, and having the full cooperation of the wife.

The ugliness of sibling relationships is presented on another level and by another generation in the relationship between the two old men in the play — Max and his brother Sam. Their conversation seems fraught with tension and nasty implications, and when Sam apparently dies in the last act of the play his final statement to his only brother is to tell him that his wife Jesse was unfaithful to him with one of their mutual friends. Max expresses no sorrow at the death of his brother at the end of the play but instead seems quite pleased.

By the end of the play, Teddy returns to his position as a college teacher in America, but his wife Ruth is surrounded by her father-in-law Max and her two brothers-in-law. She will provide sexual favors for them, plus she has agreed to let them pimp for her as she becomes a high-class prostitute. As her husband leaves to return to America, Ruth says "Eddie, don't become a stranger" — by the way, his name is Teddy, not Eddie.

Is there some misogyny here — a view of women as natural prostitutes very willing to play one man off another for her sexual favors, a woman who enjoys pitting son against son and father against son for the sake of proving her sexual power over men? Is this incest? It is certainly sexuality within one family — a reversed Oedipal complex with a father trying to seduce the wife of his son. Sexuality and seduction become part of the way the characters ignore normal family boundaries in order to torture each other — perhaps to get back at each other for previous wrongs. Or is the whole play Ruth's dream? Or Max's? Or ours?

Both the brothers, Lenny and Joey, attempt to seduce their brother's wife. She seems very willing to cooperate with this attempt to cuckold her husband. Her very name, Ruth, suggests one of the heroines of the Old Testament — a primordial name suggesting a primordial woman. There is a pattern of repetitions here as well, since Max had three sons and his first son Teddy has three sons. Max's brother Sam has been childless, as have the two brothers of Teddy. Max repeatedly refers to his dead wife Jesse as a whore, and Teddy's wife Ruth has become a whore by the end of the play — though her dialogue earlier in the play suggests that she had been a whore before she married Teddy, is bored with her middle-class life as the wife of an American professor in a small college town, and is eager to get back to her earlier trade as a prostitute on Greek Street in London. Does she enjoy being the paid sexual object of men? Does she enjoy playing men off each other in order to prove her sexual desirability as a woman? Is she eager to abandon her role as a mother in order to become a professional prostitute?

All of these questions make the audience profoundly uneasy, yet they are clearly implied in the ironically titled *The Homecoming* — where the returning son Teddy hardly finds the loving welcome of his family but instead sexual predators who enjoy stealing his wife from him. But does he mind? Is his return perhaps really his attempt to rid himself of a whorish wife? Does he want to torture his father and brothers with the fact that he has a sexual partner and they do not — and do they respond by stealing his wife? He never seems to indicate that he is sorry to lose her to the other men in his family — once again, who is torturing whom? Who is the sadist? Is Teddy a sadist wanting to torture his father and brothers, or is he a masochist who knows full well how they behave and brings his wife home to be tortured? Ruth herself has three sons back in America, but she seems in no way interested in returning to America to continue being either Teddy's wife or their mother. The play raises many interesting questions about power relationships in families and the awareness of sexual behavior as a way of torturing other members of one's family.

Pinter also implies here Konrad Lorenz's view of animal behavior. Lorenz found in his studies that animals will kill their own offspring when confronted with a possible sexual partner. He found that a rooster will attack any other rooster in the farmyard, even if that other young rooster happens to be his own son, because they are all fighting for sex. Lorenz's studies of animal behavior became famous in the '60s and '70s, and Pinter's plays reflect Conrad's studies. Pinter suggests in *The Homecoming* that human beings remain like animals in this regard, and they are all competitive with each other, particularly when a potential mate appears. Family ties are ultimately meaningless given more important male realities like power and the hunt for sexual partners.

Lorenz's famous book *On Aggression* helped him to win the Nobel Prize in 1973, though his book was first printed in Austria in 1966, around the time that Printer was writing his plays. In terms of Lorenz's theories, *The Homecoming* can be seen as the story of an aging alpha male, Max, with his three sons snarling around him and trying to become the new alpha male. Things become most intense when a female enters the ring, and both the aging alpha male and his three sons struggle for dominance and mating rights. In the beginning of the play the old alpha male Max is sitting in the main chair in the room, but by the end of the play the female Ruth has taken possession of the main chair in the room and all the males, including the dispossessed old alpha male, struggle for her attention and affection. In terms of Lorenz's theories of aggression and animal struggles for dominance, family relationships among males count for nothing in the struggle for mating rights.

And whose homecoming is occurring in this play? Is Teddy coming to his home after being absent so many years? Or is Ruth coming home to London after having lived in America apparently unhappily? Is Teddy returning home to America after the trauma of his homecoming back to his family in London, where he has been treated brutally by his wife and the male members of his own family? Or is Teddy coming to London to get rid of his wife, a former prostitute after all, and is he going home to America by the end of the play? England and America are played off against each other in the play, with the English primarily playing the role of servants to the rich Americans. Pinter seems to be suggesting that world power has shifted away from England and to America and it is the English who are serving the interests of the Americans, who have more money and power. Or is the play about the English sadomasochistic desire to torture the rich and powerful Americans? As is so often the case in a Pinter play, sadism and masochism go together, and one is left wondering who has the upper hand in the end. Is life an endless processions of torturous relationships with all people enjoying torturing the people who are closest to them? Such a cynical view of human relationships seems to permeate the theater of Harold Pinter.

Pinter's next major success in the theater was *No Man's Land,* which was first staged in London in 1974, and here too sadomasochistic relationships seem to abound. The play takes place in the home of a very wealthy and successful author, and a failed poet is trying to insinuate himself into the household. In the last act he seems to be imprisoned in the house by the wealthy author, who seems to enjoy torturing the unsuccessful author. But there are also servants in the house who seems to be controlling both men. By the end of the play the audience is wondering who is in control here. And both writers seem drunk for much of the play, and they certainly drink a lot throughout the play. Here we have two aging males, one clearly a successful alpha male, and the other clearly a failure, struggling for dominance and control.

We can call *Betrayal* a *drame à clef* because it was born of a real-life scandal — when Harold Pinter ran off with Lady Antonia Fraser, the wife of his best friend Lord Hugh Fraser. Pinter's wife, the actress Vivien Merchant, died soon afterwards, and the famous biographer Lady Fraser left her children for Harold Pinter. When *Betrayal* was first staged in 1978, the London audience was fully aware of the personal drama behind the play's dramatic situation. Since the situation in the play so resembles Pinter's own, the audience undoubtedly wondered if the play was Pinter's explanation of how the scandal occurred and who — if anyone — was to blame for it. Pinter himself ran off with his best friend's wife; does his play *Betrayal* provide the audience with his explanation of his behavior and the nature of the complex relationships between the two men and the wife? Apparently. That is certainly how most of the original audience in London responded to the play's premiere in 1978.

The same Pinteresque situation appears in *Betrayal,* and the question becomes who betrayed whom? Once again, we are presented with a rather sadistic view of women. Does the female character, Emma, enjoy betraying her husband with his best friend in order to prove her powers of seduction by manipulating both men? Does Emma get a secret thrill out of betraying her husband with her husband's best friend in order to prove her desirability as a woman? Does the lover, Jerry, enjoy torturing his best friend, Robert, by secretly having an affair with Robert's wife Emma? Though Robert and Jerry are presented as best friends in the play, there are also clearly tensions in their relationship. Is either man partially or subconsciously homosexual and enjoying some kind of sexual bond with the other man via the wife Emma? Or are both men simply very successful alpha males struggling for dominance and mating rights in this highly complicated ménage à trios?

Or does Robert secretly know about the affair, and is he having a secret thrill by torturing his wife and best friend by pretending not to know about their affair? Is Jerry sadistically enjoying having an affair for years with the wife of his best friend Robert? By the end of the affair, one must conclude that each of the three characters has betrayed the other two — and that this ménage à trios needs all three characters to continue. When Robert and Emma divorce, Jerry loses all interest in Emma despite the fact that she is now legally available to him, though he is still married to another woman. Does this weird threesome need the added sexual energy of sadomasochistic behavior to keep going? That is clearly what the play implies. Jerry does not leave his long-suffering wife by the end of the play to be with the woman he says he loves, Robert's wife Emma, though she is still with a family — and one of the recurrent questions in the play is who is the father of her children?

The title of the play, *Betrayal*, is used in many different ways during the course of the action of the play. Jerry has clearly betrayed his friend Robert by having an affair of many years of his best friend's wife. And Emma has clearly betrayed her husband by having an affair with her husband's best friend. But Robert in a way has also betrayed both his wife and his best friend, since he knows of the affair and does not confront either his wife or his friend about what is going on. Who ultimately is the greatest betrayer in this play of multiple betrayals? The audience is shown various betrayals on many levels and is left to wonder who if anyone is the most guilty of the three.

Pinter has created a new kind of drama here in which the very nature of humanity is questioned. Pinter's view of both family life and humanity in general seems to indicate a sadomasochistic view of how people operate, especially within the family. The Germans have a word for it: schadenfreude, or happiness at someone else's grief. The men in all these plays seem to enjoy more than anything else torturing someone else, particularly a member of their own family. And this behavior often has a sexual component. Pinter suggests in his theater that not only is the heart a lonely hunter but also a cruel one.

Relationships inevitably involve power, aggression, sadism, masochism, and even passive-aggressive behavior. Ultimately Pinter suggests that people are much more complicated then they know, and that their relationships are often beyond their conscious understanding.

Pinter's plays also emphasize the rivalry among people — particularly the rivalry among men, especially when a woman is present. Pinter presents men as appallingly competitive, especially with men within their own families. Often in a Pinter play we have males struggling to become alpha males. Was Pinter himself so aggressive with his male friends? Maybe, but we also know that he had many friendships with other male playwrights, especially Simon Gray and Tom Stoppard, so clearly there must be a cooperative and friendly side to Pinter as well which enables him to maintain close friendships with other men, even if on one occasion he ran off with a best friend's wife.

The theater of Harold Pinter investigates among many other things the complex nature of people and the sadomasochistic quality of many relationships. Pinter presents people as highly complex but also highly competitive and very willing to best the other people in some of the most sadistic and ugly ways possible. It is indeed a jungle out there, primarily because of Pinter's animalistic view of human nature. Here too Konrad Lorenz's theories of human aggression and the similarities of our behavior with our mammalian relatives in the animal world add to the cynical fascination of Pinter's theater. Surprisingly, the plays often gets laughs too.

In most of the Pinter plays the characters drink a lot, especially in *No Man's Land* and *Betrayal*. One of the things that is going through the audience's mind in these plays is: if any or all of these characters have a major drinking problem. In both these plays the characters seem to consume an enormous amount of drink, and by the end of the first act of *No Man's Land* the characters seem to be staggering around the stage drunk — depending of course on the director and production involved. Are these plays really about what alcoholism drives people to do that they would not do when they are sober? Or is all the drinking a way of befuddling the characters' minds to avoid the consequences of their often sadistic behavior? Or is all the drinking a way of making the characters seem more realistic in terms of the way English people socialize — often by drinking? Or, are these plays reflecting the Latin motto of "in vino veritas," in wine there is truth. Often it is only after a few drinks that Pinter's characters are able to reveal their true selves and their true motivation, and that motivation is often sadistic.

Clearly Pinter lives to pose more questions and suggest more possible interpretations than he can clarify, but that is the sign of a really interesting playwright. Pinter has a genius for creating fascinating characters and fascinating situations, and the notorious pauses and silences add to the aura of mystery in Pinter's wonderful plays. If an audience can totally understand a play, that play can easily seem dull and mechanical. But a Pinter play has a whole host of possible meanings and as a result remains very interesting and totally absorbing to an audience, and also as a result the play can be staged many different ways and give different actors and directors a variety of possible ways of approaching and interpreting these days. Those Pinter pauses are very pregnant and meaningful indeed. The audience in a Pinter play is usually left with a series of questions and a series of mysteries to contemplate. All those Pinteresque silences become quite meaningful by the end of each of these plays, and one is ultimately left with an appallingly cynical view of human relationships, especially how these relationships can be so easily sadomasochistic and useful on many different levels. Ultimately one is also left with a complex view of human motivation, and one is left wondering at the end of a Pinter play if these characters' motivations are as sadistic as they appear. Or is the whole play one character's dream?

Pinter's view of humanity and human motivation also brings up some moral questions about the rarity of goodness and kindness in the human quest for power, money, and dominance. Pinter's characters can be either poor (as in *The Caretaker*) or quite wealthy (as in *Betrayal*), yet the male desire for power, control, and mating rights pits men against each other in a fascinating way in Pinter's plays. If the view of humanity which is communicated to the audience in these plays is rather frightening, it certainly precludes boredom. Often, the audience responds with laughter — an appalled laughter, but a laugh none the less. Perhaps this is the laugh of recognition.

Bibliography

Billington, Michael. *The Life and Work of Harold Pinter*. London: Faber and Faber, 1996.

Brown, John Russell. *A Short Guide to Modern British Drama*. London: Heinemann, 1982.

Cahn, Victor I. *Gender and Power in the Plays of Harold Pinter*. Basingstoke, England: Macmillan, 1993.

Gale, Steven H. *Butter's Going Up: A Critical Analysis of Harold Pinter's Work*. Durham, N.C.: Duke University Press, 1977.

Gordon, David J. *Bernard Shaw and the Comic Sublime*. New York: St. Martin's Press, 1990.

Lorenz, Konrad. *On Aggression*. New York: Routledge, 2002.

Merritt, Susan Hollis. *Pinter in Play: Critical Strategies and the Plays of Harold Pinter*. Durham, N.C.: Duke University Press, 1990.

Peacock, D. Keith. *Harold Pinter and the New British Theater*. Westport, Conn.: Greenwood Press, 1997.

Raby, Peter, ed. *The Cambridge Companion to Harold Pinter*. Cambridge, England: Cambridge University Press, 2001.

Smith, Ian, ed. *Pinter in the Theatre*. London: Nick Hern Books, 2005.

Sternlicht, Sanford *A Reader's Guide to Modern British Drama*. Syracuse: Syracuse University Press, 2004.

8

Benjamin Britten
Pedophilia

The most recent biographers of Benjamin Britten, especially Humphrey Carpenter and Michael Oliver, have been completely candid about what many audience members and critics have long suspected, that Britten's own pedophilia often appears in his operas. Many of the operas involve relationships between grown men and young boys, often with disastrous consequences for both. His most successful operas often dramatize exclusively male relationships and often those relationships involve young men or boys. His primary compositions were in the service of the theater, and his choice of librettos indicated his fascination both with theater and with his own obsessions.

In his book on Britten, Michael Oliver has commented:

> There are two difficulties in writing about him. The first is that he was a homosexual at a time when homosexuality was illegal in the United Kingdom. Britten and his lover Peter Pears lived together openly for over thirty years, but both they and their close friends were understandably cautious about referring to their relationship. It is hard for anyone who remembers only the relatively liberal 1980s and 1990s, with much talk of "gay liberation" and with films and novels discussing the preoccupations and lifestyles of homosexual men, to imagine the prurience, censoriousness and sheer danger that surrounded homosexuals in the years before the relaxation of the law in 1967. Press reports of the arrest and imprisonment of homosexuals were frequent. So were violent assaults ("queer-bashing"), blackmail and police entrapment, though these were less often mentioned by newspapers.
>
> Britten was also attracted to teenage or pubescent boys. Some of them have spoken of his relations with them, which seem not to have gone further than affectionate caresses or the occasional kiss; both would have been seen by the law, of course, then as now, as acts of gross indecency or as sexual abuse. In such circumstances it is hardly surprising that Britten very rarely discussed his sexuality, even with his closest friends [Oliver 8–9].

Humphrey Carpenter, who has written the best biography of Britten, has also commented about Britten's relationship with Peter Pears: "He [Britten] had probably hoped that by committing himself to Pears he would be able to eliminate his powerful feelings for boys" (Carpenter 161). But the biographer reports that the relationship with Peter Pears did not accomplish this for Britten and he continued to be sexually attracted to adolescent boys, though the relationships were platonic according to his biographers.

Certainly the great love of Britten's life remained the tenor Peter Pears, and the composer wrote some of his most wonderful music with Pears's voice in mind. Indeed, Pears himself sang the premiere of most of the great tenor roles in the Britten operas — roles like Peter Grimes, Captain Vere, and Gustav von Aschenbach. Yet the evidence seems to suggest that the love between Britten and Pears soon became platonic, and that they lived together for many years in a profound and long-lasting relationship which most would call a marriage but that did not include sex, which seems to have stopped within a few years of their knowing and loving each other. Britten hoped that the relationship would cure him of his pedophilia, but he was to be sadly disappointed in this aspect of the central love relationship in his life.

One of Britten's librettists, Myfanwy Piper, has commented on this topic:

> Myfanwy Piper says that Britten "did talk to me a bit" about this friendships with boys. "He would go for long walks — I remember one occasion when he did, perhaps two — and he would say that it was very upsetting to him, worrying. He found it a temptation, and he was very worried about it." She did not know that "he's gone so far" as to kiss boys, or offer kisses, and is sure that nothing further went on — "I think he kept the rules" [Carpenter 352].

The critic John Gill has written of Britten:

> He began composing music at the age of nine, and in both junior and secondary schools developed strong attachments to other, younger, boys. These were — and, it would appear, remained throughout his life — platonic in the modern sense, although there is some hearsay evidence to suggest that, had his own reserve not got in the way, he might have consummated one or two of these relationships. It is possible that Britten was indeed a pedophile, who either did not act on his desires or managed to suppress them. With just one exception, all the young boys with whom Britten had these intense friendships attest that the composer was never more than fatherly or avuncular towards them, and that his affections never strayed into the realm of eroticism. Only one young friend, Jonathan Gathorne-Hardy, said that Britten had played an elaborate game of seductions with him. If Gathorne-Hardy had been willing, he tells Carpenter, "We would have ended up in that double bed." It is unlikely that much would have happened in the double bed, for Britten was a boy lover who had a courtly ideal of the innocent youth, even though some of his operas involved placing innocent youth in positions of extreme, and in the case of *Peter Grimes* fatal, jeopardy [Gill 14].

Such a game of seduction which Hardy experienced with Britten would still frighten and repel most parents of young boys. While earlier ages and civilizations (like the Greek and Roman) might have looked with greater toleration upon such man-boy relationships, ours would certainly not. The laws in both the United States and Britain would still see such a relationship as illegal and naturally exploitative of the child involved. Such a relationship, so often in the news with Catholic priests as the ones accused of such exploitation of children, continues to present the public with the unfortunately negative stereotype of the gay man as exploiter of children.

In any case, the composer's operatic compositions did involve man-boy relationships. Britten's first major success as an opera composer was *Peter Grimes*, which was first staged in London at Covent Garden in June of 1945 and eventually became a world-wide success. Some critics have argued that this is still his best opera, and certainly it is his most frequently performed. The main character in that work, Peter Grimes, becomes responsible for the deaths of his apprentices, young boys. The opera opens with Peter Grimes in a court room on trial for the death of one of his apprentices. He is not found guilty in the death of the boy, but he is issued a warning by the court to be more careful in his treatment of his apprentices. In the final act of the opera, another young apprentice falls to his death, and then Peter Grimes, on advice from Captain Bulstrode, a friend in the town, commits suicide. Would Captain Bulstrode have suggested to Peter that he commit suicide if those apprentices had not been victims of Grimes on some level?

While on one level the opera is about a lonely, isolated fisherman's bad luck with his apprentices, the repeated deaths of the young boys can be interpreted as a symbol of sexual molestation, and the whole opera can be seen as a product of Britten's own guilt over his sexual feelings for young boys. Britten often felt guilty about his attraction to boys, and perhaps the opera suggests that such persons should commit suicide. The famous Canadian tenor Jon Vickers (a famous Peter Grimes) has responded violently to the suggestion that this is what the opera is about, but there exists substantial evidence that this is the case from the characters and dramatic situations in the opera and from what we know of Britten's own sexual desires.

Jon Vickers and others have argued that the opera is really about the problems of isolation and what an isolated character like Peter Grimes can be driven to by the uncaring society around him. The opera ends with the chorus onstage noticing a boat sinking in the distance, probably knowing that Peter Grimes is on that boat, and not much caring. Does the opera suggest that the world is better off without Peter Grimes? Does the opera also suggest that society can be very cruel to people it has chosen to ignore? Or does the opera also suggest that pedophiles are so dangerous to society that it does not want their continued existence and wishes for their speedy extermina-

Left: *Peter Grimes*, Metropolitan Opera, 1994; Anthony Rolfe Johnson in the title role (photograph: Winnie Klotz). *Right*: *Peter Grimes*, Metropolitan Opera, 1983; Thomas Stewart as Capt. Balstrode (photograph: Winnie Klotz).

tion? The moral implications in all these questions certainly add to the fascination of Britten's opera.

Another example of the theme of pedophilia occurs in Britten's *Albert Herring,* which was first staged at Glyndebourne in 1947. This opera also involves a young boy. The central character, Albert Herring, is about fifteen or sixteen years old, and he finds himself in the comic and embarrassing situation of being elected King of the May because there are no young girls who could possibly be elected Queen of the May since he seems to be the only virgin left in the town. By the end, he too has lost his virginity — after someone spikes the punch at the village fete (while the orchestra plays love music from Wagner's *Tristan und Isolde*).

While this work is a wonderful comedy, complete with the happy ending of Albert losing his virginity and becoming independent of his possessive mother, the sex life of a young boy, although a teenager, remains the central concern of the opera — indicating yet again that one of the sources of Britten's creativity remained male adolescent sexuality. That Albert Herring seems to have become heterosexual, that his sexual initiation was with a woman rather than a man, appears satisfying enough for most audiences. Yet there is something troubling about this opera as well, since it is yet another example of the composer's apparently leering fascination with adolescent male sexuality.

Britten's next opera, *The Little Sweep*, which was first staged in Aldeburgh in 1949, is an opera written for children — all boys. Here too, the young boys are the central concern, and here as well Britten employs boys for the vocal parts. The text is based on William Blake's famous 18th century poems about the sad fate of the chimney sweeps of London at the time. Britten clearly enjoyed writing for this vocal range in both his operas and his church music, and also enjoyed rehearsing the boys before the actual premiere of the opera. Britten's *War Requiem* also uses boy sopranos to great effect. Humphrey Carpenter has suggested that Britten rarely felt comfortable around adults but often felt quite comfortable around children, especially boys. That that affection also contained a sexual component has become quite clear both in the music of Britten's operas and in the reports of his biographers.

Britten's next major opera, *Billy Budd*, which premiered in London in 1951, is now considered one of Britten's best works. The opera, based on Herman Melville's wonderful story of the same title, also involves a central male character, the very attractive Billy Budd. While he is a young man and not a child, there is a childlike quality to him. In fact, Dansker and some of the other sailors on board the ship call him "Baby Billy," but he is hanged at the end as a result of Claggert's malign fascination with him. Captain Vere's final monologue ends the opera and indicates that he too remained throughout his life obsessed with the beautiful boy/man Billy Budd. No women appear in this opera, only men and boys, and their relationships dramatize this wonderful work.

It is interesting that E. M. Forster, the main librettist for *Billy Budd*, was disappointed with Britten's music for the opera. Forster wrote to Britten about the music of the opera: "I did not, at my first hearing, feel it sufficiently important musically. I want *passion*— love constricted, perverted, poisoned, but never the less flowing down its agonized channel; a sexual discharge gone vile. Not soggy depression or growling remorse. I seemed to be turning from one musical discomfort to another, and was dissatisfied. I looked for an aria perhaps, for a more recognizable form" (Carpenter 291).

Britten dismissed Forster's musical criticisms by called him "a Wagnerian," which Forster certainly was and Britten was not. But Forster felt that the situations and attractions in the opera were clearly sexual in nature, so he wanted the music to sound sexual as well. This Britten could not do — perhaps because of his guilt over his own pedophilia. The eroticism of much of Wagner's music was needed, given the dramatic situations in Britten's *Billy Budd*, but Britten was not the composer who would write it.

Left: Revival of *Billy Budd*, Metropolitan Opera, 1997; Dwayne Croft in the title role (photograph: Winnie Klotz). *Right*: *Billy Budd*, Metropolitan Opera, 1992; Thomas Hampson in the title role (photograph: Winnie Klotz).

In *Billy Budd* all the characters are male and isolated from the rest of society. The first act of Wagner's *Tristan und Isolde* takes place on a ship, and the passion of the two central characters appears wonderfully in the sexual, passionate music of much of the opera. The homosexual passion which is the subtext of much of Britten's *Billy Budd* cannot be detected in the music, glorious though much of it remains. Forster wanted the sexual subject of the libretto to be apparent in the opera's music, but this frightened Britten. His pedophilia made him frightened of sexuality, I believe, and that left him incapable of composing music which reflected many of the main themes of his operas' libretti. Richard Wagner here makes a telling contrast to Benjamin Britten since Wagner's music is so often erotic and he became famous, often shockingly famous, for the erotic music he wrote for characters like Venus in *Tannhäuser*, Tristan, Isolde, Brünnhilde, Siegfried, and Kundry. In Wagner's operas the erotic text in his libretti clearly finds dramatic equivalence in the erotic music he wrote for these characters and situations. Perhaps it was Britten's British ancestry which did not enable him to write the kind of erotic music which many of his characters and dramatic situations seem to demand. In addition, of course, the particular nature of his own sexuality and the guilt which such sexuality produced in him incapacitated him to compose a new, modern kind of erotic music which his characters and dramatic situations seem to need.

But many musicologists would also insist that Britten was a modernist, not a Romantic composer like Richard Wagner, and had to develop a new style of musical composition. Here too Britten makes an interesting contrast with another twentieth century composer, Giacomo Puccini, whose operatic music clearly reflects much of the eroticism of his characters and dramatic situations. There is plenty of eroticism in the music of Puccini's *Manon Lescaut, La Bohème, Madama Butterfly,* and even his later operas like *Turandot.* But Puccini was not homosexual, though he may have been a bit of a pedophile given his tragic relationship with Doria Manfredi. She was a young girl whom Puccini's wife Antonietta falsely accused of having an affair with the composer. The girl become so distraught over the accusations of Puccini's wife that she committed suicide, though her virginity and innocence were eventually proven in court.

Clearly Giacomo Puccini did not have an affair with this teenage girl, though he might have had an affair with other teenage girls. His anguish over the suicide of Doria Manfredi becomes apparent in his presentation of the character of Liu in his final opera, *Turandot.* Pedophilia becomes much more ominous when homosexuality is involved, but should it? Why does society seem much more willing to forgive an older man's obsession with a 16 year old female than an equally powerful obsession with a 16 year old male?

An even better example of pedophilia remains *The Turn of the Screw,* which is based on Henry James's famous novella of 1898. Britten's opera follows the plot almost exactly. The opera premiered in Venice on September 14, 1954, and has since been staged around the world, often with great success. On the most obvious level, both the opera and the story it is based on can be seen as a ghost story, with the new governess entering a haunted house and trying to protect her two charges, Miles and Flora, from the evil influence of two ghosts — Peter Quint and Miss Jessel, their former caretakers who have both since died. On another level, the story can be seen as an example of Henry James's clever use of the technique of the unreliable narrator — in other words, the new governess becomes insane and in the end frightens the poor boy Miles to death in her effort to protect him from the imaginary ghosts that only she sees and which do not in fact exist. But on a deeper level, the opera (and the story) can be seen as a tale of sexual molestation. When Peter Quint and Miss Jessel sing that "The ceremony of innocence is drowned," they can be referring to their sexual molestation of these two children, and the opera can be interpreted as Britten's fear of what his sexual interests are doing to the boys he has become obsessed with.

The boy who sang Miles in the original production of the opera in Venice, David Hemmings, has been the subject of an interesting article by Tom Sutcliffe in the program booklet for the Welsh National Opera's production of *The Turn of the Screw*. The actor/singer has asserted that the relationship was totally platonic and that Britten never made any actual sexual advances, but he does say that he sensed that Britten has become obsessed with him and frequently wrote letters to him. Carpenter also gives many examples of Britten liking to correspond with young adolescent boys. Hemmings states that he also sensed that the tenor Peter Pears, the gay man Britten was living with, had clearly become very jealous of the boy and saw him as a rival to his love for Britten.

As Tom Sutcliffe writes in his essay:

> David Hemmings was a real find for the English Opera Group for whom Britten was writing *The Turn of the Screw*. He was aged almost 13 when he sang Miles in the original performances. But the strangest aspect of the opera's creation was the way that the composer's concern for Hemmings, whose performance was a huge bonus for the premiere, developed into an obsession that strangely matched the relationship between Miles and Peter Quint. Quint was, of course, the role the composer wrote for his intimate friend, Peter Pears.
>
> Hemmings, who later in life became even more famous as the star of Michelangelo Antonioni's cult film *Blow-up*, was not a product (as might have been expected) of the English tradition of cathedral choristers. His father had been a professional dance band pianist before the second world war who later took to playing in pubs as more profitable and secure. Hemmings had been entered for a singing competition by his father while they were on holiday; he was six, his father accompanied him, and he won.... He was chosen for the role of Miles at an English Opera Group audition at the Scala theater in Charlotte Street, London W1 when he was ten and a half in 1952.
>
> Hemmings claims his parents were entirely sympathetic to his relationship with Britten. His mother was chaperone to all the children for *Let's Make an Opera,* for which Hemmings played the Little Sweep with Michael Crawford (also destined to be a film and television star) as understudy.
>
> Hemmings did realize that the composer was, in a sense, in love with him. His parents had explained about Britten's homosexuality. Their confidence that all would be well was probably reassured by the fact that their son shown himself able to cope in a couple of molestation experiences.
>
> Peter Pears, however, was at times furiously jealous of Britten's feelings for Hemmings. There were terrible rows between the composer and the tenor. Like everybody working for Britten, Hemmings was totally aware of the situation. The openness of the pair's relationship was brave or foolhardy for the time. It didn't bother Hemmings [Sutcliffe 30–32].

Britten's next opera, *Noye's Fludde,* which premiered in Orford on June 18, 1958, is based on a Chester Miracle play and written for a tenor and boy sopranos. Most of the performers in the work are boy sopranos, and several observers have said how much Britten liked rehearsing with children, especially young boys, whom he became very friendly with. He liked talking to them and even corresponded with them, although all the biographers maintain that the relationships remained non-sexual.

Britten's next major opera, *A Midsummer Night's Dream*, was first staged in Aldeburgh on June 11, 1960. This opera is of course based on Shakespeare's famous comedy of the same title, and the opera follows the plot almost exactly. In this opera as well, we have a character obsessed with a boy. The character Oberon, husband to Titania, is determined to get possession of a little boy. This aspect of the plot comes directly from the Shakespearean play, but the boy is mentioned more often in the opera. In this opera, Puck was written for a boy soprano, and other young boys sing in the opera. Partially, of course, this would reflect the reality of actors — men and boys — during the Tudor period, but this reality also reflects, I believe, Britten's sexual interests. An obsession with a young boy operates on several levels in this opera, as it does in Shakespeare's play, and that connects rather handily with Britten's own obsession.

That a man obsessed with a young boy remains central to Shakespeare's play has given rise to a number of troubling interpretations. Given that the play was originally staged by men and boys — as was the law in Tudor England — such theaters may well have been hotbeds of homosexuality, though we can never be sure. Some critics have argued that Shakespeare himself must have been gay for he wrote a whole sonnet cycle to a young male actor. Other critics have argued that Elizabethan culture saw these man-boy relationships symbolically rather than sexually. And the Oberon in both Shakespeare and Britten seems heterosexual and happily married to Titania — but this gets even more complicated in the Britten opera since the role of Oberon is written for a countertenor, which makes him sound like a woman rather than a man. Sexual confusion seems at the heart of both Shakespeare's play and Britten's opera, and so does the theme of a man obsessed with a boy. In neither Shakespeare's play nor Britten's opera does any sexuality occur between the older man and the boy, but the presence of the suggestion of such an eventuality does leave most audience members feeling troubled by both the play and the opera.

Curlew River, first performed at a church in Orford, England, on June 12, 1964, is another work written only for men and boys, especially boys. Britten's lover Peter Pears appeared originally in the work as the Madwoman, and to great effect. Clearly here Britten is using techniques from Japanese Noh theater, where all the performers are male, but the work also reflects his sexual desires since most of the characters onstage remain boys. In Japanese Noh theater, as in Elizabethan England, all the players were male. Was there a homosexual subtext in both kinds of theater? Was man-boy love a reality in both kinds of theater? We can never be sure since the historical records are not exactly forthcoming on this issue — they could not be, given the laws in both countries at the time. But clearly what we now know about Britten's sexual interests drove his creativity into both these arenas where man-boy love may well have flourished.

The Burning Fiery Furnace is another one of Britten's church operas — based on a story from the Old Testament and written for men and boys and to be performed in a church. This opera also premiered at Orford on June 9, 1966. Here too Britten employs large groups of boy sopranos, which reflects the church setting of the opera and the church choir's frequent use of boy sopranos. The English tradition of boy choristers fascinated Britten, and he used this tradition repeatedly in his own compositions for both churches and opera houses. Was Britten's adult personality arrested in the period when he himself was a boy chorister? Did he himself dream of life among boy choristers? He certainly wrote several operas which use this musical tradition.

Another one of Britten's church parable operas is *The Prodigal Son*, which premiered at Orford on June 10, 1968. Here too the entire opera is written for men and boys, with a young boy playing the central role of the Prodigal Son — the story is of course from the Old Testament. George Balanchine choreographed a famous version of this same story, though here no children are employed in the cast.

Britten's final opera, *Death in Venice,* most centrally exemplifies the theme of pedophilia. The opera was first staged at Snape, England, on June 16, 1973, but soon afterwards appeared at the Royal Opera in London and the Metropolitan Opera in New York. This work, based on Thomas Mann's famous novella *Der Tod in Venedig* of 1912, tells the sad story of a famous German writer, Gustav von Aschenbach, and his obsession with a fourteen year old Polish boy named Tadzio. The story ends with the German writer's death. The German writer in the novella has been warned of the plague in Venice, but he cannot bear to leave his beloved Tadzio, though he never speaks one word to him throughout the story. In his final work Britten tells the sad story of an older man obsessed with a young boy — to the point where the obsession causes the German writer Aschenbach's death. He is warned by the German newspapers that there is a plague in Venice and his conscious and logical mind tells him that he should leave immediately, but he cannot tear himself away from Tadzio and dies on the Lido in Venice while gazing rapturously at the boy.

Britten's operatic treatment of Mann's *Death in Venice* remains faithful to the novella in most ways, including the repeated use of a character who

Death in Venice, as film 1971; Bjorn Andresen as Tadzio and Dirk Bogard as Aschenbach.

seems to symbolize the fate that is determined to destroy Aschenbach. Aschenbach's fatal attraction to the boy Tadzio seems clearly erotic rather than platonic in Mann's story, but here as in Britten's *Billy Budd,* the music never becomes erotic though it is evocative and interesting and Oriental sounding, often using musical instruments and musical sounds from the Far East. But one often wishes for an erotic sound to the music which Aschenbach sings as he becomes more and more fascinated with the young boy, Tadzio, who says nothing in the story — and who has not one note to sing in the opera. A writer like Aschenbach, famous for his ability to communicate, says not one word to the person whom he most adores, the Polish boy Tadzio.

Both the story and the opera have a frightening aspect to them. In both works the central character, Aschenbach, seems to have a history of heterosexuality rather than homosexuality. Does the story reflect Freud's theory that we are all bisexual? Does the story suggest that our sexuality can change in the presence of another person? Or is the story about Freud's theory of suppression, about civilization and its discontents, one of the main ones being our need to

Left: **Death in Venice**, Metropolitan Opera, 1994; Jeffrey Edwards as Tadzio (photograph: Winnie Klotz). *Right*: **Death in Venice**, Metropolitan Opera, 1994; Anthony Rolfe Johnson as Aschenbach (photograph: Winnie Klotz).

suppress our sexuality to survive in modern society? Some critics have also argued that neither the story or the opera is about sexuality at all but rather an older man's awareness of his advanced years, his ugliness, and his yearning for his former youth, symbolized by Tadzio. Yet most readers of the story feel that there is a sexual component to the story, and Aschenbach's increasingly frequent dreams also indicate a sexual component to his obsession with the young boy.

The honest biographies of Benjamin Britten, especially the best one by Humphrey Carpenter, insist that Britten's pedophilia was platonic and never actually acted upon, but that obsession remained in his life, and despite the fact that he lived with the famous gay tenor Peter Pears. He also wrote many of his best male roles with Peter Pears's voice in mind — especially the roles of Peter Grimes, Captain Vere in *Billy Budd*, Peter Quint in *The Turn of the Screw*, and Aschenbach in *Death in Venice*.

Pedophilia remains a very painful topic, especially because children always become the victims in such relationships. Gay rights groups often complain, with real justification, that anti-gay advocates accuse gay men of being pedophiles who prey on young boys, and it is distressing to find that the great composer Benjamin Britten in some ways fits that category. Britten could not

Top: Death in Venice, Metropolitan Opera, 1994; Jeffrey Edwards and Anthony Rolfe Johnson (photograph: Winnie Klotz). *Bottom: Death in Venice*, Metropolitan Opera, 1994; Thomas Allen (photograph: Winnie Klotz).

change his sexual feelings, but he kept them in control with the young boys he was attracted to, and he was also able — unlike most people — to turn his very neurosis into operas which are frequently performed around the world. It is impressive how great artists can use their very neuroses, some of them quite bizarre and dangerous, and turn them into great art which we can all enjoy.

Pedophilia as a topic frightens and disgusts most people, but Britten knew that this was part of his personality and struggled to keep it repressed. But did this take a toll on Britten's creativity? Forster's suggestion that the music in *Billy Budd* lacked the sexual passion of the situations and characters in the opera remains a valid one. Since's Britten's own sexual passion had to be repressed, did his music also fail, on some level, to address the passion in the drama of his operas' libretti? But one can also dismiss this question as a desire for Britten's music to be as erotic as Wagner's or Puccini's rather than the rather anti-erotic quality of modern, atonal music. In any case, Britten's own pedophilia remains a complicating factor in all this, as well as a major theme in most of his operas.

Bibliography

Allen, Stephen Arthur. "Britten and the World of the Child." In *The Cambridge Companion to Benjamin Britten,* ed. Mervyn Cooke. Cambridge: Cambridge University Press, 1999.

Carpenter, Humphrey. *Benjamin Britten: A Biography.* New York: Charles Scribner's Sons, 1992.

Cooke, Mervyn, ed. *The Cambridge Companion to Benjamin Britten.* New York: Cambridge University Press, 1999.

Evans, Peter. *The Music of Benjamin Britten.* New York: Oxford University Press, 1990.

Ford, Boris, ed. *Benjamin Britten's Poets: The Poetry He Set to Music.* Manchester: Carcanet, 1993.

Gill, John. *Queer Noises: Male and Female Homosexuality in Twentieth-Century Music.* Minneapolis: University of Minnesota Press, 2004.

Oliver, Michael. *Benjamin Britten.* London: Phaedon Press, 1996.

Palmer, Christopher, ed. *The Britten Companion.* London: Faber and Faber, 1984.

Sutcliffe, Tom. "Haunting Parallels Between Art and Life." In "The Turn of the Screw," program booklet for the production of this opera by Welsh National Opera. Cardiff, 2000.

Williams, Jeannie. *Jon Vickers: A Hero's Life.* Boston: Northeastern University Press, 1999.

9

Caryl Churchill, Joe Orton, Tom Stoppard
Sexual Dysfunction

While sexual problems were a taboo in theater for most of its history, by the end of the twentieth century this topic could be presented in contemporary theater. In the traditions of the Victorian theater and for most of the early twentieth century, given the force of Victorian culture, sexual problems were seen as a taboo and not a fit subject for the theater. The censorship of the period in both Britain and America ensured that sexual matters were kept off the stage by and large. By the late 1960s most forms of censorship were eliminated in the British and American theater — although the case of *My Name Is Rachel Corrie* indicated that Zionist censorship still often occurred in America. This wonderful play had to struggle to be staged in New York, proposed but ultimately censored by the one New York theater but ultimately staged in the fall of 2006 by the Minetta Lane Theater in New York's Greenwich Village despite Zionist efforts to halt its production.

But if all British and American theater is a footnote to Shakespeare, we can clearly see that the bard also addressed sexual problems in his plays, despite Elizabethan censorship. Clearly the Elizabethan period was a very earthy one, much more comfortable with sexual topics than the Victorian period. One has to think only of *Othello* and his neurotic jealousy which ultimately drives him to murder his faithful wife Desdemona and then commit suicide. Hamlet's love of Ophelia is full of sexual frustration, to the point where he even suggests that she get herself to a nunnery. The comedies also present the sexual frustrations of humanity, for example in the sexual complications of *A Midsummer Night's Dream*, where people seem doomed to love people who used to love them back but are suddenly no longer interested in them. More problematic, of course, is Oberon's obsession with a young boy — an obsession which certainly angers his wife Titania. Such an obsession has sexual implications which the Elizabethan stage seemed more comfortable with than contemporary audiences.

One of the revolutionary plays in terms of discussing the whole topic of sexual taboos and sexual dysfunction was certainly Caryl Churchill's *Cloud 9*, which premiered in London in 1979, and was soon also staged New York in 1981, very successfully directed by Tommy Tune — also in New York's Greenwich Village, an American home of the avant-garde in both personal lifestyles and in the arts.

All sorts of sexual problems and sexual taboos were addressed in this play, the most prominent being repression and trying to live with Victorian taboos and Victorian hypocrisy. The first act of the play is set in Africa under British colonial rule and the second act is set in London one hundred years later, though the characters have only aged 25 years. Clearly, Churchill is using this rather complicated mechanism to imply that the tradition of Victorian prudery and hypocrisy remains quite alive in contemporary British life despite the passage of one hundred years and the sexual revolutions of the '60s. Churchill presents sexual repression and sexual problems as alive and well in modern-day London and despite the women's liberation and gay liberation movements of the '60s in both America and Britain.

In the first act, we have the problem of gay characters who cannot admit to their homosexuality. We have the explorer Harry Bagley, who has to lie about his sexuality, and his friend Clive's family governess Ellen, who also has to lie about her sexuality. Ellen is clearly in love with Clive's wife Betty, while Betty remains obsessed with Harry Bagley. That the audience knows that he is a gay or bisexual man adds to the dramatic irony of the situation. That these two characters (Harry Bagley and Ellen, both gay) are married to each other at the end of the first act adds to the comedy of the situation — the Victorian solution to homosexuality was marriage, which was supposed to cure both males and females of their decadence. Of course the audience laughs at this happy ending since they know thanks to dramatic irony that both Ellen and the explorer Harry Bagley are gay and doomed to a very frustrating sexual life in their marriage. There are still people in contemporary times who feel that homosexuality can be cured through marriage, and the religious right wing in both Britain and America still propose their own solution to what they see as the problem of homosexuality through heterosexual marriage.

The play *Cloud 9* also presents us with the problem of the sissy-boy; in the first act this is the boy Edward, played by a woman in the first act, by a man in the second act. Edward in the first act is a sissy boy who is always

Cloud 9, New York, 1981; E. Katherine Kerr as Betty and Zeljko Ivanek as Gerry (photograph: Martha Swope).

stealing his mother's jewelry and his sister's dolls and who is sexually attracted to Harry the explorer (aptly named). That boy Edward becomes a gay man in the second act, attracted to his lover of the time, Gerry, who is very promiscuous and who seems to be able to enjoy sex only with total strangers in public places, like compartments in trains. Clearly *Cloud 9* was a play which tried to attack every taboo in the theater, coming as it did so soon after the end of theatrical censorship in England in 1967, and after the decriminalizing of homosexuality a year earlier.

In the second act of *Cloud 9*, we are presented with the character of Lin, a radial feminist and lesbian who has a little girl called Cathy who likes very feminine things like makeup and jewelry despite her mother's giving her guns to play with. Both acts present us with frustrated parents who have children who are not what they want — in act 1 a sissy boy and in act 2 a normal little girl. Lin, as a liberated woman and a radical lesbian, does not want a typical little girl, but that is precisely what she gets in her daughter. That the daughter Cathy is played by a grown man in a dress adds to the comedy of the situation, though the mother Lin does not ever see the situation as comic but rather as very frustrating.

Lin makes an interesting foil to Victoria, Clive's daughter, now a grown-up woman. Victoria is married, but her marriage seems to be falling apart

Cloud 9, New York, 1981; Zeljko Ivanek as Betty, Don Amendolia as Cathy, Concetta Tomei as Edward (photograph: Martha Swope).

and she is very unsure of herself and why her marriage is falling apart. The audience soon realizes that the marriage is falling apart because she is a lesbian who can find sexual fulfillment only with other women, though Victoria does not seem to understand this clearly for most of the act. By the end of the second act of the play Victoria seems to have accepted her lesbianism and divorced her husband to be with her lover Lin (and her brother Edward). An incestuous ménage à trois seems to make Victoria fulfilled — sort of. One of the central ironies of this play remains the sad reality that not one character ever seems to have experienced "Cloud 9" — that image of total happiness which all the liberation movements of the '60s promised.

Clearly Victoria's own desire to role-play as a "normal" heterosexual woman becomes at odds with her sexual attraction to another woman, Lin. By the end of the play she seems very content to be involved with a ménage à trois with Lin and her brother Edward and seems to be thriving in this strange atmosphere. Where are the sexual boundaries? this play seems to be asking. In the first act pedophilia becomes apparent in the sexual liaison of the boy Edward and the Victorian explorer Harry Bagley, and the ménage à trois appears in the second act in the strange triangular relationship between Victoria, Lin, and Edward. *Cloud 9* clearly wants to make audiences uncomfortable by looking into the few taboos left in the contemporary world, and pedophilia is one of the few taboos among contemporary audiences. Caryl Churchill has become one of the few female playwrights who is comfortable shedding light into this dark and dangerous area of modern supposed liberality in sexual relationships.

The first act also presents us with the problem of pedophilia since Edward, the sissy boy, wants to have sex with the explorer, who is a grown man. This taboo topic is balanced in the sex act, with incest occurring between Victoria and her brother Edward, who had been gay but is sexually interested in his sister — in addition to his former lover Gerry. As Edwards comments by the end of the play, "I think I'm a lesbian."

Caryl Churchill presents us with a very complicated world of sexual confusion and sexual dysfunction — no one ever seems to find Cloud 9, a supposed never-never land of happy sexuality. One would think that with the end of Victorian taboos and inhibitions, personal happiness would result, but Churchill suggests that sexual problems persist despite the alleged liberation of the late twentieth century — or maybe even that women's liberation or gay liberation create their own sexual problems. Ultimately, Churchill asks, is sexual liberation — or Cloud 9, as it is called in the play — even possible? Perhaps one is being naïve to think that the fantasy of total happiness that we all have is ever going to be achieved in our own lifetime. Churchill has written a play full of sexual problems which occur in the Victorian period in the first act and in supposedly liberated Britain in the late twentieth century in the play's second act — but many sexual problems plague the characters in both acts of her fascinating play.

In 1982 Churchill had another major success with *Top Girls,* which has two very contrasting acts as does *Cloud 9.* In the first act, we have a fantasy situation of the character of Marlene meeting a group of friends for lunch at a restaurant in contemporary London. But the friends turn out to be historical figures of very unusual women, in some cases very liberated women — women like Pope Joan, Griselda, a literary figure, a famous Japanese courtesan. Some of these women are historical characters, some are literary characters, and some are fantasy characters — since there is no documented evidence that Pope Joan ever really existed. One character, Dull Gret, is even a figure from a Brueghel painting from the late medieval period.

Clearly what Churchill remains interested in is how women survived in earlier, much harsher times. Some, like Pope Joan, were murdered. But these women do not think of themselves as victims — instead they have incorporated the prejudices of their period. While the modern reader would view the husband of Griselda as a male chauvinist pig who treated her sadistically, that is not how Griselda sees herself. Male and female role-playing, sado-masochistic relationships, and sexual problems are all investigated and dramatized in this play.

In the second act of *Top Girls* we are placed in the offices of the Top Girls employment agency and see its owner, Marlene, in action. Alcoholism remains a major theme here as well since by the end of the first act, most of the women are drunk; Marlene too may be an alcoholic since she herself says she drinks too much. But we soon learn that she cannot seem to connect with anyone sexually and in fact has abandoned her daughter to her sister, who has raised her. But clearly Marlene is a very rejecting mother who has no sympathy with people who are not as bright and aggressive as she is. And when Marlene discovers that her own daughter, raised by his sister Joyce, is not so bright, Marlene, as a modern politically conservative Thatcherite woman, is ready even to reject her own daughter in her determination to defend this conservative vision of the world as a place for only winners and with no regard for or even sympathy for the "losers," as Marlene would be the first to call such people, including her own daughter Angie. The question which Churchill poses is what to do about the less bright and less accomplished of society's members; while the political left has always argued that society has an obligation to help them, the Thatcherite Marlene clearly feels that society has no obligation to help such people since by doing so society is getting in the way of the "winners," as she would call them, and blocking their path to success with excessive taxation.

Such an approach has created both personal and sexual problems for Churchill's Marlene and she is isolated at the end, isolated even from her own daughter.

Churchill here too presents us with a world in which all the liberation movements of the '60s in both Britain and America have not produced the sexual and social liberation and happiness which they promised. Those movements argued that if people were free from the closet and the hypocrisy which society forces on them, then they would find fulfillment and even happiness. Both Churchill's plays suggest instead that human happiness remains a social goal and even a social fantasy.

Joe Orton also investigated in his theater the problem of sexual problems, though here it is Victorian hypocrisy which is usually the culprit. In one of Orton's early plays, *Entertaining Mr. Sloan*, we are presented with the horrible image of a brother and sister fighting over the same man, Mr. Sloan, whom they incite to kill their father. Orton suggests that patricide can be forgiven and even encouraged when sexual desire is involved. Both Kath and her

Entertaining Mr. Sloan, original New York production, 1965; Lee Montague as Ed, George Turner as the Dadda, Sheila Hancock as Kath, and Dudley Sutton as Sloan.

brother are clearly obsessed with the highly attractive Mr. Sloan, and they fight each other for his sexual favors, which certainly creates a new and unusual variant of sibling rivalry on a very literal level for the modern stage.

Not only is Victorian repression being presented and by implication attacked, but also a kind of incestuous taboo, as brother and sister fight for the same sexual partner. And that sexual partner, the very attractive and desirable Mr. Sloan, is not naïve but clearly someone who knows the reality about his power to attract and also his ability to fleece his victims. That he seems to be the one fleeced by the end of the play indicates the complexities of sexual desire and sexual power-plays which Orton is trying to portray in this highly cynical but also highly amusing and perceptive play.

In Orton's later play *Loot* (1965), we also see sexual repression and sexual hypocrisy. Characters try to hide their sexual obsessions, and even incest is the result. In *What the Butler Saw* a mental hospital becomes a real looney bin since the psychiatrist in charge of the place is clearly sexually obsessed with anyone but his wife. The farcial sexual shenanigans are quite comic, with most of the characters denying their sexual interests, whether they be heterosexual, homosexual, or both. In one sense, the play is trying to attack British prudery (due to the Victorian tradition in British culture) and also British hypocrisy, an unwillingness to be open and honest about one's sexual feelings. Orton often presents in this play his authority figures as sexual renegades, liars, and hypocrites. Since he himself was jailed by society, he felt that he was treated very unfairly by the pillars of English society.

Sexual dysfunction certainly operated in the life of Joe Orton since he was a gay man in the '40s and '50s before the gay liberation movement of the '60s and '70s. His lover Halliwell was obsessively possessive and ultimately murdered the playwright, then committing suicide himself. The sexual dysfunction that operated in their relationship was anything but gay and ultimately cost both of them their lives thanks to the murderous lover Halliwell. On August 9, 1967, Orton's brilliant career as a playwright came to a bloody and tragic end when his skull was smashed by his lover Halliwell, who then committed suicide.

Sexual dysfunction and sexual problems in general also occur in the theater of Tom Stoppard. In *The Real Thing* we have a playwright as a central character — always a hint of autobiography. We also know that Tom Stoppard himself went through several divorces and emotional separations, so clearly this is a topic that is close to his heart — a broken heart perhaps.

In *The Real Thing* we have a search for the real thing — a pun that is used in many ways in the play. The concept of reality is central to this play, but what is reality? Clearly, that problem appears in the first scene, which is a scene from a play by the playwright in the play—and often the audience is confused about what is really happening in the life of the playwright character and the other central characters and what is happening in the internal play by the playwright character.

"The real thing" is also used as a phrase to describe true love—when people have fallen in love, they often say they have found "the real thing," though given the divorce rate in both America and Britain one wonders what this reality really is or at least how long it lasts. But the search for the real thing—or true love—is central to the play. The latest national statistics on marriage in both America and Britain in the 21st century are pretty grim—half of these marriages end in divorce and the other half end in death.

In the beginning, the playwright Henry is having an affair with Annie, who happens to be married to someone else, his friend, another actor in his play. When Annie finally tells this character the truth, that she is having an affair with someone else, he says "I thought we had a commitment! What ever happened to our commitment??" But she says, "These days there are no commitments, only bargains which have to be negotiated every day." What Annie is saying here is that a new kind of relationship has developed in modern life and that this is the new reality—that permanent commitments just do not exist any more, only bargains, which she says have to be negotiated every day. But why did this couple split up? Sexual problems seem to be the implication.

After Annie and the playwright are finally together, one would think that "the real thing" has been found and happiness will result—and it does, but only for a short while. Then stuff happens—as the playwright David Hare would say in the title to one of his most recent plays about the Bush presidency and the war in Iraq.

The playwright's wife Annie—formerly his mistress, now his legal wife—remains an actress and gets cast in a play in Edinburgh. The play is Ford's famous play *Tis Pity She's a Whore*, and that title is hardly coincidental since from the playwright's point of view, his wife starts playing the whore and having an affair with someone else. In the beginning of the play the playwright was having an affair with someone else's wife, and that was ok; now that his own wife is having an affair with someone else, the playwright really begins to suffer. Is he not satisfying her sexually? There must be some sexual dysfunction in the relationship or else why would she begin an affair with another man? She continues the affair even after the playwright finds out about it—clearly she had tried to keep her affair clandestine. This mirrors the situation in the playwright's play, where the wife is also having an adulterous affair.

Is there a misogynistic subtext in this play, suggesting that women are all whores and tis a pity, to use Ford's play and title? Or is Stoppard suggesting that while society is used to the idea of the male as not capable of being monogamous and faithful, the new kind of liberated woman is just as incapable of being faithful and monogamous in relationships? Perhaps it is not only women but all people who are whores ultimately, and these are the new social realities which modern society has to adjust to. There is a lot of bed-hopping which occurs in the play. When Henry's wife is talking to their daughter, the wife seems to be referring to Henry as a modern-day Victorian, unaware of the promiscuous behavior of their own daughter. Henry is apparently unable to adjust to the modern accommodation to young people's sexual needs, the lack of any desire to impose marriage upon relationships among the young which seem to be based only on sexual adventures and even promiscuity.

The play may also be suggesting that monogamy is a dated concept, which the young people in the play realize but which the older generation has much more trouble accepting. The older characters in *The Real Thing* believe that monogamy is the basis of marriage, but the younger characters like Henry's daughter seem to have a more relaxed view of both sexuality and marriage and do not seem to need monogamy as the basis of love and marriage.

Is Victorianism still alive and well in contemporary England — at least in the case of the playwright Henry in this play? Henry has problems both as a husband and a father since he cannot adjust well to the sexual realities of his daughter's generation and her own demands for sexual liberation and sexual experiences outside of marriage. In any case, the play does have a happy ending and Henry and Annie are reunited at last, though one wonders for how long. Are there really no longer any commitments in relationships but only bargains, as one of the female character says early in the play? That is precisely what Stoppard is suggesting about sexual relationships and sexual problems and their effect on marriage.

We see sexual problems again in Tom Stoppard's next big hit, *The Invention of Love* (1995), centrally concerned with the character of Alfred Housman. One of the major sexual problems in his life is that he is a gay man during the Victorian period and as a result a criminal. If he is open about his sexuality, he risks exposure and jail. He can never be honest about his sexuality given the period he was born in. But another sexual problem he develops is that while he is a student at Cambridge he falls madly in love with a heterosexual man, Moses Jackson. As another character tells Housman, "He is never going to want what you want."

In life, Moses Jackson finally moved to Vancouver, Canada, primarily to get away from Alfred Housman. When Jackson married, Housman actually moved into a nearby apartment building so that he could be near him — which of course was seen as very peculiar behavior, and Jackson's wife objected. Housman's obsession with Moses Jackson continued after his marriage and caused problems in his marriage — ultimately Jackson moved to Canada, in part to get away from Housman's obsessive interest in him. But Housman continued to write to him frequently and dedicated several books to him, to his wife's annoyance. As the character of Housman says to Moses Jackson at one point in the play, "I would have died for you but I never had the luck." It is significant as well that Housman's first line in the play is "I am dead then. Good." Obviously the frustration of Housman's desire and obsession with the heterosexual Moses Jackson led to many suicidal thoughts on the part of the poet and classics scholar Housman.

Clearly these playwrights (Chruchill and Stoppard, in addition to Orton) present multiple problems, sexual dysfunction being arguably the main one, but also including alcoholism. Homosexuality is not viewed these days as a sexual problem — though the adjustment to homosexuality can cause problems. In the Churchill and Stoppard plays, a lot of drinking seems to be occurring, and one often wonders which characters are drunks and which characters are merely social drinkers. These drinking problems undoubtedly add to the sexual problems which playwrights like Churchill, Orton, and Stoppard have investigated in these fascinating plays.

That the theater of the 21st century can address problems of sexual dysfunction and sexual problems directly and not so delicately and obliquely helps to make the theater a vibrant and relevant art form. As Victorian repression and prudery have begun to disappear, sexual realities and sexual complexities can be examined by contemporary playwrights in an honest and forthright manner. Even nudity onstage has become a commonplace on the stages of both London and New York, and the provinces have become even more corrupt than the capitals, as Oscar Wilde predicted.

Bibliography

Billington, Michael *Stoppard the Playwright*. London: Methuen, 1987.
Coppa, Francesca, ed. *Joe Orton: A Casebook*. New York: Routledge, 2003.
Fleming, John. *Stoppard's Theatre: Finding Order Amid Chaos*. Austin: University of Texas Press, 2002.
Kelly, Katherine E., ed. *The Cambridge Companion to Tom Stoppard*. Cambridge: Cambridge University Press, 2001.
Kritzer, Amelia Howe. *The Plays of Caryl Churchill: Theatre of Empowerment*. New York: St. Martin's Press, 1991.

Lahr, John. *Prick Up Your Ears: The Biography of Joe Orton.* New York: Alfred A. Knopf, 1978.

Nadel, Ira. *Tom Stoppard: A Life.* New York: Palgrave Macmillan, 2002.

Orton, Joe. *The Orton Diaries.* Ed. John Lahr. New York: Da Capo Press, 1996.

Randall, Phyllis R., ed. *Caryl Churchill: A Casebook.* New York: Garland, 1989.

Rusinko, Susan. *Joe Orton.* New York: Twayne Publishers, 1995.

_____. *Tom Stoppard.* Boston: Twayne, 1986.

Sternlicht, Sanford *A Reader's Guide to Modern British Drama.* Syracuse: Syracuse University Press, 2004.

10

David Hare
Transference

Transference can be described as moving an emotional reaction from one area where it belongs to another area that is less painful for a person. Freud first described the phenomenon when dealing with his initial patients, and their ability to deal with difficult situations in their personal lives by transferring the feeling from one area or person where it belonged to another area or person where it would be more manageable. Transference can occur in any interchange between two people, especially when one of them is an authority figure. Transference also occurs when a patient transfers his feelings for a person who was very significant in his life onto his therapist. Thus Freud describes his patients transferring their feelings for their mother or father onto him, their doctor. Freud felt that transference occurred inevitably in therapy and that it was central to the value of the therapy, and believed the therapist needed to help the patient to see where he was transferring his feelings to people or situations where it was not appropriate. Transference can also occurs when a patient transfers his feelings from one situation where they are appropriate to another where they are not — for example, feelings for a therapist are not appropriate for another person in another situation outside therapy. A patient can also transfer his personal conflicts onto political conflicts — thus a complex and difficult relationship with a parent can be played out in a political arena.

Freud also talked about counter-transference, when the therapist could transfer feelings he had for someone else onto his patients, something the therapist had to be very aware of and try to avoid. Freud also felt that transference can occur in any human interaction when we are capable of transferring onto another person feelings which are more appropriate for our own needs and from our own past relationships with other people.

Transference can also occur in politics, especially when politics is connected with religion. Thus one's action, no matter how irreligious or even immoral, can be justified by transferring that action onto God and religion. Thus, during the Crusades in the Middle Ages, supposed Christians killed hundreds of thousands of non–Christians in the Middle East, all under the guise of religion. In trying to capture the "Holy Land" for Christians, the place of Christ's birth after all, Crusaders killed and raped and pillaged, and all responsibility for this immoral behavior was transferred onto God and the Christian religion. Other religions of course also massacred in the name of their God, all claiming that God gave the land to them. Most religious people do not believe that God is in the real estate business, and the whole idea seems immoral and racist to most people — a painful and bloody example of transference on a grand scale.

It seems to me that various types of transference occur in the theater of the British playwright David Hare. In an interview Hare once said that he felt that his theater was a search for a moral order, a search for morality in general. Such a search for morality in areas where that morality might not exist can result in real frustrations, but also in some great theater and some wonderful plays. In any case, the search for a moral code has led David Hare to some very interesting situations where transference occurs. To suggest that morality governs human behavior can easily be seen as transference from the playwright's human need for morality onto a political reality where morality does not function, except as a PR technique after an action has been taken.

One of Hare's first successes, *Teeth and Smiles* (1972), involves a rock group performing at a college campus for a group of students in England. The rock group and its singer become the central focus of the play, and their various drug, alcohol, and sexual problems — especially those of their lead singer — become the focus of the play. Hare's own search for a moral order in this drug-infested mess of a world in some ways interferes with his ability to see and portray these characters. They too often present us with David Hare's own moral problems, and displacement is occurring. But that is allowable, since the play is very interesting and if well done will entertain an audience and keep them riveted to their chairs. The play also reflects the relative positions of England and America onto the characters so that they are affected by English subordination to American dominance, which may explain all the addiction problems in the play. Here Hare shows us how international politics transfers onto the feelings of his central characters in a very interesting way. The play implies that in a universe where there is no religious belief by any of the characters, dissolution will occur — an example of transference since moral and religious values are being transferred onto politics, an area which does not provide religious or moral values except through transference.

One of his major successes as a playwright was undoubtedly his play

Plenty, which was first staged in 1978 and later filmed in 1980. The title comes from one of the slogans of World War II — "peace and plenty" was what people were fighting for during the war. Susan Traherne is on the winning side, but her life after World War II spirals into suffering and ultimately emotional collapse. She was a British spy for the Free France movement stationed in rural France during the war — and by the end of the play we see that her three years' fighting in World War II were the happiest in her life. She had moral certainty — she was a moral person fighting for a good and just cause, the defeat of Hitler and the Nazis. After she and the Allies win the war, things fall apart for her since she no longer has moral certainty. She marries unhappily and gets involved with the wrong people — and repeatedly she acts utterly irrationally. With the war she was on the right side, but with peace and plenty — and she gets both — she suffers in a world of ambiguous morality. By the end of the play she has become a very wealthy woman who is quite self-destructive and psychologically on the brink of collapse. The peace and plenty she yearned for during World War II she got, but they drove her insane.

By the end of the play she has not only become psychologically deranged, but has done terrible harm to the people around her, especially her poor husband, who is trying to develop a career in foreign diplomacy. His wife's lack of diplomacy has ruined his diplomatic career for him. Susan Traherne seems to be searching for a moral order in the Britain of her time but becomes angry that her society did not provide her with one. To seek religious order in political realities seems dim at best, though Susan's work as a British agent during World War II provided her with that sense of value and worth while she was part of a war that attempted to destroy an obvious evil, Hitler and the Nazis.

We see this theme yet again in Hare's play *Licking Hitler*; here too we have a contrast but this time right during the war. We are in a foreign office in London during World War II, and while the people are all doing the right things and fighting for a good and just cause, some of the actions of some of the people are appalling. One of the women gets raped by one of the officers, and he gets away with this appalling behavior, all because he is involved in the more glorious work of licking Hitler — and the female victim feels she cannot press charges. The moral force of the war — all these characters are fighting against a real evil, Hitler — does not create a moral goodness in their lives. Instead, some of these heroic warriors in the fight against Nazism and Fascism themselves do some appallingly evil things. Their own needs transfer onto their behavior and result in a new form of personal evil. The audience finds itself in the difficult situation of rooting for a very good officer who does his job very well, but who has also just raped a woman under his command. What

Plenty, Broadway, 1983; Kate Nelligan and Edward Hermann (photograph: Martha Swope).

should a superior officer do in a situation like this? To court-martial the man would mean a very valuable officer would not be able to do his job, but not to court-martial him would result in his getting away with raping one of the women under his command — and perhaps he will do that again if he is let off the hook. These complex moral issues, by being transferred onto the situation of World War II, let us see into the complex inner workings of a large and crucial institution, the British Army during World War II.

In Hare's *Racing Demon* we have the world of morality and the world of the Anglican clergy confronting each other. Here too we would think that in the world of the Anglican Church morality would not be able to be transferred, but in point of fact it is. We see the church hierarchy as a monolithic power, and the average minister trying to survive with the high powers of the church manipulating priests and parishes for various reasons that do not seem to reflect morality at all. In addition, the play inevitably asks if transference is possible in such a clerical setting — and the answer seems to be that morality and church power are not necessarily the same thing. Political realities occur even here, within the Anglican Church, and they seem to violate the moral basis of the organization. Racing Demon becomes chasing the demons within as well as without. Hare is obviously very interested in the inner workings of an allegedly benign institution, the Church of England, and he discovers the same examples of personal power plays and competition for career development in the Church that he found in politics or business. Careerism among the clergy becomes a major example of the transference of personal power onto the Church of England. Why would such a transference disturb David Hare?

Hare looks at a complex reality, careerism in the Church of England, and how careerism operates within a religious community. Clearly the bishop and clerical hierarchy have real power over the lowly priests and curates in contemporary England, but how does that power connect with the religious vocation which they all profess to be part of? Can religion be both a powerful moral force and a career path? For these clerics it is both, but the play presents the viewer and reader with situations which question how this juggling act is possible given the professed aims of Christianity, and indeed all religions.

In *In the Absence of War* David Hare looks at politics in Britain during the period after World War II. Hare implies in this play that in the absence of war, modern politics because a very ugly game with the media — involving personalities and innuendos rather than moral issues. The moral issues brought up during a war get transferred into issues that are really non–issues. The prime minister becomes centrally concerned with appearances on television rather than substantial issues — transference of what Hare feels politics should be about. Hare suggests that in the absence of war the political parties have no substantive issues to disagree about, and so politics becomes the game of how the candidate appears on television and how the polls tell the politicians what the people want them to say. In such a televised world real sincerity is transferred to the sidelines and media coverage becomes all important.

Hare seems to be questioning how politics can occur in the absence of war in contemporary Britain. But his suggestion that without a just war, politics becomes just a front for careerism and manipulating the media suggests that politics needs a moral order. But does it? In a democracy, separation of church and state is basic, and asking contemporary political leaders to provide a moral order and a moral justification for what they are doing suggests transferring religious needs onto political realities. President George W. Bush has tried to do that with his "moral majority" and trying to justify his actions by his alleged daily conversations with God, but that dialogue has lead to an imperialist war in Iraq and Afghanistan, the denial of rights to a trial and statement of accusations in Guantanamo, and Bush's defense of torture. Is this what his religion is all about? Could any truly Christian leader justify such actions as part of the Christian religion, or indeed any religion? Is Bush transferring his needs for political power onto the religious susceptibilities of many Americans?

Hare also questions in this play the human need for a leader and whether that need is really about a search for a religious figure, perhaps a messiah. What are people looking for in their political leaders? Is part of our infatuation with political leaders a search for a religious leader that our own religions cannot provide for us? Hare suggests in *In the Absence of War* that political leaders and how the media present them remain very complicated indeed. The human interest in the sexual lives of political leaders suggests that we are somehow transferring our own prurient interest in leaders onto a quasi-religious plane since we want to turn them into the kind of cult figures which one would expect in a religious rather than a political arena. Have the lives of contemporary politicians become a substitute for what has traditionally been provided by the lives of the saints?

In *Skylight* (1995) we also see this issue in terms of politics, since we have the classic confrontation of right versus left. A leftist, liberal woman (Kyra Hollis) is trying to break off an affair with a very conservative former lover (Tom Sergeant). She works at a school for minority students, while he is a very successful restaurant owner. She cares passionately about helping poor people — in fact her life as a teacher does exactly that. But he does not care at all about poor people and feels that she is wasting her life. He clearly feels that the poor are poor because of their own shortcomings and that only they can help themselves, if indeed they are capable of that. She is transferring her feelings for the poor to her feelings for him — and the relationship dies as a result. The audience is left to wonder if she did the right thing — or indeed if it is fair to separate yourself from people if they do not share your view of morality or even your politics. But, Hare suggests, political differences can easily be transferred to moral differences which affect the way we behave and the way we see the world. Why should political differences separate people who obviously love and need each other in this play? Hare may be suggesting that the political discussions are attempts to avoid the more painful topics that divide the main characters.

What are our moral obligations to the poor, if any? Most people on the political left feel that society needs to help the poor, while most people on the right do not seem to feel any such need. Is the economic policy of laissez-faire all that we should be doing for the poor? Hare's play *Skylight* itself provides a skylight view of this complex problem and shows how love and politics can be mixed in the pursuit of moral truth and righteousness. By the end of the play, the two lovers are separated, but the main female character is having a jolly breakfast with Edward Sergeant, the son of her lover, suggesting that some reconciliation, some family — type bond, will remain in her love of her former lover.

Eating itself becomes a major concern, and indeed a major metaphor in this play. The female lead spends most of the first act of the play making an Italian dinner for her friend, and indeed in the little Cottlesloe theater in the National Theater in London the whole area smelled of an Italian tomato sauce since the actress was clearly really doing the actual cooking of the sauce and pasta. And the play ends with a happy breakfast when the young son, Edward, brings in an entire breakfast from the Ritz Hotel for them to share. Is the human desire for food and enjoyment in eating a metaphor then for the human desire for a morality that can be shared by the entire community? And can that moral order include all peoples despite their various races and religions? These are the main concerns in *Skylight*. Hare provides his audience with a fascinating play which examines some of the major human needs and their connections with the political realities of the day.

Amy's View was first performed in 1997. It involves an actress, Esme, and her relationship with her daughter Amy. The title of the play comes from Amy's view that if you do the moral thing, good things will happen. But Amy is dead by the end of the play — dead at an early age. Her major conflict with her mother is over her husband, a man she loves and marries though her mother loathes him. We see transference occurring over and over again in the play, as Esme transfers her feelings of hatred for films to Dominic, the film critic who has married her daughter Amy. We also see that Dominic's hatred for the theater gets transferred to his new hatred for his actress mother-in-law, Esme. Poor Amy gets caught between them and dies (indirectly) as a result of this horrible conflict between the two people she loves the most. She is trying to do the right thing, but somehow that does not solve the problems or end the conflicts. Amy has this optimistic view that if you try to do the right thing and stand by the people you love, things will work out. By the end of the play Amy is dead, done in part by her pain at seeing all the most important relationships in her life fall apart. Her relationship with her mother is very strained and her marriage to Dominick is falling apart too — despite her optimistic belief that emotional honesty will solve all problems. Dominick has started a relationship with a Swedish actress despite all Amy's efforts to love and nurture him and their children, and the audience suspects that her subsequent heart attack or stroke occurs as a result of her efforts to save her marriage and her relationship with her mother, and to keep her family intact and stay with her husband.

Hare looks very directly at the connections between politics and religion in his hit play *Via Dolorosa*, which was first staged in London in 1998 and became a hit on Broadway the following year — and then was revived again in London five years later. There David Hare wrote a one-act play for one actor, and then not really an actor at all, really for himself. In that play Hare describes his trip to Israel and the consequences of that trip. He begins by being deeply interested in Israel and eager to get there — for one thing, Israel is as old as he is, both having been born in 1948, and for another thing, a playwright, Theodore Herzl, started the Zionist movement.

As he says early in the play, Israel is more than anything else a cause — the cause being the suffering of the Jewish people as a result of the Holocaust. But while he is eager to visit Israel and to see the many realities of Israel, he soon becomes totally disillusioned and finally returns by the end of the play to his home in Hampstead, a suburb of London. Hampstead is a small town with many literary connections; it was where John Keats was born and lived most of his life, and Freud moved to Hampstead after being driven out of Vienna by the Nazis before World War II. By extension, the town has become a haven for Hare as well from the horrors and injustices he sees in Israel. Hare also repeatedly mentioned an Israeli friend who always loves to go to Hampstead Heath because it has an air of freedom and religious toleration lacking in his own country. While England does not provide the religious and moral fervor of the Jewish cause, as does Israel, there is freedom of religious and political expression there, and people are not forced into refugee camps as a result of their race or religion. There are no Rachel Corries there — the American peace activist who was murdered with a bulldozer in Israel.

But what Hare sees in this religious state of Israel horrifies him and implies that the transference of politics into religious fervor results in war, bloodshed, and most of all racism and injustice. Hare visits Palestinian refugee camps and sees the suffering of the Palestinian people, who have been pushed into those refugee camps as a result of Zionism. The Jews keep insisting that

God gave that land to them, and their God wants that land only for Jews and believes in ethnic cleansing and driving non–Jews out. Is this moral behavior — to expel people from a land they have occupied for hundreds of years because of God and the Jewish religion? The moral question becomes whether God is in the real estate business. To most religious people that sounds ridiculous, but not to Zionist Jews. The resultant lying becomes increasingly clear in the play, and increasingly horrifies David Hare. Hare cannot understand why Israel cannot become a secular state like England with full civil rights for people of all religions, but when he suggests this in the play, he is accused of being anti–Semitic.

Hare spent some time with Danny and Sarah, Americans who are also Israeli settlers, who want to follow their version of the Torah literally — and that means occupying Palestinian land, pushing Palestinian Arabs into refugee camps (since, Danny says, God did not give the land to them, only to the Jews). Hare also describes the repeated acts of torture which Israelis have done to Palestinians — that every year Amnesty International reports Palestinians being subjected to Jewish torture, always justified by the Jews' God. Clearly, Hare implies, religion has been transferred into racism, torture, and bigotry. Rather than encouraging justice for all the people of the Middle East, the Jewish religion has created a Jewish state that has turned six million Palestinians into refugees. The horrors of the Jewish Holocaust have generated another horror, the tragic fact that the Holocaust itself has been used to justify making millions of Palestinians refugees by stealing their property and denying them civil rights in the Jewish state. And what is used to justify such immoral behavior? God, of course — ironically enough.

In the final scene in Israel in the play, Hare quotes an Abraham Cohen, who says of the Jewish quest for a homeland in Israel: "Fuck the land. Fuck it. The Jewish religion is about moral values, not real estate. Fuck the land. Israel is a complete deformation of what the Jewish religion is about." That person clearly expresses David Hare's view of what transference has done to the Jewish religion — transferring its moral values into lying for the sake of real estate. But not many Jews would agree with David Hare's summary of the situation, though the play was seen by many Jews during its highly successful runs in both London and New York. Most rabbis would undoubtedly disagree with Hare's moral vision — probably calling him anti–Semitic. But Hare would undoubtedly call Zionism anti–Semitic since Palestinians are Arabs, also a Semitic people. Hare would also say that while Jews claims to be the victims of terrorism, they themselves have used terrorism and torture to push millions of Palestinian Arabs out of their homes and into refugee camps — and once they are there, Israel drops cluster bombs on them. And these cluster bombs are provided free to Israel by the United States, under the government of the very religious Bush family, plus other very religious leaders. Israelis have also created an apartheid wall to separate Jews from non–Jews in the "Holy Land," and that wall itself has become a symbol of Jewish apartheid.

By the end of *Via Dolorosa*, Hare is very happy to be back home in Hampstead and with his wife and family. In the beginning of the play, Hare describes England as a place where people do not believe in anything. The settler Daniel says that Memorial Day in the United States means only a good day to buy mattresses since they go on sale on Memorial Day weekend. Daniel argues that America is a land without religious meaning, but when he goes to Israel he finds true religious feeling — but that religious feeling gets transferred into racism and apartheid. Clearly, Hare seems to be implying, the search for morality must not necessitate the brutal treatment of other people. The settler Danny sees no contradiction between his religion and his moral fervor, both of which find expression in his politics in his homeland, Israel. But Hare clearly implies that Danny and Sarah's behavior strikes him and most other people as appallingly immoral and racist — and Hare notes that Danny and Sarah's religion, the Jewish religion, is not about to point out any contradiction to them. Has religious fervor been transferred into racism and apartheid and crimes against humanity? They have indeed, Hare suggest in this play.

Former American president Jimmy Carter seems to have learned from David Hare's writing on the topic of Israel. His book *Palestine: Peace Not Apartheid* clearly reflects the implications in David Hare's play *Via Dolorosa*. As a person very concerned with morality, Jimmy Carter clearly shows the immorality of Zionism's apartheid policies and its brutal treatment of the Palestinian people — killing thousands of them and forcing millions into refugee camps so the Jewish settlers could steal their land. While Israel claims to be a victim of terrorism, Carter clearly shows that Israel itself uses torture and terrorism against the Palestinian people, a Semitic people.

Morality is a very tricky issue, but David Hare has created some very fascinating theater out of the search for morality. One of his main tools is his own and his characters' inevitable uses of transference. Moral issues can easily be transferred into other issues, but the lack of moral issues can also be horrible, leading to an empty life. But a life of religious fervor, as with the settlers in Israel, can lead to appalling racism, apartheid, and immorality. These are all important issues which David Hare examines in his plays. Transference remains a tricky issue — both in Freudian psychotherapy and in David Hare's theater. Both Freud and David Hare imply that moral certainty is not really always possible but that theater can be a fascinating medium for examining those very issues of morality and transference.

Speaking of transference, Alan Ryckman's play *My Name Is Rachel Corrie*, based on the writings on Rachel Corrie, has been a major success in London. The show was supposed to transfer to New York in the spring of 2006, but somehow the show was postponed, though it was finally staged at the Minetta Lane Theater in New York's Greenwich Village for a successful run of performances which had to be extended due to a positive public response despite mediocre reviews. Clearly, the forces of censorship in New York did not want Americans to see that show. It is based on the life and writings of Rachel Corrie, an American college student who was trying to prevent the Israeli army from bulldozing Palestinian homes. Members of that army crushed Rachel Corrie to death with one of their new bulldozers — bulldozers transferred for free to Israel from America. Luckily for New York, the brave little Minetta Lane Theater in Greenwich Village did finally stage this important play after another New York theater announced it but then backed out of staging it because of Jewish pressure. Clearly, transference can easily become censorship.

David Hare's more recent play *Stuff Happens,* which first appeared at the National Theater in London in 2006 and then moved later than spring to the Public Theater in New York, exemplifies yet again the moral transference Hare has become famous for in his plays. This play tries to recreate the Bush presidency's involvement in Iraq and the start of the Iraqi war, and Hare defends his presentation in terms of actual quotes from the press reports on the historical events. We see a group of people slowly and inexorably dragging the American people and the world into a war into Iraq, and the play ends with the horrifying statement about the suffering of the Iraqi people as a result of thousands of them being slaughtered by the coalition forces, primarily American and British soldiers.

As is dramatized in this play, President George W. Bush begins most of his meetings with a prayer — he and his wife Laura are very religious people who go to church every Sunday, and are often photographed there shaking hands with the presiding minister. Bush has often said very encouraging and supportive things about Israel and its religious mission to bring the Jews back to the Holy Land, though he has also asserted the right of the Palestinian people to a homeland as well. Why not a democratic solution for both people? Doesn't his religion or the Jewish religion allow for a democratic state which tolerates all religions and has separation of church and state, surely the basis for any real democracy? Why can't Israel/Palestine become another United States of the Middle East with separation of church and state and toleration of all religions? Many very religious Jews would not want such a state since they insist that their religion demands a Jewish state, Israel, with only one state religion, their own. This would remind most people of the aims of the Crusaders in the medieval period, who wanted a Christian state in the Holy Land despite the millions of Muslims living there. But religious transference onto politics can enable religious leaders to defend torture, racism, theft, and religious intolerance.

Hare ends the play by suggesting the horrible suffering and the horrible immorality involved in this series of actions which resulted in so many mistakes, so many lies, and so much human suffering. But here too transference is occurring since Hare implies that moral decisions have been made, and immoral actions have occurred which resulted in horrendous suffering. But was morality ever a concern of the Bush presidency or was morality used simply as a PR stunt to justify actions that were taken for other purposes more involved with political and economic realities?

Hare's concern with morality, while the result of transference, however, remains a human concern as Americans, the British, and peoples around the world question the morality of an American-initiated war and its purpose and its cost in human suffering.

The transferring of one topic or one feeling onto another occurs frequently in the plays of David Hare, and that is precisely what makes them so interesting. Transference is a common human occurrence, as Freud pointed out, and it is part of our daily lives. But if we can spot it and handle it, perhaps we can control it so that it does not distort our perception and our own grip on reality.

In any case, David Hare's obsession with transference allows us to see characters and political issues in a new way, and also enables us to see Hare's characters operating in a different way. While using rather traditional forms for his plays, Hare has nevertheless been able to create a new form of exciting theater by showing how the human tendency to transfer painful ideas and people onto less painful targets can have both comic and tragic consequences on both people and ideas.

I have used the word transference in many different ways in this chapter, but the basis for my usage of this word is Freud's concept of transference — transposing one meaningful relationship or idea onto another area, all done subconsciously. David Hare's plays use this Freudian mechanism very cleverly and subtly to expose some of the conflicts and political horrors of our own time. David Hare's own search for morality shows how transference can generate some wonderful theater which analyzes our own concept of morality.

Bibliography

Boon, Richard. *About Hare: The Playwright and the Work.* London: Faber and Faber, 2003.

Carter, Jimmy. *Palestine: Peace Not Apartheid.* New York: Simon and Schuster, 2006.

Dean, Joan Fitzpatrick. *David Hare.* Boston: Twayne, 1990.

Donesky, Finlay. *David Hare: A Moral and Historical Perspective.* Westport, Conn.: Greenwood, 1996.

Fitzpatrick, John. *David Hare.* Boston: Twayne, 1990.

Fraser, Scott. *A Politic Theatre: The Drama of David Hare.* Atlanta, Ga.: Rodopi, 1996.

Hare, David. *Obedience, Struggle and Revolt.* London: Faber and Faber, 2005.

_____. *Writing Left-Handed.* London: Faber and Faber, 1991.

Homden, Carol. *The Plays of David Hare.* New York: Cambridge University Press, 1995.

Mearsheimer, John and Stephen Walt. *The Israel Lobby and U.S. Foreign Policy.* New York: Farrar, Straus and Ginoux, 2007.

Oliva, Judy Lee. *David Hare: Theatricalizing Politics.* Ann Arbor, Mich.: University of Michigan Research Press, 1990.

Pappe, Ilan. *The Ethnic Cleansing of Palestine.* Oxford: Oneworld, 2007.

Sternlicht, Sanford *A Reader's Guide to Modern British Drama.* Syracuse: Syracuse University Press, 2004.

Zeifman, Hersh, ed. *David Hare: A Casebook.* New York: Garland, 1994.

11

David Mamet
and Harvey Fierstein
Gender Roles and Role Playing

Gender roles and role playing do not seem to be major concerns for most people. One thinks of these things as fixed, but transgendered people are there to remind us that these things can be changed, and that some people feel that they were born in the wrong body with the wrong gender. Most people go through some form of role-playing and some gender insecurity — and indeed some people spend their entire lives role-playing and not being aware that they are playing a role rather than being themselves.

One sees this issue immediately when one looks at photos of David Mamet. Usually he is smoking a very large and prominent cigar. Also he is usually photographed in blue jeans and a tee-shirt, with a Marine-like short haircut. He usually looks like a very masculine Marine or army general — very short hair, very large, prominent cigar. General Tommy Franks looks similar to David Mamet — at least in terms of haircut, cigar, and facial expression.

One cannot help wondering why David Mamet is trying to look so much like the macho American military man. He is the most masculine-looking writer in America since Ernest Hemingway, who also made sure that he was always photographed doing very masculine things like boxing or fishing or going big game hunting. Hemingway, too, always tried to maintain a very prominent and even pugnacious image of masculinity, and one can't help wondering if that was why he finally killed himself — was the effort to maintain such a masculine persona too much for him? Was he really this masculine or was he role-playing — and if so, why did he feel the need to role play the part of the hyper-macho male?

So, too, David Mamet is always photographed doing very masculine things. Why does he find this necessary? Is he insecure about his masculinity?

Does he want to counter-attack the image of the writer or playwright as a big sissy? Does he want to dissociate himself from homosexuality in a very pronounced way? Why?

Mamet makes a very marked contrast to another Jewish playwright, Harvey Fierstein, who usually performs in a dress. He was a big star on Broadway in a very successful musical called *Hairspray*, where he plays a woman, Mrs. Greenblatt. He first became famous for a play about a transvestite, and indeed Harvey Fierstein has become most famous in his dress rather than trouser roles. In his first Broadway role, in his own play *Torch Song Trilogy*, he played a drag queen — a man in a dress — which he himself was for many years. He was the lead in *Fiddler on the Roof* on Broadway in the spring of 2006 but got very mixed reviews — clearly both the critics and his audience were not used to seeing him perform in pants. Both Jewish playwrights look at gender roles and role-playing not only in their personal appearance but also in their respective plays.

Mamet's first major success in the theater was *Sexual Perversity in Chicago*, and that play involved two couples who were trying to relate to each other. And role-playing was constantly occurring in the play, with men trying to act like men and women trying to act like women — as one of the woman thoughtfully comments, "Men all want just one thing, but it's not the same thing."

David Mamet, circa 1983 or 1984 (photograph: Nobby Clark).

Torch Song Trilogy, 1982; Harvey Fierstein as Arnold and Estelle Getty as Mrs. Beckoff in the Broadway production (photograph: Hunt/Pucci).

In her role as a preening woman, she feels she has to generalize in a sweeping way about men. Clearly she is finding the situation very confusing, and most of the characters seem not very authentic, clearly what the playwright intended.

Mamet also examines these same issues *A Life in the Theater.* This is a two-character play involving an older actor and a younger actor, and one wonders if these two men are sexually interested in each other, but apparently they are not. But one of the things one wonders about these two is what roles they are playing — appropriate for a play about two actors. Another issue the play questions is how masculinity and acting come together — or indeed whether they do. Many uninformed American have the suspicion that most men who are interested in the theater are gay — and Harvey Fierstein reasserts this old stereotype in many ways.

Real men in both America and Britain are not supposed to want a life in the theater. So what is the sexuality of these two men in David Mamet's play? How does the old actor relate to the young actor and vice versa, and when are they acting and when (if ever) are they really themselves? One can't help wondering about these things, and they are central issues in the play itself. Role-playing becomes a profession in acting, and the play also queries whether these actors are acting or are ever themselves while playing their assigned roles and in real life as well — whatever that is.

In *Glengarry, Glen Ross* — perhaps Mamet's biggest success so far, running for a long time on Broadway and also becoming a highly successful movie with Jack Lemon — masculinity remains a constant presence on stage. All the characters are men, and part of their strategy as highly successful real estate salesmen is their hypermasculinity. In fact, when one of the secretaries in the office tells a customer the truth for once, the salesman who has lost a sale as a result becomes enraged and viciously yells at him, "you cunt." Mamet has become famous for his obscene language on stage, which is part of his masculine front, though not many people are shocked by this any more. But the accusation of being "a cunt" is clearly a way of denying a man his masculinity, and masculinity is clearly at a premium among the characters in *Glengarry, Glen Ross*. All of the vulgar language also serves as a method of male bonding, as it does in real life — ugly, vulgar language being the sign of a hypermasculine man, which all these salesmen clearly want to project to each other. Why, one wonders, if they are so secure about their own masculinity?

In this play, Mamet suggests that the sign of a real man in this society of real estate agents remains making a lot of money. The manager of the office these salesmen work from boasts of his salary, his possessions, his wealth — a real man, in other words, makes more money than the men around him, who are by definition less masculine.

Is Mamet also suggesting that capitalism, especially when we see capitalism at its most naked in selling, specifically real estate sales, is itself a method of asserting one's masculinity by fleecing someone else? These salesmen are an unscrupulous lot, desperate to

Torch Song Trilogy, 1983; Harvey Fierstein as a transvestite.

Glengarry, Glen Ross, 1984; Joe Mantegna as Richard Roma (photograph: Brigitte Lacombe).

sell their real estate and make their fat commissions, and their manager keeps very accurate records of their monthly sales to post on the company's bulletin board. Is capitalism itself based on the most aggressive form of role-playing — a hypermasculinity? Now that more and more women exist in the business world, one wonders how they function in such a masculine environment, an issue that Caryl Churchill investigates in several of her plays, especially *Top Girls*.

Mamet suggests in *Glengarry, Glen Ross* that capitalism and masculinity seem to go hand in hand, that there is something predatory about real estate sales and that these men, highly successful in their field, are using their masculinity to dominate and subjugate their naïve customers in the play — they are especially brutal to their male secretary, who as a secretary has a rather dubious and questionable masculinity since real men do not do secretarial work. In fact, it is this male secretary who is called — the ultimate put-down for a man —"a cunt." His masculinity is attacked because of the mistake he made. Part of being a man in this play is being able to fleece customers out of their money by selling them worthless real estate at inflated prices. Being a real man, a really successful man, in this play means being able to sell and make big profits. A bad salesman is a sissy, a fruit, not a real man.

Is this the American concept of masculinity? Mamet suggests that it is, at least in the world of real estate, which he is clearly presenting as a microcosm of capitalism itself. But a look at the photos of the playwright indicates that he is trying to present himself in the role of the hyper–male of contemporary America.

Because Mamet has often been accused by the critics of being unable to write a good role for a woman, Mamet then wrote *Boston Marriage*, in which three women are the only characters in the play. Significantly, this was not one of Mamet's major successes. But "Boston Marriage" was a term for lesbianism in the 19th century—a situation when two women were living together and did not want to marry a man. Some of these relationships were undoubtedly lesbian relationships, and that is what is centrally examined in *Boston Marriage*. Two women in the play, the major characters, seem to be lesbian lovers of the classic division of butch/fem—or very masculine versus very feminine lesbian partners. But the roles keep switching and one wonders if these women are playing roles or really fall naturally into these two roles.

Are they lesbians? One cannot be sure, but that seems to be the case. And these two women, in their efforts to be really masculine, are often very cruel to each other and especially to their maid. Mamet implies in this play that one of the characteristics of true masculinity is the ability to be cruel and inflict pain and suffering on others. He seems to suggest that these lesbians are in some ways crueler than the "real men" sales men in *Glengarry, Glen Ross*. His concept of masculinity includes an element of sado-masochism, rather as in the plays of Harold Pinter. Both playwrights present us with sometimes sadistic relationships, as in Mamet's *Boston Marriage*.

Oleanna, which was a major success off–Broadway in New York and also succeeded admirably in London, is also centrally concerned with roles and role-playing. The male teacher in that play is clearly role-playing the macho man, and to prove how masculine he is to his female students he often treats them sadistically. He is often very cruel to them, letting them wait for him while he chats on the phone to his wife and colleagues. He is likewise insensitive to Oleanna, and when he becomes victimitized by her in the second act, he responds in the brainless macho way by hitting her. Attacking and pummeling her physically satisfies his sadistic needs as a man, though it also destroys his career by the end of the play.

In *Oleanna* Mamet has written a very good role for a woman, a role with many complex possibilities for a great actress. In the first act Oleanna seems like a very naïve and victimized woman, but is she playing a part in pretending to be so naïve? In the second act Oleanna seems like a vengeful, determined woman — determined to destroy the career of her male teacher. Is she a symbol of victimized womanhood determined to get revenge? Or is she a symbol of a duplicitous woman who pretends to be a victim in the first act to destroy sadistically an innocent man in the second act? Is she a symbol of female liberation gone amuck? Or is she a symbol of a woman becoming the kind of predatory male which we found so clearly in *Glengarry, Glen Ross*? Is Mamet suggesting that a liberated woman has to become a new kind of animal, the kind of hyper-aggressive, vengeful male that we have seen in several of Mamet's earlier plays?

Of course, the recurrent question in *Oleanna* is who the real victim is. In the first act it seems that the female student has become a victim, while in the second act the male teacher looks like the victim. Clearly there is a sado-masochistic relationship going on in the play as these two characters react to each other. Is Mamet suggesting that there is something sadistic in the role of the teacher? Ionesco's very famous play *The Lesson* also presents us with the male teacher as sadistic rather than helpful and nurturing to the female student. Some students who really hate school think of teachers as sadistic, though such a student's definition of sadism might be assigning the student something to read in an English class. Most teachers would not consider that sadism, but is the very role of teacher essentially sadistic since teachers do make assignments and other requirements of students? I do not think so, but some students undoubtedly do — but such students might also think of any future employer, in fact any authority figure, as essentially sadistic. Most people are not so cynical, even so paranoid, about authority figures and realize that one can learn from such people, even through the work that they assign to students or employees. Most people would not see this as sadism but as how one learns and how work gets done.

Mamet's world is very different from Harvey Fierstein's. His first major success in the theater was *Torch Song Trilogy*, and he played the lead role — that of a transvestite nightclub performer. Each act of the play has a different locale; in fact, it was like three one-act plays. In all these three acts, Fierstein is clearly a gay man who is confronting problems with partners and even problems with his mother and his son, but his homosexuality is never doubted or even in question. Fierstein's theater is centrally gay, unlike Mamet's — but even with gay people, role-playing can easily occur. We see in the first act of *Torch Song Trilogy* the main character playing the role of a female cabaret singer and even singing in drag for the audience. Fierstein himself worked as a drag performer and clearly exults in this role, which he did so well in the first act of *Torch Song Trilogy* — thereby questioning not only his own masculinity but his determination to flaunt his homosexuality and transvestite reality. To dress as a woman pleases Fierstein since he does it so often and with obvious pleasure rather than any embarrassment.

Clearly Harvey Fierstein, as a liberated and openly gay character, wants to exalt the gay experience and write the kind of new plays which will investigate and dramatize this formerly taboo topic. While Shaw presents the topic of role-playing and homosexuality in a very oblique way — he had to given the legal realities in England during his lifetime — Fierstein can be quite open about gay realities like transvestitism and transgendered people in his plays. Clearly his brand of homosexuality contradicts the politically correct view of homosexuals as people like everyone else, not transvestite queens.

Fierstein also wrote a very successful one-act play — *On Tidy Endings* — about the death of a gay man and the attempt of his wife to deal with his former lover. The play was also staged as part of three one-acters entitled *Safe Sex*. Here too the wife seems like the most masculine and unforgiving of people, while the male lover has what used to be called a feminine sensitivity to characters and situations. By the end of the play the female character becomes less stereotypically male and more stereotypically female in being able to adjust to the reality of her former husband's lover and even allowing him to know her son, and the son of her dead husband who of course was also gay. The husband-father died of AIDS, thanks to his homosexual lifestyle and his deception of his wife. By the end of *On Tidy Endings* we can see that there are no tidy endings but that people can deal humanely with other people if they deal honestly with each other and avoid role-playing. By the end of the play the wife has come to accept her husband's lover and his rights as the person her husband loved most and left her for.

Gender bending seems to be a central issue in the plays of Harvey Fierstein, while rather rigid concepts of gender roles seem more central to the theater of David Mamet. Since Harvey Fierstein has been very vocal about his homosexuality, one would expect his view of sexual roles and role playing to be that of a liberated gay man who tolerates very flexible concepts of masculinity. David Mamet, on the other hand, as a heterosexual male, seems more interested in rigid sexual roles, especially in his earlier plays like *Glengarry, Glen Ross*. But in his later plays like *Boston Marriage* he too shows greater interest in fluid and more complicated sexual roles, as the two lesbians indicate, though they are often grotesque and cruel, defining masculinity in terms of sadism. But gender roles clearly remain important to both writers.

When one is presenting and discussing gender roles, one naturally brings up the whole issue of role-playing. Are gender roles natural or manufactured? Are these characters role-playing to make themselves appear as masculine or feminine as they are?

All this brings up a book by one of the revolutionaries of the modern stage, Luigi Pirandello. In his book *Maschere Ignudi,* or *Naked Masks,* one is confronted with the whole issue of role-playing, and Pirandello suggests repeatedly that if one is playing a role one is not being real. *Naked Masks* suggests that behind the masks which we present to others there is no reality but just another series of masks. Very confusing indeed.

Role-playing and gender roles are particularly confusing for adolescents, who are trying to define their sexualities while living in a highly homophobic situation: most high schools in America and Britain. Jonathan Harvey's *Beautiful Thing* tries to present these very issues with teenage characters and succeeds very well in showing the problems gay teens face, even when they have cooperating and realistic parents who do not want them to role-play a heterosexual self that is actually foreign to them. Life is more complicated and difficult for these teens — and in fact gay teens have a higher than average rate of suicide.

All these writers dramatize role-playing but imply that it is a very complicated phenomenon. Often people are unaware themselves of when they are playing a role and when they are themselves. Our society's concepts of masculinity and femininity affect all members of that society, and most people mold their behavior in such a way as to conform to social concepts. Even if one denies and defies social concepts of sexual roles, that too indicates a response, a personal response, to a social reality.

Some of the new gay theater of the late 20th and early 21st centuries seeks to investigate these complex and often very personal issues. Transgendered people have to face these complexities most frontally, but most people — at least in adolescence — are painfully aware of gender roles and trying to fit into society's concepts of what is normal and what is acceptable for oneself. For most people this is a bit difficult but not very difficult, but some people find it impossible to fit themselves into society's preconceived conceptions of proper gender roles. Playwrights David Mamet and Harvey Fierstein, among others, have created a new kind of theater which looks at these very personal and complex issues for the contemporary stage — issues that can create both tragedy and comedy in their characters' lives. Both playwrights imply that there are no tidy endings in life, just as there are no tidy endings in the human personality. Where does role-playing begin and reality intrude on the complexities of the human personality? Both Mamet and Fierstein are curious about the boundaries here and write a new kind of theater to investigate those boundaries.

Bibliography

Bigsby, C. W. E. *David Mamet*. New York: Methuen, 1985.
_____. *Joe Orton*. London: Methuen, 1982.
Bigsby, Christopher, ed. *The Cambridge Companion to David Mamet*. Cambridge: Cambridge University Press, 2004.
Carroll, Dennis. *David Mamet*. New York: St. Martin's Press, 1987.
Dean, Anne. *David Mamet: Language as Dramatic Action*. Rutherford, N.J.: Fairleigh Dickinson University Press, 1990.
Kane, Leslie. *Weasels and Wisemen: Ethics and Ethnicity in the Works of David Mamet*. New York: St. Martin's Press, 1999.
Kane, Leslie, ed. *David Mamet: A Casebook*. New York: Garland, 1992.
Sternlicht, Sanford. *A Reader's Guide to Modern American Drama*. Syracuse, N.Y.: Syracuse University Press, 2002.

12

Stephen Sondheim
Perfectionism

One of the things which early distinguished many of Sondheim's musicals was perfectionism and an unwillingness to use the traditional structure of a musical, a usual plot of a story, with the action stopping for the major characters to sing a song. The typical structure of a Broadway musical generally involved the old format of boy meets girl, boy loses girl, boy gets girl. Oscar Hammerstein, Stephen Sondheim's mentor, used variations of this form for most of his musicals with Richard Rodgers. *Oklahoma, Carousel, The Sound of Music, The King and I, Cinderella,* and *Flower Drum Song* used variants of this traditional theatrical formula, and those shows were major Broadway successes. Stephen Sondheim became a personal friend of Oscar Hammerstein, who in turn become his mentor as a writer and composer of Broadway musicals.

There is clearly an obsessive-compulsive force in Sondheim to create something new and in a new format in each of his musicals and not repeat the traditional forms of the Broadway musical. Sondheim was rarely happy using traditional forms; instead, he sought new, original forms which he felt were organic to the material rather than inherited from the genre. Such an approach seems more typical of opera than the Broadway musical, usually looking for the hit musical number to sell tickets rather than musical experimentation to confuse audiences. With varying degrees of success Sondheim tried to create a new kind of form for a new kind of Broadway musical, and as a result he created some of the most original shows ever seen on the Broadway stage. Perfectionism remained at the core of his work as a composer of musical theater for the Broadway stage, and his mentor Oscar Hammerstein encouraged this aspect of his creativity.

But Sondheim's determination to create something completely new in each show created problems for him as well since some of his shows were flops,

and their unorthodox approach remained part of the reason for those failures
in many cases. A more traditional approach to musical comedy can often produce more predictable results — as with the shows of Rodgers and Hammerstein, Jerry Herman, and Lerner and Loewe. These Broadway composers
produced more bankable Broadway hits, though with duller and more predictable results for the theater. Sondheim's mad desire for originality has generated more theatrical and musical excitement, and has resulted (undoubtedly
much to his chagrin) in the staging of his musicals in more and more opera
houses around the world. Sondheim shows such as *Sweeney Todd* and *A Little Night Music* have become operatic staples around the world, despite Sondheim's often professed dislike of the art form of opera. He has often said that
he finds traditional operas too long and boring — and how ironic that his own
shows are now being converted into opera house successes.

Meryle Secrest, in her excellent biography of Stephen Sondheim, repeatedly points out his perfectionism. Collaborators Leonard Bernstein and James
Lapine have both commented on the perfectionism which characterized both
his personality and his works, though he was also willing to compromise to
get works staged. But Sondheim remained uncomfortable with traditional
forms for the Broadway musical, a theatrical genre which he clearly adored
and which he liked to create. Yet his perfectionism has driven him to give
each of his own shows a structure which differs from his other shows and all
other Broadway musicals.

He started with a very traditional plot and story-line when he began as
a librettist rather than a composer. *West Side Story,* which premiered at the
Winter Garden Theater in New York on September 26, 1957, had a book by
Arthur Laurents and music by Leonard Bernstein. Stephen Sondheim contributed only the lyrics, but the show became a major hit on Broadway and
then became a very popular movie. *West Side Story* ran for 732 performances
and closed, then soon reopened for 249 more performances within two sea-
sons. Using the plot of Shakespeare's *Romeo and Juliet* was certainly a daring
idea for a musical, but it was hardly the first Shakespearean adaptation for
Broadway; earlier there had been *The Boys from Syracuse* plus *Kiss Me Kate,*
by Cole Porter, to mention the two most prominent Broadway musicals based
on Shakespeare — though these were comedies rather than tragedies, which
indicates how experimental the Bernstein/Sondheim show really was when it
first appeared in 1957. There were other Broadway shows with sad endings,
such as *Pal Joey,* but these were real rarities. Leonard Bernstein's use of jazz
in the show's music also marked it as revolutionary at the time, in addition
to its tragic rather than up-beat ending. Hell's Kitchen in Manhattan with
all its racial tensions and resultant gang violence seemed at the time like a

revolutionary place to set a Broadway musical as well. The show succeeded in both its theater and film formats despite being considered box office poison by many people at its inception.

Certainly *West Side Story* connects in interesting ways with both its Shakespearean source in *Romeo and Juliet* and with Puccinian opera. The tragic love presented in Puccini operas like *La Bohème, Tosca,* and *Madama Butterfly* connects musical tragedy with hit musical numbers in a wonderful way. Puccini's absolute genius for the great aria for his major characters, the kind of aria which one cannot forget, the musical tune which remains haunting in the listener's mind, characterizes some of Sondheim's shows as well, especially *West Side Story.* Songs such as "Maria," "Tonight, Tonight" and "America" became quite popular at the time of the show's premiere and have entered the tradition of popular American songs, something which Sondheim has clearly sought. Unlike some avant-garde composers, who feel that popular music is innately and inevitably junk, Sondheim has always sought to achieve popular success with his shows, which he of course has often achieved.

Sondheim's next show, *Gypsy,* first appeared at the Broadway Theater in New York on May 21, 1959, and here too Sondheim was the librettist — with music by Jule Styne and book again by Arthur Laurents, suggested by the memoirs of Gypsy Rose Lee. Sondheim hated that he again was librettist rather than composer since he also wanted to compose a Broadway musical. Here too the format for the show was experimental since it was based on the memoirs of an actual historical figure, something quite new and unusual for a Broadway show. But here again Sondheim's lyrics were clever and dramatic, though without the original music which Sondheim was clearly aching to write. *Gypsy,* though, was a major hit and ran for 702 performances, and the show has also been revived several times on Broadway, most recently for Tyne Daly and Bernadette Peters (in 2003). The show centers around a grotesque mother figure who uses her children for her own aims and pursuits — and since Sondheim had such a bad relationship with his own mother (he did not attend her funeral), this theme probably first attracted him to the idea for the show. Yet here the format of most of his songs for this show use the traditional musical forms of the time, though with increasing irony on Sondheim's part. The opening song, "Let me entertain you," which is first sung by the innocent theater children in the beginning, becomes the song to which Gypsy Rose Lee strips off her clothes by the end of the show. This show hardly contains the typical musical finale and happy ending which one expects in a Broadway hit, but the show was still a major hit and has been revived about every fifteen years on Broadway; it has also been staged very successfully in London and elsewhere around the world. *Gypsy* attempted to create a musical with ideas, a musical for adults rather than a childish and brainless musical entertainment.

The first show of Sondheim's for which he wrote both music and lyrics was *A Funny Thing Happened on the Way to the Forum,* which premiered at the Alvin Theater in New York on May 8, 1962, and ran for 964 performances — another big hit. The search for an organic form, for something different from the typical plot for a Broadway musical, was apparent in the fact that the show was based on the Roman comedies of Plautus. Zero Mostel turned Pseudolus, the slave yearning for his freedom, into one of his most famous roles, and Nathan Lane was also very comic and effective in a revival of this show. But though theater historians like Oscar Brockett had pointed out that these Roman comedies of Plautus and Terence were similar to the spoken text and songs of a Broadway musical, Sondheim used that very format to create a new form of Broadway show. Interestingly enough, a subplot involved the familiar boy meets girls, boy loses girl, boy gets girl form, but the central character remained a slave yearning for freedom. But this show does include the typical Broadway ending — marriage and a happy musical finale. The show enjoyed the kind of Broadway hit success which most producers yearn for. The traditional ending of comedy in Western theater, a marriage, does appear in the final scene of this show, too — a bit of a disappointment in this otherwise experimental show.

But after three major successes within five years on Broadway — *West Side Story, Gypsy,* and *A Funny Thing Happened on the Way to the Forum* — Sondheim was due for a flop, and the flop he developed was *Anyone Can Whistle.* This show premiered in New York at the Majestic Theatre on April 4, 1964, and ran for nine performances after very negative reviews. Despite the presence of Angela Lansbury, Lee Remick, and Harry Guardino, and some interesting songs, the play failed to generate much approval from either audiences or critics and died a quick death. It has never been revived on Broadway.

After this flop, Sondheim's confidence suffered, so he went back to being a lyricist, writing lyrics for the music of Richard Rodgers in *Do I Hear a Waltz;* but the collaboration with the rather rigid Rodgers turned out to be a very painful experience for Sondheim, who felt he could not create a new kind of form working with this elderly and rather conservative composer even though Rogers was his mentor Oscar Hammerstein's famous collaborator. The show premiered at the 46th Street Theatre on March 18, 1965, and ran for 220 performances. While this show was not a total flop, it was not a major success, either, though it did play for most of one season. But this show also indicates Sondheim's unwillingness to write a show that typified the Broadway musical.

After two non-hits, Sondheim's confidence as a composer had built up enough so that he began working on his own score, *Company*, with a book by George Furth. This show premiered on April 26, 1970, at the Alvin Theatre in New York, and ran for 690 performances. This was a very clever and experimental show, again showing Sondheim's perfectionism and search for an organic form rather than the typical musical plot. The book resembled a television sit-com, centering on a main character, Bobby, and his relationship with various friends, especially married couples. Robert, the main character, is a thirty-five year old man, apparently heterosexual, who cannot find a person to marry, though all his friends are married. Robert was suspected by some critics of being homosexual (as Sondheim himself is) and seeking parental figures in all the married couples who become his friends, but the difficulties and crises in all the marriages of all the couples onstage indicate something about the difficulty of marriage, and even the difficulty of intimacy in general, a thoroughly modern theme.

While the show was not the great hit of that season, its experimental use of form, and the ironic sophistication of its music and lyrics in songs like "Could I Leave You" indicate the revolutionary show it really was. Some critics said the show attacked marriage and was guilty of misogyny in its presentation of women, and other critics argued that the central character of Robert remained a mystery and a cipher. The show had a truly organic and original form which fit the story perfectly, and its success is seen in the revivals of the show in London, New York, and elsewhere, despite its lack of a happy ending with a marriage and a musical fanfare. Marriage is the traditional ending of comedy in Western theater, especially in Shakespeare and Moliere, but Sondheim's attack on marriage in this show precludes such an ending. The central character, Bobby, his thirty-fifth birthday and his state of still being a bachelor become the central focus of this show, though *Company* also dramatizes the problems of alcoholism. One of the recurrent suggestions in this show is Bobby's possible alcoholism. And a song like "The Ladies Who Lunch" clearly indicates the alcoholism of those women, whose own excessive drinking has become both a joke and a tragedy in this show. Clearly, Sondheim's perfectionism drove him to redefine the American musical in an intelligent and original way.

Follies appeared next, and here too the structure of the show was original. Sondheim wrote both music and lyrics, with a book by James Goldman, choreography by Michael Bennett, and direction by Harold Prince and Michael Bennett. Michael Bennett became more famous for *A Chorus Line* and *Dreamgirls*, but his choreography impressed in this show as well. The whole idea of a reunion of a group of dancers — all of whom were in a Broadway review rather like the Ziegfeld Follies of the 1920s — gave the show its wonderfully enigmatic Pirandellian title. The show premiered in New York at the Winter Garden Theater on April 4, 1971, in a truly lavish production by Boris Aronson. Using time jumps and flashbacks, the show presents us with middle aged and old people as they are now, attending a reunion, and also shows us the same people thirty years earlier when they were in a Broadway review.

Several have married, and the unhappiness of all the marriages, a recurrent theme in Sondheim, is shown here as well. But the form of *Follies* remains absolutely unique, and wonderfully experimental and different. The show received mixed review but some raves and ran for 522 performances — and lost money. It was not an unqualified hit — rather a succès d'estime, and has been revived on Broadway. But the idea of turning a class reunion into a Broadway show remains daringly original and created a new kind of Broadway musical. Eschewing the happy Broadway ending — marriage and a musical finale for everybody to sing and dance at the end — Sondheim's *Follies* managed to say profound things about human relationships and the passage of time, though still within the setting of a Broadway stage and starring a group of Broadway babies, boys and girls from the chorus who have become old but are still vibrant and exciting onstage. But the singing and dancing often indicate the personal tragedy of unhappy marriages, as in *Company*, and clearly reflects the divorce and resultant trauma of Sondheim's own parents.

More successful was *A Little Night Music*, again with both music and lyrics by Stephen Sondheim, but with a book by Hugh Wheeler. This show, also directed by Harold Prince, opened in New York at the Schubert Theater on February 25, 1973, and ran for 601 performances. Based on Ingmar Bergman's film *Smiles of a Summer Night*, the show included Sondheim's most famous and popular song, "Send in the Clowns," and was quite successful. The idea of using a movie — originally of course in Swedish — was a very clever and original idea, though used after that in shows like *Nine* and more recently *Hair Spray*. Even before that, the musical *42nd Street* was also based on a Hollywood movie of the same title. Since Sondheim wanted a real Broadway hit, he avoided the bleak vision of many of his earlier shows like *Company* and *Follies* and provided a crowd-pleasing happy ending with all the couples happily in love, though "Send in the Clowns" suggests a modernist, cynical view of intimacy and marriage which the happy ending of this show belies. Though Sondheim has repeatedly stated how much he dislikes opera, this show has an operatic quality and has been adapted for opera houses in Europe and America. The New York City Opera Company revived their operatic version of this Sondheim show in the spring of 2003. The happy ending of mar-

A Little Night Music, original Broadway production, 1973; Glynis Johns and Len Car-iou in Sondheim's version of an Ingmar Bergman film (photograph: Martha Swope).

riage and a happy musical finale, while surely a crowd pleaser, does seem a bit mechanical and even simple-minded in light of the complexities of the male-female and parent-child relationships in the show. Though the happy ending in this musical seems forced, it did give the show its success and the frequency of its revivals and even its movement toward an opera format.

Even more experimental was Sondheim's *Pacific Overtures*. Here too he wrote both the music and the lyrics, using a book by John Weidman and based in part on the memoirs of Commodore Matthew Perry. This show had its premiere in New York at the Winter Garden Theater on January 11, 1976, and Harold Prince directed the brilliant production. Boris Aronson designed the lavish Kabuki-style set for this highly original show. A Japanese company, the New National Theatre, did a version in Tokyo using Noh rather than Kabuki theatre and then brought it to New York in the summer of 2002. This story also dispensed with the typical plot of boy meets girl, etc., of the Broadway musical, but is instead based on Commodore Perry's entry into Japan and forcing it to trade with America and other Western powers.

The whole topic of European and American imperialism in Asia is the real subject matter of this musical, and I know of no other musical which uses such an original form for a show. The show was written during the period of the Vietnam war, which remained in the original audience's mind so that they clearly had an example in the current world of American imperialism in Asia. This is a musical about ideas, and there is no central plot other than the American Perry's invasion of Japan and its consequences for Japan. The music is very clever as well — parodying haiku poetry in "Welcome to Kanagawa." This song was cleverly performed by men costumed as Japanese female prostitutes (the geishas). In "Hello Please" Sondheim parodies the musical styles of the various imperialist powers in this song — the American sings to a Sousa march, the British to a Gilbert and Sullivan patter song, the Russian uses a Russian folk rhythm, and the Frenchman uses a can-can musical background. The form of this musical, that of an investigation of imperialism in Japan, is done in the style of Japanese Kabuki theater, all the parts played by men, as in that native Japanese form of theater. Seeing the arrival of Commodore Perry and the Americans from a Japanese point of view serves to create a

A Little Night Music, original Broadway production, 1973; Hermione Gingold as Madame Armfeldt and Glynis Johns as Desiree (photograph: Martha Swope).

Pacific Overtures, original Broadway production, 1976; Japanese prostitutes awaiting the Americans (photograph: Martha Swope).

unique point of view for this show. The Commodore's lion dance on his arrival in Japan creates a wonderful finale for the first act of the show and cleverly presents his momentous appearance from a Japanese perspective. Although the play does not really have a central character that one can identify with or remain interested in, the ideas remain fascinating, as is the whole

Pacific Overtures, original Broadway production, 1976; Sondheim's look at American imperialism in Japan (photograph: Martha Swope).

concept of the musical of ideas rather than hit tunes. Richard Wagner would have liked this show because of the many interesting ideas in it dramatized both theatrically and musically, but many theater-goers at the time did not.

Pacific Overtures got very mixed reviews. Some reviewers enjoyed the experimental nature of this very Japanese show, but others felt that much of it was dull because of a lack of a central plot or even a central character. There was a political urgency about the show, since it was first staged during the period of the war in Vietnam and the theme of American imperialism in the East appeared constantly in the headlines of the time. That a Broadway musical about ideas bored many members of the audience remains a depressing fact but perhaps indicates a reality of audience expectations and even demands. The show had a decent run of 193 performances, but it was hardly a hit and it lost its backers a lot of money. The rumor began to spread that a Sondheim show would be original but lose money for its backers, that Sondheim's very perfectionism created losses rather than financial gains for the shows' backers — that Sondheim had become box office poison. This show has been revived, though much more simply than in its original elaborate production, and has generated repeated successes. *Pacific Overtures* has remained a musical for adults which does not repeat the stale old Broadway musical formats.

Sweeney Todd: The Demon Barber of Fleet Street was Sondheim's next show. He again wrote both the music and the lyrics, though the book was by Hugh Wheeler and it was based on a version of the Victorian play *Sweeney Todd* by Christopher Bond. Sondheim's musical first appeared in New York at the Uris Theatre on March 1, 1979, and was directed by Harold Prince, obviously Sondheim's favorite director at the time. The show ran for 558 performances, a major success, though the lavish, realistic production probably did not make much money for its backers.

Here again, Sondheim experiments with form, using a Victorian melodrama of the Grand Macabre genre with characters having their throats slit on stage by a lunatic barber. The plot is obviously Marxist, presenting the image of the rich abusing the poor, and survival depending on the exploitation of others. Mrs. Lovett adds the metaphor of cannibalism when she turns Todd's murder victims into meat pies, pies which eventually become the most popular dish in London at the time. This show is Brechtian theater, a style of theater rarely done for the Broadway musical, though *Cabaret* and *Chicago* have become rare exceptions and do use the Brechtian style of musical and political theater.

This gruesome, Marxist melodrama, with the grotesque elements of cannibalism and human exploitation, was hardly typical Broadway musical fare.

Once again the experimenter Sondheim found a new organic form for a new kind of musical — musical tragedy rather than musical comedy. Sondheim also has great fun parodying the bravura arias of traditional operas in the song "Pirelli's magical elixir," where a singer plays an Italian barber who tries to sell Londoners his worthless medicine with a Rossini aria rather like Figaro's "Largo al Factotum." Len Cariou and Angela Lansbury turned the parts of Sweeney Todd and Mrs. Lovett into real tour de force roles, captivating the audience even though many of them were repelled by the carnage onstage. Bryn Terfel, the great Welsh bass-baritone, had a major success in the role of Sweeney Todd at the Lyric Opera of Chicago in the fall of 2002.

A London revival of the show moved to Broadway in the fall of 2005 with Patti Lupone and Michael Cerveris playing the lead roles with great success. John Doyle directed this production in a minimalist style with only one set, and with each character also playing a musical instrument. The comic and grotesque qualities of this show were emphasized in Doyle's minimalist and cynical production and succeeded with audiences. This same director used the same approach, with each actor also playing a musical instrument, in the 2006 Broadway revival of Sondheim's *Company*. Clearly *Sweeney Todd* could be played in a variety of styles from Harold Prince's elaborate Victorian sets in the original production to more minimalist and Brechtian approaches. And opera companies like the Royal Opera in London and the New York City Opera in New York have been repeatedly staging Sondheim's perfectionist shows as operas despite the fact that Sondheim has said how much he dislikes the art form.

Merrily We Roll Along, Sondheim's next show, for which again he wrote both music and lyrics, though the book was by George Furth, appeared at the Alvin Theatre in New York on November 16, 1981, and ran for 16 performances. This show flopped rather badly (and quickly). Harold Prince also directed this show, but all his showmanship could not save it from the bad reviews it got. The show was based on a play of the same title by George S. Kaufman and Moss Hart, and was the closest to the format of a typical musical, but perhaps for that very reason Sondheim failed to be inspired by the material and the music was not interesting enough to keep the audience's interest, though future revivals may alter the general impression of this show.

Sunday in the Park with George, Sondheim's next show, was a partial success and enjoyed a long run. Once again Sondheim wrote the music and lyrics, but the book was written by James Lapine, who also directed. The show opened at the Booth Theatre in New York on May 2, 1982, and ran for 540 performances, surely indicating a success with the public.

Bernadette Peters and Mandy Patinkin impressed all the critics, but the structure of the show also impressed for its very originality. Sondheim based the show on Georges Seurat's famous painting "Sunday Afternoon on the Island of La Grand Jatte" in the Art Institute of Chicago, though New York's Metropolitan Museum owns a preliminary drawing Seurat did for the painting. The first act of the show shows Georges trying to finish the painting with his new theories of pointillism, with the stage becoming an image of the painting in the finale of the first act, while the second act shows the artist's grandson in contemporary Paris trying to create an entirely new kind of art with laser beams. Most critics felt that the first act worked absolutely brilliantly, both musically and in terms of the text, but most also felt that the second half fell apart and that Sondheim had not produced a compelling second act for this show either musically or dramatically.

The pointillism of the French painter became a kind of musical pointillism in the music of the first act. The artist Georges Seurat is presented as obsessed with trying to create art from only dots of color and trying to understand and control how the eye perceives these dots. The artist even calls his mistress "Dot," adding a comic element to his artistic obsessions. Even the fancy laser beam in the second act, though, could not counteract the boredom that set in with most members of the audience since the music did not remain very interesting. While the first act of the show seemed riveting and wonderful, the second act did not sustain the first act's fascination. One of the major themes in this show is the obsessive narcissism of the artist Seurat, who uses and abuses even the woman he loves for the sake of the production of his unusual and highly original art. Sondheim's perfectionism once again drove him to create a new kind of musical, a musical based on a painting with a musical style also based on a painting.

Next came Sondheim's *Into the Woods*, which premiered at the Martin Beck Theatre in 1987 and got mixed reviews. Sondheim wrote both the music and the lyric, but the book was once again by James Lapine, who also directed. Despite its mixed reviews *Into the Woods* had a year-long run, and in 2002 it was revived on Broadway. Bernadette Peters starred in the original production to glowing reviews, and Vanessa Williams starred in the 2002 revival on Broadway, and she too earned very positive reviews. Here again, Sondheim's show had an organic form unique to its subject matter rather than a formulaic format. The first half presents a retelling of some very familiar Grimm's fairy tales — Little Red Riding Hood, Jack and the Beanstalk, Rapunzel in the tower, etc. The first act ends quite happily with the proverbial fairy tale ending we are all familiar with, but the second act follows the characters after the fairy tale ends when some have made horrible marriages and died, despite Grimm's original happy endings for most of the tales.

Bruno Bettelheim's famous book on fairy tales, *The Uses of Enchantment: The Meaning and Importance of Fairy Tales,* was reflected in the sombre interpretations of the famous tales. The show was originally criticized for a brilliant first act but a disappointing second act, but the 2002 revival had a much better second act, Sondheim obviously having rewritten some of the music to make the second act more compelling musically. The idea of a musical starting off with familiar fairy tales but ending with sad, realistic endings continued the Sondheim theme of the difficulty of human relationships, especially marriage. As Prince Charming tells Cinderella in the second act, after she finds out he has been unfaithful to her, "I was raised to be charming, not sincere." Perhaps this remains the ultimate fate of all prince charmings — it certainly does in this show. Sondheim's perfectionism drove him to create a musical out of the weaving together of various popular fairy tales and then taking a realistic view of their possible versus their more realistic endings. His innate cynicism about human relationships, probably the result of his very difficult relationships with both his parents, who divorced while he was still a young child, has repeatedly influenced his view of how people connect with each other and develop these human connections. Marriage has become the central tragedy in most (but not all) of his shows.

Sondheim's more recent show, *Passion,* opened on May 9, 1994, and also got very mixed reviews. This show is based on an Italian novel called *Fosca* by the writer Iginio Ugo Tarchetti. The novel also became a film by the Italian filmmaker Ettore Scola, who titled his film *Passione D'Amore.* Both the novel and the film involve the obsession of a very sick woman for a handsome officer in her garrison town in northern Italy. *Passion* was done as one very long act running over two hours, and many audience members felt trapped in a show that lasted at least a half an hour too long. The main female character failed to ignite much interest, and the music seemed operatic in the worst sense and also very repetitive. Perhaps because of its Italian source, the music was through-composed like a traditional opera, but many critics felt that Sondheim's music failed to maintain the required interest of the viewer, though this point is of course debatable. This Pucciniesque score lacked that composer's genius for creating the great aria for each of the main characters.

In any case, the show yet again indicated Sondheim's search for new forms for a Broadway musical, an organic form to fit the material rather than the traditional forms of musical comedy. That Sondheim would use a format of Italian opera after saying repeatedly how much he disliked the genre indicates that he was rethinking his previous positions and trying a new form for his new show. Many critics felt that the show's music could not sustain its length of almost two hours. The difficulty and pain of yet another human relationship, initiated and controlled by the main female character (Fosca) and her obsession with a military officer stationed in the same town where she lives, hardly ends with the happy musical finale one would expect in a Broadway musical. Death has the finale here, as of course he always does in real life, and despite the happiness of those theatrical Broadway finales.

Sondheim's next show, *Assassins* (2000), tried to create a show from the stories of various assassins in American history, people such as John Wilkes Booth and Lee Harvey Oswald. Here too Sondheim and his perfectionism tried to create a new kind of show, but this show did not have a Broadway production though its off–Broadway version succeeded with some of the critics and some Sondheim fans. Using the format of a musical review, Sondheim tried to take a cynical look at the many assassins in American history and how their lunacy controlled American history for their own time periods. The examination of violence and murder as components of history remains a distinctive approach to the Broadway musical, but this show remained an off–Broadway phenomenon, perhaps for that very reason. But Sondheim's look at the anti-hero, the assassins in history, created a perfectionist's view of history.

Experimentation and innovation in both musical and theatrical forms have remained basic characteristics of Stephen Sondheim's Broadway shows. While some theater-goers have missed the older forms of Rodgers and Hammerstein or Lerner and Lowe, many others have been very happy to see a new form of experimental musical theater which contains so much originality. It was undoubtedly Sondheim's innate perfectionism which drove him to create so many fascinating experiments in the forms of the American musical and to write so much intriguing music in the process of creating exciting musical theater. Sondheim's cynical view of human relationships, especially marriage, also helped to give his shows a uniquely modern viewpoint. At a time when fifty percent of American marriages end in divorce, such cynicism found a responsive chord with many theater-goers by the end of the 20th century.

But is Sondheim obsessive-compulsive in his determination to avoid writing the typical American musical? Here he reminds me of Richard Wagner, who also could not write the same kind of opera over and over again — all his works have a unique sound and a unique style and they were constantly changing, perhaps the sign of most revolutionary artists. Perhaps Sondheim has an obsessive-compulsive approach to his art since each show differs markedly from the typical Broadway musical, and each of his shows differs from his other shows. There is a perfectionism about the shows, and though they do not always succeed they clearly have become models of a new kind of experimental, daring Broadway musical which has changed the genre forever.

Sondheim seems to be suggesting that is not enough for a Broadway composer to write a musical hit, since the theatrical format has to be original as well if the show is to become truly memorable. Is this a product of Sondheim's personal neurosis? Is this a product of his own musical and theatrical genius? In any case, such an approach has created a distinctive and often highly successful form of musical theater, and in a world of cheap success, there is much to be said for an interesting failure, which has been the sad fate of some of Sondheim's most interesting shows.

Bibliography

Goodhart, Sandor, ed. *Reading Stephen Sondheim: A Collection of Critical Essays.* New York: Garland, 2000.

Gordon, Joanne Lesley. *Art Isn't Easy: The Theater of Stephen Sondheim.* New York: Da Capo, 1992.

Gordon, Joanne Lesley, ed. *Stephen Sondheim: A Casebook.* New York: Garland, 1997.

Gottfried, Martin. *Sondheim.* New York: Abrams, 2000.

Secrest, Meryle. *Stephen Sondheim: A Life.* New York: Knopf, 1998.

Zadan, Craig. *Sondheim and Co.* New York: Harper and Row, 1986.

13

Tom Stoppard
Logomania

Logomania, or the obsession with words and wordplay, remains the major theme in the theater of Tom Stoppard. This is also a part of his very personality as well. The following story was told of an encounter between Stoppard and an actress at the party after the Broadway premiere of his *Rosencranz and Gildenstern Are Dead*. The actress asked the playwright exactly what the play was about. Stoppard responded that the play was about to make him a very rich man—a prediction which turned out to be true. The quip tells us much about Stoppard's fondness for wordplay, as well as his greed and ambition. He is a man who clearly cannot resist a pun, and punning and wordplay have become central themes in all his plays. Since Stoppard's main obsession is clearly language, that has advantages and disadvantages. In a great Stoppard play, the wordplay adds to the comic effect of the play, but the characters remain sympathetic and real. In a less successful Stoppard play, the characters never seem to become alive onstage and instead the audience only gets the wordplay—and in some cases the audience can become confused and bored by the whole show. Confusion itself has become a hallmark of the Stoppard plays, with some audiences liking the mystery and trying to understand it, while other people do not enjoy becoming confused and as a result become hostile to Stoppard's shows. Many people find his plays hopelessly confusing and purposely obfuscating and off-putting and as a result avoid his plays, though other audience members are attracted to these same qualities.

Many would argue that this was the result of the British playwright's rather insane childhood since it involved so much moving around and the horror and trauma of World War II. He was actually born in Czechoslovakia of Czech-Jewish parents, but his father died trying to escape the Japanese in Singapore during World War II. His mother remarried an Englishman, and when the playwright was six, the family moved to Britain. Was he English or

British or Czech or Jewish — or all of the above? In several interviews Stoppard has called himself a bounced Czech — so he himself makes puns about his background. This remained a crucial question for him for his childhood. But he received a typically English education at totally British schools, and English became his primary language. While studying at the University of Oxford, he quickly developed a keen interest in writing and English literature. In fact, his plays contain many references to the history of English literature, especially Shakespeare. He early determined to out–English the English by constantly referring to the classics of English literature and by becoming a prominent English playwright. And he succeeded in his pursuit of such a career, beginning as a critic and journalist and quickly becoming a very successful playwright with long-running successes both in the West End in London and on Broadway in New York. Perhaps because of the trauma surrounding his early childhood, he was eager to become a real Englishman — obsessed with all things English, like cricket and Shakespeare.

He started his career as a writer as a journalist and dropped out of college before getting his degree, working as a journalist in small towns in northern England. But he was soon transferred to a newspaper in London and quickly made London his home, though now he also has homes in rural England and even France. He had some success as a drama critic, but soon switched to playwriting. His early success as a playwright meant that he no longer had to work as a journalist and could devote himself full time to playwriting, where he continues to experience significant renown. He has become within the past thirty years arguably Britain's greatest playwright, and certainly one of the major themes in his work is insanity and insane behavior, often indicated through puns. This theme appears in many of his most important works, and indicates his concern for people who suffer from mental problems.

Of course, insanity is often a tricky term to define, but the term and the phenomenon recur in Stoppard's theater. Stoppard's first major success in the theater was *Rosencrantz and Guildenstern Are Dead.* The play first appeared in London at the Old Vic Theater in April of 1967 and moved to the Alvin Theater on Broadway in October of that same year; the play succeeded with both London and New York theater audiences. Insanity plays a major theme in the play. The most obvious use of insanity is in the mad appearances of Shakespeare's Hamlet. The play, of course, takes two minor characters from Shakespeare's *Hamlet* and turns the situation into the Beckett-like situation of waiting, as the two keep waiting for something to do, keep waiting for orders from the more powerful, royal characters in the play. Now and again, characters from Shakespeare's *Hamlet* appear, using the lines from Shakespeare's play, and making not much sense. They seem only to add to the

Rosencrantz and Guildenstern Are Dead, New York, 1967; Brian Murray as Rosencranz and John Wood as Guildenstern.

confusion. By the end of the play both Rosenkranz and Guildenstern are in
fact dead, the title of the play itself being a quote from Shakespeare's *Hamlet* and the play's final reference to these characters.

Using many of the same techniques from Beckett's theater of the absurd,
the whole idea of waiting for something significant to happen, the whole
absurd concept of waiting for something that ultimately turns out to be death,
occurs significantly in Stoppard's play. In this way the play reflects the absurdist situation of Beckett's *Waiting for Godot.* The situation of Rosencrantz and
Guildenstern remains ultimately absurd since they are awaiting orders from
Prince Hamlet and the royal family. But whenever Prince Hamlet does appear
on stage, he seems insane. Rosencranz and Guildenstern are in the insane situation of awaiting orders from a lunatic, a lunatic who ultimately causes their
deaths. In *Rosencrantz and Guildenstern Are Dead*, Stoppard suggests that life
is ultimately absurd and insane; that our actions — like those of the doomed
Rosencrantz and Guildenstern — remain idiotic and insane rather than rational.

The characters spend much of their time punning to kill time until time kills them. They reflect many of the same actions of Vladimir and Estragon in Beckett's famous *Waiting for Godot*— these characters also use punning and wordplay to kill time while waiting for the mythical Godot, who of course never appears.

In the very next year, specifically June of 1968, Stoppard experienced his next successful premiere — that of his comedy *The Real Inspector Hound*. This play premiered at the Criterion Theater in London and is a wonderful spoof of an Agatha Christie murder mystery, especially her play *The Mousetrap*. Most of the characters in this play seem insane. The play functions very cleverly on two levels: that of the play itself and that of the two critics, Moon and Birdboot, who are witnessing and reviewing the play. Both Moon and Birdboot display various examples of obsessive-compulsive behavior. Birdboot remains obsessed with women, though he is already married to his homely wife Myrtle (as he refers to her). Birdboot has established a reputation as a theater critic who will give an actress a good review if she sleeps with him first, and he is obsessed with the actress playing Cynthia in the play. In fact, one of the high points of the play is when Birdboot actually leaves his seat and enters the play in his pursuit of Cynthia. When Birdboot does this, Moon says: "Have you taken leave of your tiny mind?" That one critic questions the sanity of the other — as he leaps onto the stage and enters the world of the play on stage — adds to the complex and subtle comedy of this play.

But Moon himself is also obsessed in this play, in his case obsessed with his position as second-string critic. In fact, when Moon appears in the theater, people generally say, "Where's Higgs?"—who is the first-string critic. Moon has a long speech in which he bemoans the fact that he is the second-level critic, and he is in fact killed by Puckeridge, who is the third-string critic. Clearly status and pecking order are central concerns to the careers of these two terrible, corrupt critics, and these themes appear central to the play as well. That neither critic seems to understand much about the play they are witnessing and reviewing adds to the comedy of Stoppard's spoof.

Madness enters the plays as well in terms of the "whodunit" being staged in the play within a play in *The Real Inspector Hound*, because a madman has escaped and everyone in the play is afraid he is the murderer on the loose who is terrorizing the neighborhood. The recurrent radio bulletins refer to a "madman on the loose," which of course has the comic effect of parodying the typical Agatha Christine murder mysteries. In some of her plays, a murder is committed by a person who has escaped from a mental hospital. In Stoppard's play, the police are searching for a suspect named McCoy, who turns out to be the real McCoy — Stoppard cannot resist a good pun. And in Stoppard's play, as in a typical Agatha Christie play, the events occur in a wealthy but isolated country location somewhere in the wilds of England. And insane characters and insane situations repeatedly have generated comedy in the theater — from Aristophanes to Shakespeare down to contemporary times.

Stoppard returns to the theme of insanity most clearly in his *Every Good Boy Deserves Favor*, one of his strangest and most ambitious plays. The play was written for six characters and an entire symphony orchestra. André Previn wrote an original score for the orchestra to play at various intervals in the play. The play was first performed at the Festival Hall in London with the London Symphony Orchestra, conducted by André Previn. The play was also staged at Lincoln Center several years later with the New York Philharmonic. The play centrally involves a political prisoner in the former Soviet Union who is placed in a mental hospital with real mental patients. And the situation in this play involves the characters Alexander, the political prisoner, and Ivanov, a genuine mental patient, who are both housed together in the same room. Of course, Stoppard was especially sensitive to this issue because of his own Czech background. He also developed a friendship with the Czech dissident writer Václav Havel, another political prisoner and dissident writer who ultimately became the president of his country after the collapse of the Soviet Union and communism in general.

The real heart of this play is the predicament of Alexander, the political prisoner. He has a very significant speech early in the play:

> The KGB broke my door and frightened my son and my mother-in-law. My madness consisted of writing to various people about a friend of mine who is in prison. This friend was twice put in mental hospitals for political reasons, and then they arrested him for saying that sane people were put in mental hospitals, and then they put him in prison because he was sane when he said this; and I said so, and they put me in a mental hospital. For the politicians, punishment and medical treatment are intimately related. I was given injections of aminazin, sulfazine, tritazin, haloperiodal, and sinsul, which caused swellings, cramps, headaches, trembling, fever, and the loss of various abilities including the ability to read, write, sleep, sit, stand, and button my trousers.

Stoppard used the play to analyze the relationship between political dissent and alleged insanity in the former Soviet Union. Stoppard obviously sympathized with writers in these countries and how they were treated by the Communist regime. Telling the truth and writing about it were dismissed as insanity by these regimes, and Stoppard wanted to point out the injustice of this position. *Every Good Boy Deserves Favor* remains his clearest testament to the coupling of political dissent and insanity. Dismissing the truth as insane can have horrendous political consequences — but also comic ones. More than one comic theoretician has said that telling the truth can be the funniest thing in theater. Stoppard is also fascinated by the paradox that when Havel was a forbidden playwright he had a large following of readers and audience, but once the Soviet Union and communism collapsed and people in the Czech Republic were free to read what they wanted to, Havel's creative writings failed to generate much interest there.

In 1968 Stoppard's play *Jumpers* appeared and had a successful premiere at the Royal National Theatre. Here Stoppard combines moral philosophy, logic, and acrobatics with a murder mystery, and the result is quite comic, though the human element does not come through very frequently in most productions of this play. With acrobats jumping and somersaulting around stage for most of the piece, the audience often laughs but is often confused by George Moore, the philosopher who is at the center of the stage. That there was another real philosopher and a novelist of that same name adds to the confusion of the play. But the whodunit quality of the play and the sudden appearances and disappearances of the gymnasts flying around the stage add to the appeal of this play, with the punning more often adding to the confusion. If the results seem like insanity, it is a comic insanity which includes Stoppard's typical uses of punning and wordplay.

Stoppard uses the theme of insanity again in his play *Travesties*. Here the play operates on repeated allusions to Oscar Wilde's *The Importance of Being Earnest*. In fact, Stoppard borrows the names of Gwendolyn and Cecily from Wilde's play. Stoppard's play was first staged at the Aldwych Theater in London on June 10, 1974, and the play was one of the major successes of that season in London. The play appeared the following season on Broadway, where it succeeded as well.

Stoppard uses the fact that James Joyce, Vladimir Lenin, and Tristan Tzara were all in Zurich in March of 1918. Stoppard also uses the fact that an English amateur actor, Henry Carr, was also in Zurich at the time, performing in a production of *The Importance of Being Earnest*, and that James Joyce was a managing director of the Zurich theatrical company. Henry Carr felt that Joyce had cheated him, and he sued Joyce twice, and ultimately won a small financial settlement from Joyce. Needless to say, puns on James Joyce appear repeatedly in the play, with many characters assuming the Irish author is a woman named Joyce, much to the writer's annoyance.

But the theme of insanity enters *Travesties* most clearly in terms of senile dementia. The play presents Carr both as a young man, a young amateur acting in Zurich in 1918, and as an old man, recalling the events of that period, when he was suing the great writer James Joyce. One of the sources of comedy in the play is Carr's senile dementia, when he is recalling what the audience knows has not occurred, and when he is forgetting what the audience knows has occurred. Seeing an old codger repeatedly confusing and forgetting the truth can be both comic and tragic, though in *Travesties* it repeatedly generates comedy.

The play also fascinates as it presents the shenanigans of the Dadaist writer Tristan Tzara, as he composes poems by writing individual words on separate pieces of paper, tossing them in a hat, and then pulling out the words one by one to create poetry. The play puns on sugar cubes and Cubism, Dadaism and, as one character says, "My heart belongs to dada"—a comic reference to Cole Porter's song of the same title. Stoppard parodies the lunacy of some modernist writers who can reduce composition to the point where a person without literary talent can still become a writer. Since Tristan Tzara's absurdist and Dadaist poetry occurs in this play, Stoppard can add to the lunacy of the proceedings by creating his own kind of Dadaist situation in the play, with characters moving from one period to another, and calling for surreal visual effects. That several of the characters in the play think that "Joyce" is James Joyce's character's first name instead of his last name adds to the comedy of the situation and the hilarity of the word playing which so often occurs.

As with most Stoppard plays, this one too assumes a knowledge of Zurich and Communism and other revolutionary activities occurring in Zurich right before and after World War I. After a Stoppard play, audience members frequently feel like spending a month in a library to do research on the period of the play. Such a reaction excites and attracts some audience members but annoys others who do not feel that they go to the theater for a homework assignment. One often feels that one needs a Ph.D. to understand a Stoppard play, which adds to their attraction for some people but which annoys and offends others. But this is part of the insanity of a typical Stoppard play which most people have come to expect.

Stoppard made fun of this same kind of pseudo-writer in his next play, *The Real Thing.* The insanity of modern marriage and love relationships, however, becomes the central theme in this work, which premiered in New York at the Plymouth Theater on January 5, 1984. Glenn Close's and Jeremy Irons's performances, plus the fascinating quality of the play itself, made the play one of the hits of that Broadway season, and it opened in London the following year. In the beginning of the play Henry is married to Charlotte, but he is having an affair with Annie. Annie is married to Max, but she has lost all interest in him and is enjoying her affair with Henry. Soon afterwards, Henry and Annie marry and are happy for a while, but then Annie begins an affair with another actor, Billie. The central character, the playwright Henry, is looking for love—or "the real thing," as it is called in the play. First he thinks he has the real thing with Charlotte, and then he thinks he has it with Annie. In the midst of all these marital infidelities, one of the cuckolded husbands complains, "I thought we'd made a commitment!" But his former wife patiently explains: "There are no commitments, only bargains. And they have to be made again every day." Through all these conflicts the characters are constantly drinking as well so one begins to suspect that alcoholism adds to the confusion onstage.

As Stoppard presents modern marriages in *The Real Thing*, the situation is truly insane, especially for anyone who thinks that marriage is a permanent commitment. Instead, argues Stoppard, all that is possible in modern relationships is bargains, temporary arrangements which have to be renegotiated on a daily basis. Such an insane situation, argues Stoppard, remains the reality of love relationships in the modern world and explains the multiple divorces and emotional separations which have come to characterize modern love. And despite such an anarchic situation, the real thing, or true love, is still possible. But the actress Annie cheats on the playwright Henry while playing the lead in Ford's *'Tis Pity She's a Whore*, suggesting a pun on the character of Annie, though ultimately she does return to Henry. Some misogyny enters this play; though the men are more often the victims, they do not appear blameless, either. Stoppard himself has been married and divorced twice and now seems to prefer living alone.

The Real Thing, 1984; Jeremy Irons as Henry and Glenn Close as Annie.

The Real Thing, 1984; Jeremy Irons, Glenn Close, Christine Baranski as Charlotte, and Kenneth Welsh as Max.

But Stoppard cannot resist complicating a supposedly real situation in *The Real Thing* by writing some scenes that are supposed to be "really happening" and some scenes which are scenes in a play by the playwright character Henry—so that the audience can easily become confused by what is really happening or what is supposed to be a scene in a play from another play. Confusion adds to the insanity of the situation, but this is clearly what Stoppard wants to create in his theater, and this complexity adds to the play's fascination. These very elements of complexity and multiple meanings add to the attraction of a typical Stoppard play, though that very complexity can annoy some audience members who have been confused so often by a Stoppard play that they refuse to attend another one.

Presenting insanity on an international level is clearly one of the main points in Stoppard's *Hapgood*; the play first appeared at the Aldwych theater in London on March 8, 1988, where it received mixed reviews. The play appeared three years later in New York at the Lincoln Center Theater. There too the play received mixed reviews and was attacked for confusing the audience.

Confusion becomes the central theme in this difficult play about international espionage. The character of Hapgood, a British woman in charge of espionage for the British government, directs all the men under her in a complex and confusing world of British agents, American agents, Russian KGB agents, and double and triple agents. The play becomes even more confusing when Hapgood's twin sister appears in some of the scenes so that the audience does not know if the real Hapgood or her twin sister is appearing in the scene, and which is the spy and which the ordinary citizen.

Clearly Stoppard's *Hapgood* spoofs international espionage. In the confusion caused by agents, double agents, and triple agents (not to mention twins), the alleged principles of a just government that the various foreign offices are fighting for get lost in the scuffle. What good, finally, does international espionage achieve, Stoppard asks, and does not the whole effort seem ultimately like insanity? Of course, this is an insanity that is not only comic but also bloody — for some of the agents on both sides are killed in the process. The very title "Hapgood" suggest a punning combination of happenstance and goodness, implying that neither real happiness nor goodness is possible in international relations or even domestic governance.

Stoppard's *Arcadia* uses the theme of insanity in a completely different way. The play was first staged at the Lyttleton Theater of the Royal National Theater on April 13, 1993, where it got very good reviews. The play appeared the following year on Broadway — at the Vivian Beaumont Theater at Lincoln Center — where it also succeeded. The character Thomasina, an inquisitive teenage girl, opens the play by asking her tutor, "Septimus, what is carnal embrace?" The tutor informs her that it is "throwing one's arms around a side of beef." The play begins with a comic and sexual pun and thereby introduces the audience to its central theme, the power of love throughout the centuries, and its often animalistic nature. Though the tutor ultimately becomes more honest with his student Thomasina about the realities of carnal embrace, the play opens with a comic pun.

The play itself is rather schizophrenic in construction since it operates on two levels. Half of the play is set in Regency England during the period of Romanticism, and in fact the poet Byron is referred to. When the play opens, we are in the orangery of a large, 18th century country estate in Derbyshire in April of 1809. This part of the play centrally involves the literary squabbles of the period, especially those involving Lord Byron. But the second half of the play is set in the same setting — the orangery of an 18th century estate — only now we are in contemporary England — the England of 1993. Here too we have literary squabbles among writers, and especially the squabbles of some literary critics who are trying to piece together what actually happened in the house in 1809 when Byron visited it. Different critics, all of whom seem to hate each other despite a surface politeness, are trying to find evidence for their theory of what happened in the house during the Regency period. Academic careerism and competition become the targets of the satire in the second act of this play.

The academic sleuths who enter the play in the second act and try to understand what actually happened to Byron and his friends in the Regency period add to the comedy. Here Stoppard can poke fun at academic careerism and one-upmanship. These professors at one point actually physically attack each other in their efforts to obtain academic control and absolute power over each other.

Another kind of schizophrenia occurs in that the characters in the Regency period are building a hermitage on the estate — something fashionable in the early 19th century in Europe — and in the hermitage there has to be an authentic hermit. This character never speaks on stage, but is constantly referred to. And this character is reflected in the modern period part of the play in the character of Gus Coverly, a modern version of a hermit. He too never speaks a line, though the audience sees him observing the other characters. Schizophrenia, or being cut off from society, is reflected in the two hermits in the play — not to mention in the very construction of the play. And is the hermit a schizophrenic mental patient or a wise man who has wisely withdrawn from the madness of both Regency and contemporary social conflicts? The search for a peaceful and safe arcadia, as the very title of the play indicates, has remained a constant in European art from Roman pastoral poetry. The search for both a hermit and a hermitage reflect the human desire for an asylum from the ugly realities of the world — what the classical world of ancient Greece and Rome would have called an arcadia.

Some kind of union is achieved at the end, when the characters in Regency costume as well as the characters in contemporary costume dance around the stage at the end. But the union is visual rather than thematic and logical since none of the conflicts and many confusions in the play have been resolved, though the complications have been fascinating and often comic — primarily because of all the puns. By the end of the play characters from both periods dance together to try to achieve a kind of unity.

Stoppard's next hit, *The Invention of Love*, also involves puns — like admiring art, as in a male nude (with legs apart). The invention of love referred to in the play can be interpreted on many levels. On one level, the love that was invented was homosexuality, since the play is about the poet and classical scholar A. E. Housman, and it was during the Victorian period that the words heterosexuality and homosexuality appeared — an invention of a new kind of love that before had only slang terms to define it. One of the comic incidents in the play occurs when Housman first hears the word "homosexuality" and is horrified. As a classicists scholar he would be horrified because the word is a combination of a Greek word and a Latin word, as indeed it is. It was the Germans who invented the word in the 19th century, which perhaps explains the confusion. Perhaps it was intentional, and perhaps reflects the many references to homosexuality in ancient Greece and ancient Rome. Their concept of normal sexuality was quite different from the modern one, especially in ancient Greece, where it was assumed that all normal men were bisexual, though women were not accorded as much freedom and flexibility.

In this play, Stoppard operates with a kind of juxtaposition of two Victorian homosexuals: the closeted man (A. E. Houseman) and the more openly gay writer (Oscar Wilde). Ultimately, who is the luckier one? One would think that Houseman was, since he lived a very long life and became a famous teacher, scholar, and poet while poor Oscar Wilde became a public scandal and was dead by the time he was 46. But Stoppard gives the character of Wilde a long speech in which he feels that he was the luckier one since he avoided the horrors of the closeted gay man, Houseman, who led a life of long silences and secrets. As Wilde says, "Better a rocket spray than one never spent." Houseman paid a terrible price for his discretion about his homosexuality—falling madly and hopelessly in love with a heterosexual fellow student, Moses

The Invention of Love, original Broadway production, 2001; Robert Sean Leonard and Richard Easton as the young and old Housman (photograph: Paul Kolnik).

Jackson, while they (and Wilde) were students at Oxford, and living a life of secrets and frustrations, though a long life at that. Who was the more sane man?

Stoppard's most recent plays have centered on political and historical problems in Russia and Czechoslovakia, though the logomania persists. In *The Coast of Utopia* Stoppard has become his most ambitious theatrically and has written a trilogy of plays (*Voyage*, *Shipwreck*, and *Salvage*) which was the first staged during the 2005-2006 theater season at London's National Theatre and then at New York's Lincoln Center. These three lays presented the historical character Alexander Herzen (along with Bakunin, Belinsky, and other writers and artists) and his place in the intellectual history of Russia and Europe in the middle of the 19th century. Here Russian intellectuals and aristocrats involved in Russia's political problems like the ending of serfdom meet in various parts of Russia and Western Europe to discuss current issues like Marxism and serfdom, at a time when most of these intellectuals are leading very comfortabe lives with multiple servants and houses, thanks to the serfs on their Russian estates. They pun away their time, as revolutions (like those in 1848 and 1849) are occuring around them in western Europe.

In *Rock 'n Roll* (2006), Stoppard creates wonderful levels of irony in the history of Czechoslovakia during its Communist period when western Rock 'n Roll was deemed decadent, capitalist music and forbidden by the Communist authorities. In many ways this is Stoppard's most autobiographical play since it reflects what might have happened to him if his mother had not married his step-father Stoppard and moved the family to England. If she had returned to Czechoslovakia instead, Tom Stoppard might well have been the central character in this play, a young journalist called Jan who fell in love with British and American Rock music and been persecuted by the Communist authorities, especially with its Ministry of the Interior, generating multiple puns. The madness of such political lunacy as the censorship of music is central to this play, and the puns indicate a yearning for a political and social (and musical) liberation which Communism did not allow, though this does occur when the regime collapses and people are at last allowed to hear the kind of music they want to hear. The play's finale presents Rock music being played in 1997 at the central palace in Prague, thanks to Vaclav Havel ending communism there, which also results in the country being split in two. This play also includes the character Max Morrow, the British intellectual who defends communism long after most other people have come to hate the insanity of its resultant oppression of dissidents.

Insanity has been a major theme in the theater of Tom Stoppard. I have used the term "insanity" is a rather loose way, covering a whole series of conditions from insane situations to insane characters to using the charge of insanity as a method of imprisoning people. But in all these varying situations and cases, Stoppard has used the theme of insanity and a logomaniacal writing style to create some fascinating contemporary theater. He is arguably the greatest contemporary British dramatist, and his career has been amazingly long and productive. He even won an Oscar award for his wonderful script for *Shakespeare in Love*. He has been able to sustain a literary career of amazingly range and longevity. If the world of theater is itself insane, Stoppard has managed to survive and succeed in its insane atmosphere. The kind of insanity he is most characterized by is certainly logomania — and he will pun to his dying day. As Oscar Wilde said on his deathbed in a cheap Parisian hotel: "I am dying beyond my means, and either this wallpaper goes or I go." Stoppard would certainly have understood Wilde's comic compulsion to pun to the bitter end.

Does Stoppard suggest that his obsession with punning and other word plays remains the only reality he (or we) can trust? Is he suggesting that language itself is the only reality we can count on in a world gone insane with various political, ethical, and social realities? Is logomania a neurosis or a method of protecting oneself in a world that remains essentially crazy? Of course a play is, more than anything else, a group of words. A playwright can naturally be subject to logomania, though Stoppard has taken this obsession to new heights and some would even say to new depths because of his own repeated use of punning and wordplay. Since many audience members share his fondness for wordplay, this is a very forgivable mental failing in a playwright; though in a great Stoppard play that wordplay includes characters who become real human beings and attract audiences to their very human problems and resultant suffering. Even Shakespeare included multiple puns in both his comedies and tragedies.

Stoppard has a genius for combining his own sense of the fun of playing with language with larger issues like madness, insanity, and comedy. He is essentially a comic writer, since audiences generally laugh their way through most of his plays, at least if they have graduate degrees.

Bibliography

Corballis, Richard. *Stoppard: The Mystery and the Clockwork*. New York: Methuen, 1984.
Delaney, Paul. *Tom Stoppard: The Moral Vision of the Major Plays*. London: Macmillan, 1990.
Fleming, John. *Stoppard's Theatre: Finding Order Amid Chaos*. Austin: University of Texas Press, 2002.
Gussow, Mel. *Conversations with Stoppard*. New York: Grove Press, 1995.
Hayman, Ronald. *Tom Stoppard*. London: Heinemann, 1977.
Londre, Felicia Hardison. *Tom Stoppard*. New York: Frederick Ungar, 1981.
Nadel, Ira. *Tom Stoppard: A Life*. New York: Palgrave Macmillan, 2002.
Rusinko, Susan. *Tom Stoppard*. Boston: Twayne, 1986.
Sammells, Neil. *Tom Stoppard: The Artist as Critic*. London: Macmillan, 1988.
Stoppard, Tom. *Every Good Boy Deserves Favor* and *Professional Foul*. New York: Grove Press, 1978.

14

Stages of Struggle,
a Wagnerian Conclusion

For purposes of analysis, I have categorized these playwrights under a particular personal, societal or mental problem. But even so I have discussed other problems within the playwrights' lives and plays. Mental troubles do not come in ones, do not appear singly, but more often appear as multiple problems that have to be separated to be analyzed, which is precisely what I have attempted to do. But there is something artificial about singling problems out since they appear in clusters rather than singly, though the advantages of such an approach enable greater analysis of a particular problem.

We can conclude by asserting that there is a logic to the divisions but also something arbitrary as well. Since Tennessee Williams was himself an alcoholic, perhaps we should have centered his chapter on this problem rather than sibling rivalry. But alcoholism or at least alcohol-related problems also appear in the plays of Pinter (*Betrayal*) and Stoppard (*The Real Thing*) as well as in those of Eugene O'Neill and Brian Friel. Sibling relationships occur often in Tennessee Williams plays, but in Shakespeare as well (particularly in *Hamlet* and *King Lear*) for this is a recurrent theme in literature in general.

But is theater essentially about mental anguish? That depends on the play under analysis. In some plays these are the central issues, but certainly not in all plays. One of the things which occurs in contemporary theater is a willingness to look at formerly taboo topics — such as homosexuality and sexual dysfunction. These topics could be referred to only very delicately and obliquely for most of the history of the drama. There has been a liberation of the theater, although there are still taboo topics particularly in political theater, but modern and contemporary theater focus on mental issues in a way that previous theater did not.

Many of these issues were originally addressed in 19th century opera of all places, especially in Germany. When we look at the influence of Richard

Wagner on the contemporary British and American stage we can see that he has made a major contribution to world theater. His experimental theater in Bayreuth, in Bavaria, still exists and is still in operation during the festival time in the summer.

When Wagner designed his own theater at Bayreuth, that theater's design had a wide-ranging influence on theater. Wagner's theater opened in the summer of 1876 with his own staging of his *Ring* cycle of four operas. He was the first person to eliminate the house lights during a performance, and he designed chairs with straight backs and no upholstery to demand that the audience be distracted by nothing — so that it could look only at and see only the stage itself and respond to it with their full attention. Wagner did not want purely escapist theater, not a fairy-tale theater about old European fairy tales like the Nibelung myth. Instead Wagner used mythology to address the important social, political, psychological and philosophical issues of his day.

Surely most serious theoreticians of the theater still want it to address those very same issues, instead of being what theater has often been, a means of silly escapist entertainment. The spoken theater of most of the 19th century is now considered some of the worst in the history of the art form, though at the very end people such as Ibsen, Wilde, and Shaw were doing more interesting things with the stage and turning it into something worthy of serious attention.

But in the late nineteenth century, theatrical revolutions were being fomented by playwrights like Ibsen, which would point the theater in the direction of a revolutionary new modernism. The concept of the artist as madman appeared in France in the late 19th century — the *poète maudit*, the mad poet. Even in the late 20th century Foucalt in his study on madness pointed out the connection between perceived madness and the arts, the creative artist as madman.

But of course the 19th century was considered one of the golden ages for opera — with both Verdi and Wagner composing operas during this period. The spoken theater of the period was primarily Victorian melodrama or poetical drama. Wagner wanted to change all that and did. And his influence was immense in changing the direction of both spoken and sung theater. Theater would never be the same again. And that change facilitated the kind of presentation of modern neuroses that we have been examining in this book.

Wagnerian opera often seemed to mirror a bipolar reality which dominated the life of Richard Wagner. One of his greatest tragedies, *Tristan und Isolde*, presents us with a classic example of a bipolar reality — the lovers are either exulting in the physical passion of their love or planning to commit suicide. Tristan attempts suicide at the end of every act of that opera, succeeding at the end of the final act, after which Isolde sings the famous "Liebestod," or love-death music. Wagner's masterpiece, his *Ring* cycle, also includes manic highs and suicidal lows, with the whole cycle ending with Brünnhilde's suicide, glorified by the wonderful final music at the end of *Götterdämmerung*.

As Freud said, neurosis is the human condition, and addressing problems of neurosis on the contemporary stage becomes a way of addressing the human condition. Clearly the implication here is that psychological realities become in some ways more important than philosophical realities since the psychological problems are what we are most immediately dealing with in everyday life. A theater which addresses those realities can more immediately connect with an audience dealing with those very same psychological realities on a daily basis. At a time when religious convictions generate suspicion and political conflicts in most people, the artistic concern with personal psychological problems remains as valid and as captivating in our own lives as we live them now.

But I have defined psychological issues very generally to include the realities of the closeted homosexuality in Shaw's plays, the schizophrenia of Pirandello's, the sibling rivalry in Tennessee Williams's plus the alcoholism there and in the theater of Eugene O'Neill and Brian Friel, and the sexual dysfunction of Caryl Churchill's plays. Even Stoppard's logomania has been analyzed in terms of psychological dysfunction. I have defined psychological troubles so generally as to include all the playwrights I have examined. I have defined my terminology so generally as to include us all.

Bibliography

Allen, Stephen Arthur. "Britten and the World of the Child." In *The Cambridge Companion to Benjamin Britten,* ed. Mervyn Cooke. Cambridge: Cambridge University Press, 1999.

Ames, Louise and Carol Haber. *He Hit Me First: When Brothers and Sisters Fight.* New York: Dembner Books, 1982.

Bair, Deirdre. *Samuel Beckett: A Biography.* New York: Harcourt Brace, 1978.

Barbina, Alfredo. *La Biblioteca di Luigi Pirandello.* Rome: Bulzoni Editore, 1980.

Bassnett, Susan, and Jennifer Lorch, eds. *Luigi Pirandello in the Theatre: A Documentary Record.* Switzerland: Harwood Academic Publishers, 1993.

Bassnett-McGuire, Susan. *Luigi Pirandello.* New York: Grove Press, 1983.

Bentley, Eric. *The Pirandello Commentaries.* Evanston, Ill.: Northwestern University Press, 1986.

Berst, Charles. *George Bernard Shaw and the Art of Drama.* Urbana: University of Illinois Press, 1973.

Bigsby, C.W.E. *David Mamet.* New York: Methuen, 1985.

_____. *Joe Orton.* London: Methuen, 1982.

Bigsby, Christopher, ed. *The Cambridge Companion to David Mamet.* Cambridge: Cambridge University Press, 2004.

Billington, Michael. *The Life and Work of Harold Pinter.* London: Faber and Faber, 1996.

_____. *Stoppard the Playwright.* London: Methuen, 1987.

Bini, Daniele. *Pirandello and His Muse: The Plays for Marta Abba.* Gainsville: University Press of Florida, 1998.

Blackwell, Louise. "Tennessee Williams and the Predicament of Women." *South Atlantic Bulletin,* March 1970, 9–14.

Bloom, Harold, ed. *Luigi Pirandello.* New York: Chelsea House, 1989.

Boon, Richard. *About Hare: The Playwright and the Work.* London: Faber and Faber, 2003.

Brater, Enoch. *Beyond Minimalism: Beckett's Late Style in the Theater.* New York: Oxford University Press, 1987.

Brown, John Russell. *A Short Guide to Modern British Drama.* London: Heinemann, 1982.

Cahn, Victor I. *Gender and Power in the Plays of Harold Pinter.* Basingstoke, England: Macmillan, 1993.

Cambon, Glauco, ed. *Pirandello: A Collection of Critical Essays.* Englewood Cliffs, N.J.: Prentice-Hall, 1967.

Caputi, Anthony. *Pirandello and the Crisis of Modern Consciousness.* Urbana: University of Illinois Press, 1988.

Cardullo, Bert. "The Role of the Baby in *A Streetcar Named Desire.*" *Notes on Contemporary Literature,* March 1984, 14–24.

Carpenter, Humphrey. *Benjamin Britten: A Biography.* New York: Charles Scribner's Sons, 1992.

Carroll, Dennis. *David Mamet.* New York: St. Martin's Press, 1987.

Carter, Jimmy. *Palestine: Peace Not Apartheid.* New York: Simon and Schuster, 2006.

Castle, Terry. *Noel Coward and Radclyffe Hall: Kindred Spirits.* New York: Columbia University Press, 1996.

Cole, Lesley. *Remembered Laughter: The Life of Noel Coward.* New York: Knopf, 1976.

Cometa, Michele. *Il Teatro di Pirandello in Germania.* Palermo: Novecento, 1986.

Cooke, Mervyn, ed. *The Cambridge Companion to Benjamin Britten.* New York: Cambridge University Press, 1999.

Coppa, Francesca, ed. *Joe Orton: A Casebook.* New York: Routledge, 2003.

Corballis, Richard. *Stoppard: The Mystery and the Clockwork.* New York: Methuen, 1984.

Coward, Noel. *Autobiography* (consisting of *Present Indicative, Future Indefinite,* and the uncompleted *Past Conditional*). London: Methuen, 1986.

Cronin, Anthony. *Samuel Beckett: The Last Modernist.* London: HarperCollins, 1995.

Davis, Tracy. *George Bernard Shaw and the Socialist Theatre.* Westport, Conn.: Greenwood Press, 1994.

Day, Barry. *Coward on Film: The Cinema of Noël Coward.* Lanham, Md.: Scarecrow Press, 2005.

Dean, Anne. *David Mamet: Language as Dramatic Action.* Rutherford, N.J.: Fairleigh Dickinson University Press, 1990.

Dean, Joan Fitzpatrick. *David Hare.* Boston: Twayne, 1990.

Delaney, Paul. *Tom Stoppard: The Moral Vision of the Major Plays.* London: Macmillan, 1990.

DiGaetani, John Louis. *Richard Wagner and the Modern British Novel.* Rutherford, N.J.: Fairleigh Dickinson University Press, 1978.

_____. *A Search for a Postmodern Theater: Interviews with Contemporary Playwrights.* Westport, Conn.: Greenwood Press, 1991.

_____. *Wagner and Suicide.* Jefferson, N.C.: McFarland, 2003.

_____, ed. *A Companion to Pirandello Studies.* New York: Greenwood Press, 1991.

_____, ed. *Inside the Ring: Essays on Wagner's Opera Cycle.* Jefferson, N.C.: McFarland, 2006.

Donesky, Finlay. *David Hare: A Moral and Historical Perspective.* Westport, Conn.: Greenwood, 1996.

Dunn, Judy. *Sisters and Brothers.* Cambridge, Mass.: Harvard University Press, 1985.

_____, and Carol Kendrick. *Siblings: Love, Envy and Understanding.* Cambridge, Mass.: Harvard University Press, 1982.

Evans, Peter. *The Music of Benjamin Britten.* New York: Oxford University Press, 1990.

First, Michael B., et al. *Diagnostic Criteria from DSM-IV-TR. Diagnostic and Statistical Manual of Mental Disorders.* Arlington, Va.: American Psychiatric Association, 2005.

Fishel, Elizabeth. *Sisters: Love and Rivalry Inside the Family and Beyond.* New York: Morrow, 1979.

Fisher, Clive. *Noel Coward.* New York: St. Martin's Press, 1992.

Fitzpatrick, John. *David Hare.* Boston: Twayne, 1990.

Fleming, John. *Stoppard's Theatre: Finding Order Amid Chaos.* Austin: University of Texas Press, 2002.

Fletcher, John. *Beckett: A Study of His Plays.* New York: Hill and Wang, 1972.

Floyd, Virginia. *The Plays of Eugene O'Neill: A New Assessment.* New York: Frederick Ungar, 1985.

Ford, Boris, ed. *Benjamin Britten's Poets: The Poetry He Set to Music.* Manchester: Carcanet, 1993.

Fraser, Scott. *A Politic Theatre: The Drama of David Hare.* Atlanta: Rodopi, 1996.

Gainor, J. Ellen. *Shaw's Daughters: Dramatic and Narrative Constructions of Gender.* Ann Arbor: University of Michigan Press, 1991.

Gale, Steven H. *Butter's Going Up: A Critical Analysis of Harold Pinter's Work.* Durham, N.C.: Duke University Press, 1977.

Gassner, John. *Eugene O'Neill.* Minneapolis: University of Minnesota Press, 1965.

Gautier, Judith. *Wagner at Home.* Translated by Effie Dunreith Massie. London: John Lane, 1911.

Gelb, Arthur, and Barbara Gelb. *O'Neill: Life with Monte Cristo.* New York: Applause, 2000.

Gill, John. *Queer Noises: Male and Female Homosexuality in Twentieth-Century Music.* Minneapolis: University of Minnesota Press, 2004.

Giudice, Gaspare. *Pirandello: A Biography.* Trans. A. Hamilton. London: Oxford University Press, 1975.

Goodhart, Sandor, ed. *Reading Stephen Sondheim: A Collection of Critical Essays.* New York: Garland, 2000.

Gordon, David J. *Bernard Shaw and the Comic Sublime.* New York: St. Martin's Press, 1990.

Gordon, Joanne Lesley. *Art Isn't Easy: The Theater of Stephen Sondheim.* New York: Da Capo, 1992.

_____, ed. *Stephen Sondheim: A Casebook.* New York: Garland, 1997.

Gordon, Lois, ed. *Pinter at Seventy: A Casebook.* New York: Routledge, 2001.

Gottfried, Martin. *Sondheim.* New York: Abrams, 2000.

Gussow, Mel. *Conversations with Stoppard.* New York: Grove Press, 1995.

Hare, David. *Obedience, Struggle and Revolt.* London: Faber and Faber, 2005.

_____. *Writing Left-Handed.* London: Faber and Faber, 1991.

Hayman, Ronald. *Tom Stoppard.* London: Heinemann, 1977.

Hoare, Philip. *Noel Coward: A Biography.* London: Sinclair-Stevenson, 1995.

Holroyd, Michael. *Bernard Shaw.* 3 vols. New York: Vintage, 1993.

Homan, Sidney. *Beckett's Theaters: Interpretations for Performance.* Madison, N.J.: Associated University Presses, 1984.

Homden, Carol. *The Plays of David Hare.* New York: Cambridge University Press, 1995.

Innes, Christopher, ed. *The Cambridge Companion to George Bernard Shaw.* Cambridge: Cambridge University Press, 1998.

Kane, Leslie. *Weasels and Wisemen: Ethics and Ethnicity in the Works of David Mamet.* New York: St. Martin's Press, 1999.

Kane, Leslie, ed. *David Mamet: A Casebook.* New York: Garland, 1992.

Kelly, Katherine E., ed. *The Cambridge Companion to Tom Stoppard.* Cambridge: Cambridge University Press, 2001.

Kiel, Norman, ed. *Blood Brothers: Siblings as Writers.* New York: International Universities Press, 1983.

Knowlson, James. *Damned to Fame: The Life of Samuel Beckett.* New York: Simon and Schuster, 1996.

Kritzer, Amelia Howe. *The Plays of Caryl Churchill: Theatre of Empowerment.* New York: St. Martin's Press, 1991.

Lahr, John. *Prick Up Your Ears: The Biography of Joe Orton.* New York: Alfred A. Knopf, 1978.

Leary, Daniel. *Shaw's Plays in Performance.* University Park: Pennsylvania State University Press, 1983.

Londre, Felicia Hardison. *Tom Stoppard.* New York: Frederick Ungar, 1981.

Lorenz, Konrad. *On Aggression.* New York: Routledge, 2002.

Matthaei, Renate. *Luigi Pirandello.* Trans. Simon and Erike Young. New York: Frederick Ungar, 1973.

Mayberry, Susan Neal. "A Study of Illusion and the Grotesque in Tennessee Williams' *Cat on a Hot Tin Roof.*" *Southern Studies,* Winter 1983, 359–65.

Mearsheimer, John, and Stephen Walt. *The Israel Lobby and U.S. Foreign Policy.* New York: Farrar, Straus and Ginoux, 2007.

Meisel, Martin. *Shaw and the Nineteenth Century Theater*. Princeton, N.J.: Princeton University Press, 1962.

Melman, Lindy. "A Captive Maid: Blanche DuBois in *A Streetcar Named Desire*." *Dutch Quarterly Review of Anglo-American Letters*, 1986, 125–144.

Mencken, H.L. *George Bernard Shaw: His Plays*. New Rochelle, N.Y.: E.V. Glaser, 1959.

Merritt, Susan Hollis. *Pinter in Play: Critical Strategies and the Plays of Harold Pinter*. Durham, N.C.: Duke University Press, 1990.

Mignone, Mario, ed. *Pirandello in America*. Rome: Bulzoni, 1988.

Milioto, Stefano, ed. *Le Donne in Pirandello*. Agrigento: Edizioni del Centro di Studi Pirandelliani, 1988.

Morash, Christopher. *A History of Irish Theater: 1601–2000*. Cambridge: Cambridge University Press, 2002.

Morella, Joseph, and George Mazzei. *Genius and Lust: The Creative and Sexual Lives of Noel Coward and Cole Porter*. New York: Caroll and Graf, 1995.

Morley, Sheridan. *A Talent to Amuse: A Biography of Noel Coward*. Garden City, N.Y.: Doubleday, 1969.

Nadel, Ira. *Tom Stoppard: A Life*. New York: Palgrave Macmillan, 2002.

Nelson, Benjamin. *Tennessee Williams: The Man and his Work*. New York: Ivan Obolensky, 1962.

Newman, Ernest. *The Life of Richard Wagner*. 4 vols. Cambridge: Cambridge University Press, 1976.

Nichols, Nina DaVinci, and Jana O'Keefe Bazzoni. *Pirandello and Film*. Lincoln, Neb.: University of Nebraska Press, 1995.

O'Connor, Sean. *Straight Acting: Popular Gay Drama from Wilde to Rattigan*. Washington, D.C.: Cassell, 1997.

Oliva, Judy Lee. *David Hare: Theatricalizing Politics*. Ann Arbor: University of Michigan Research Press, 1990.

Oliver, Michael. *Benjamin Britten*. London: Phaedon Press, 1996.

Oppenheim, Lois, and Marius Buning. *Beckett On and On*. Madison, N.J.: Fairleigh Dickinson University Press, 1996.

Orton, Joe. *The Orton Diaries*. Ed. John Lahr. New York: Da Capo Press, 1996.

Palmer, Christopher, ed. *The Britten Companion*. London: Faber and Faber, 1984.

Paolucci, Anne. *Pirandello's Theater: The Recovery of the Stage for Modern Art*. Carbondale: Southern Illinois University Press, 1974.

Pappe, Ilan. *The Ethnic Cleansing of Palestine*. Oxford: Oneworld, 2007.

Payn, Graham. *My Life with Noel Coward*. New York: Applause, 1994.

Payn, Graham, and Sheridan Morley, eds. *The Noel Coward Diaries*. London: Weidenfeld and Nicholson, 1982.

Peacock, D. Keith. *Harold Pinter and the New British Theater*. Westport, Conn.: Greenwood Press, 1997.

Pennica, Gilda, ed. *Pirandello e la Germania*. Palermo: Palumbo, 1984.

Peters, Sally. *Bernard Shaw: The Ascent of the Superman*. New Haven, Conn.: Yale University Press, 1996.

Pirandello, Luigi. *The Late Mattia Pascal*. Trans. William Weaver. New York: Marsilio Publishers, 1995.

Raby, Peter, ed. *The Cambridge Companion to Harold Pinter*. Cambridge, England: Cambridge University Press, 2001.

Rader, Dotson. *Tennessee: Cry of the Heart*. Garden City, N.Y.: Doubleday, 1985.

Ragusa, Olga. *Pirandello: An Approach to His Theatre*. Edinburgh: Edinburgh University Press, 1980.

Randall, Phyllis R., ed. *Caryl Churchill: A Casebook*. New York: Garland, 1989.

Reynolds, Jean. *Pygmalion's Wordplay: The Postmodern Shaw.* Gainesville: University Press of Florida, 1999.

Rusinko, Susan. *Joe Orton.* New York: Twayne Publishers, 1995.

_____. *Tom Stoppard.* Boston: Twayne, 1986.

Sammells, Neil. *Tom Stoppard: The Artist as Critic.* London: Macmillan, 1988.

Secrest, Meryle. *Stephen Sondheim: A Life.* New York: Knopf, 1998.

Shaw, Bernard. *Bernard Shaw and Alfred Douglas: A Correspondence.* London: J. Murray, 1982.

Sheaffer, Louis. *O'Neill: Son and Artist.* Boston: Little, Brown, 1973.

Silver, Arnold. *Bernard Shaw: The Darker Side.* Stanford, Calif.: Stanford University Press, 1982.

Smith, Ian, ed. *Pinter in the Theatre.* London: Nick Hern Books, 2005.

Smith, Warren Sylvester. *Bishop of Everywhere: Bernard Shaw and The Life Force.* University Park: Pennsylvania State University Press, 1982.

Spoto, Donald. *The Kindness of Strangers: The Life of Tennessee Williams.* New York: Ballantine, 1985.

Sternlicht, Sanford. *A Reader's Guide to Modern American Drama.* Syracuse, N.Y.: Syracuse University Press, 2002.

_____. *A Reader's Guide to Modern British Drama.* Syracuse, N.Y.: Syracuse University Press, 2004.

_____. *A Reader's Guide to Modern Irish Drama.* Syracuse, N.Y.: Syracuse University Press, 1998.

Stoppard, Tom. *Every Good Boy Deserves Favor* and *Professional Foul.* New York: Grove Press, 1978.

Sutcliffe, Tom. "Haunting Parallels Between Art and Life." In "The Turn of the Screw," program booklet for the production of this opera by Welsh National Opera. Cardiff, 2000.

Tharpe, Jac, ed. *Tennessee Williams: 13 Essays.* Jackson: University Press of Mississippi, 1980.

Tischler, Nancy M. *Tennessee Williams: Rebellious Puritan.* New York: Citadel Press, 1965.

Turco, Alfred. *Shaw's Moral Vision: The Self and Salvation.* Ithaca, N.Y.: Cornell University Press, 1975.

Valency, Maurice. *The Cart and the Trumpet: The Plays of George Bernard Shaw.* New York: Oxford University Press, 1973.

Weber, Eugen. *France Fin de Siecle.* Cambridge, Mass.: Harvard University Press, 1986.

Weintraub, Rodelle, ed. *Fabian Feminist: Bernard Shaw and Women.* University Park: Pennsylvania State University Press, 1977.

Whitman, Robert F. *Shaw and the Play of Ideas.* Ithaca, N.Y.: Cornell University Press, 1977.

Williams, Dakin, and Shepherd Mead. *Tennessee Williams: An Intimate Biography.* New York: Arbor House, 1983.

Williams, Edwina, and Lucy Freeman. *Remember Me to Tom.* New York: G.P. Putnam's Sons, 1973.

Williams, Jeannie. *Jon Vickers: A Hero's Life.* Boston: Northeastern University Press, 1999.

Woolf, Virginia. "Impressions at Bayreuth." *London Times,* 1909; rpt. in *Opera News,* 41 (August, 1976), pp. 22–23.

Yacowar, Maurice. *Tennessee Williams and Film.* New York: Frederick Ungar, 1977.

Zangrilli, Franco. *Pirandello: Le Maschere del "Vecchio Dio."* Padova: Edizioni Messaggero, 2002.

Zadan, Craig. *Sondheim and Co.* New York: Harper and Row, 1986.

Zeifman, Hersh, ed. *David Hare: A Casebook.* New York: Garland, 1994.

Index

193